DISTANCE
Cycling

John Hughes
Dan Kehlenbach

HUMAN KINETICS

Library of Congress Cataloging-in-Publication Data

Hughes, John, 1949 Apr. 22-
  Distance cycling / John Hughes.
      p. cm.
  Includes bibliographical references and index.
  ISBN-13: 978-0-7360-8924-1 (soft cover)
  ISBN-10: 0-7360-8924-1 (soft cover)
  1. Cycling--Training. I. Title.
  GV1048.H84 2011
  796.6--dc22
                                            2011009480
  ISBN-10: 0-7360-8924-1 (print)
  ISBN-13: 978-0-7360-8924-1 (print)

Acquisitions Editor: Tom Heine; **Developmental Editor:** Carla Zych; **Assistant Editors:** Tyler Wolpert and Claire Gilbert; **Copyeditor:** Bob Replinger; **Indexer:** Nan N. Badgett; **Permissions Manager:** Dalene Reeder; **Graphic Designer:** Bob Reuther; **Graphic Artists:** Nancy Rasmus and Julie L. Denzer; **Cover Designer:** Keith Blomberg; **Photographer (cover):** Helen Budinger/Alaska Digital Visions; **Photographers (interior):** Rob O'Dea and Neil Bernstein, all photos © Human Kinetics unless otherwise noted; **Photo Asset Manager:** Laura Fitch; **Visual Production Assistant:** Joyce Brumfield; **Photo Production Manager:** Jason Allen; **Art Manager:** Kelly Hendren; **Associate Art Manager:** Alan L. Wilborn; **Illustrations:** © Human Kinetics; **Printer:** United Graphics

Human Kinetics books are available at special discounts for bulk purchase. Special editions or book excerpts can also be created to specification. For details, contact the Special Sales Manager at Human Kinetics.

Printed in the United States of America   10 9 8 7 6 5 4 3 2 1

The paper in this book is certified under a sustainable forestry program.

Human Kinetics
Website: www.HumanKinetics.com

United States: Human Kinetics
P.O. Box 5076
Champaign, IL 61825-5076
800-747-4457
e-mail: humank@hkusa.com

Canada: Human Kinetics
475 Devonshire Road Unit 100
Windsor, ON N8Y 2L5
800-465-7301 (in Canada only)
e-mail: info@hkcanada.com

Europe: Human Kinetics
107 Bradford Road
Stanningley
Leeds LS28 6AT, United Kingdom
+44 (0) 113 255 5665
e-mail: hk@hkeurope.com

Australia: Human Kinetics
57A Price Avenue
Lower Mitcham, South Australia 5062
08 8372 0999
e-mail: info@hkaustralia.com

New Zealand: Human Kinetics
P.O. Box 80
Torrens Park, South Australia 5062
0800 222 062
e-mail: info@hknewzealand.com

E5013

We dedicate this book to Carol Garnand, LuAnn Kehlenbach, and our families, whose love, support, and encouragement have been invaluable. We also dedicate it to you—the endurance riders who want to go just a little bit farther...and farther.

CONTENTS

Preface **vii** ● Acknowledgments **ix** ● Introduction **xi**

CHAPTER 1   Going the Distance 1

CHAPTER 2   Selecting Your Event 9

CHAPTER 3   Baseline Conditioning 19

CHAPTER 4   Fueling the Distance Cyclist. 57

CHAPTER 5   Gearing Up for the Long Haul 73

CHAPTER 6   Preparing Your Body to Go the Distance. 99

CHAPTER 7   Conquering the Century and 200K 129

CHAPTER 8   Ultimate Training for Ultra Events 147

CHAPTER 9   Mastering the Multiday 173

CHAPTER 10   Ultradistance Riding 195

CHAPTER 11   Preventing Injury. 225

Resources **243** ● Works Consulted **249** ● Index **251** ●
About the Authors **259**

PREFACE

Afew years ago my 16-year-old friend Kira told me (John) that she wanted to ride the Buff Classic, our local century in Boulder, Colorado, with me. Cool—but it was just seven weeks away!

Kira had only a mountain bike (MTB), and on the first weekend we rode 20 miles (32 km), farther than she'd ever ridden. We stopped a couple of times to admire the view (I didn't call them rest stops), and after a dozen miles (20 km) we ate snacks at a deli. Looking back at Boulder, she was pleased with how far we'd come.

The next weekend we rode 30 miles (48 km), still on our MTBs, stopping every hour to eat granola bars. Afterward she asked, "Is there any way I could get a road bike?" A woman friend in the Rocky Mountain Cycling Club loaned her a classic Bianchi seven-speed with down-tube shifters, and I put on pedals with toe clips.

At the start of our third ride, she rode around the block practicing getting in and out of the toe clips. We then headed north. After a few miles she let her front wheel kiss my rear wheel, but she didn't go down. We stopped and talked about group riding skills. On our two previous rides I'd given her tips on riding in traffic but hadn't lectured her on safety.

During week 4 we added a midweek 25-mile (40 km) ride that included some short climbs and downhills to work on climbing out of the saddle and cornering on descents. On the weekend we rode 50 miles (80 km), practicing nutrition (eating every hour) and pacing (riding at a conversational pace). So far, Kira had chosen to ride in running shorts, a T-shirt, and running shoes. After the ride she decided that the running shorts were uncomfortable, and she asked her sister whether she could borrow a pair of cycling shorts.

The Buff Classic includes a 3-mile (5 km), 6 percent climb to Carter Lake, so during the week we climbed Olde Stage, which features 2 miles (3 km) of 7 percent grade. She climbed steadily, and from the top we coasted home, where she proudly told her mom, "I climbed Olde Stage!"

On the fifth weekend, we headed for Carter Lake. Approaching the climb Kira could see the switchbacks. "This is nothing; I've done Olde Stage," she said. That became our mantra. We rode 48 miles (77 km) that day, stopping every hour to eat. I kept my food in my jersey pocket; she kept hers in her seat pack. When we got back, she asked if she could borrow one of my cycling jerseys, noting, "Those pockets are handy."

For our final training ride we first drove north about 25 miles (40 km). We then climbed to Carter Lake again and previewed the northern part of the Buff Classic route, another 50-mile (80 km) ride.

Kira was ready. She'd learned what and when to eat. She'd decided to upgrade to a road bike and to wear cycling clothes. She'd practiced climbing and descending. She knew how to ride with others and how to ride in traffic. She was mentally prepared; she'd ridden the entire course and had climbed to Carter Lake twice. She knew how to pace herself, how to listen to her body. We had a great ride, and during the last half she was chasing down riders on fancy bikes, riders who didn't understand pacing and nutrition.

Although Kira wasn't aware of it because I mixed in plenty of fun, I'd planned from the start how to teach her all the necessary skills over those seven weeks, and I'd allowed her to make her own decisions along the way.

Dan and I wrote *Distance Cycling* because we would like to share our knowledge and enjoyment of the sport with you, too, and help you reach your endurance cycling goals, whatever they may be.

ACKNOWLEDGMENTS

Writing a book is an endurance process similar to preparing for and riding a long-distance event, and we could not have reached our goal without the help of many people! First we are very grateful to our significant others for their support over the three years from conception to publication. Thank you Carol Garnand and LuAnn Kehlenbach—now we can spend more time together!

We each have significant influences in our athletic careers. John is the person he is today because of his coach, Michelle Grainger—Michelle, this book wouldn't exist without you. Lon Haldeman and Susan Notorangelo led John on his first transcontinental PAC Tour over 20 years ago—Lon and Susan, thanks for your ongoing friendship and support. Dan is particularly grateful to Richard Shumway who guided him through his studies and provided him with invaluable clinical experience.

Writing the book was a team effort, and the result is better because of our teammates who contributed sidebars and reviewed specific sections: Ken Bonner, Paul Carpenter, John Lee Ellis, Julie Gazmararian, Michelle Grainger, Lon Haldeman, Jenny Hegmann, Dan McGehee, Pete Penseyres, Muffy Ritz, and Lulu Weschler.

Many volunteers provided information on specific points, especially the lists of rides: Jamie Andrews, Marko Baloh, Susan Barr, Michael Bentley, Fabio Biasiolo, Fritz Blindenbacher, Chuck Bramwell, Dan Driscoll, Rex Farnsworth, Kim Freitas, Matt Haigh, Bill Ingraham, Kevin Kaiser, Peter Leiss, Doug MacKenzie, Warren McNaughton, Sven-Erik Olsson, Dave Parker, Dessa Paris, Michael Simon, Merry Vander Linden, and Joel Voelz.

Our friends at Alaska Digital Visions provided action photos: Helen Budinger, Peter Lekisch, and George Stransky. These friends modeled for the photo shoot: Tim Feldman, Michelle Grainger, Andrea Koenig, Elizabeth Weiss, Mark Swartzendruber, and Rebecca Ray. We are grateful to Rick Barron and John Elmblad for loaning their equipment, Rob O'Dea and Neil Bernstein for taking photos, Jim Groh and Don Walker for assisting, and RallySport in Boulder, Colorado, for allowing us to shoot there.

Finally, we are grateful to our coaches, Dick Hughes, who over the years has taught John how to write well, and Tom Heine and Carla Zych, our editors at Human Kinetics.

As you prepare for and ride an endurance event, we hope that you have the same support from family, mentors, friends, and volunteers and that you find our coaching is helpful.

INTRODUCTION

You may have started with a journey down the block. Then, before long, you rode around the neighborhood, and then across town. The bike was your ticket to freedom, allowing you to explore and discover new nooks and crannies of your young world. As an adult with ever-increasing responsibilities, you may use the bike for only a few hours on weekend club rides or relegate it to a dusty corner of your garage, bringing it out occasionally for a ride with friends or family on a sunny afternoon. Sound familiar?

Allow us to rekindle that sense of adventure and the pleasure of traveling great distances under your own power, enjoying the sun, the breeze, and the feeling of accomplishment. Long-distance cycling is much more than sitting on a bike and grinding away at the distance. It's about the journey, about planning new adventures. The journey is deeply personal. It can be a way to enjoy the camaraderie of fellow riders, develop new relationships, and discover greatness within yourself.

We both ride because we love riding! We aren't (primarily) racers; we just enjoy going places on our bikes. If you share our love of riding and want to become a better endurance rider, this book is for you. We are writing for

- cyclists who are preparing for a first long ride, the metric century (100 km, or 62 miles), a regular century (100 miles), or a 200-kilometer event;
- endurance riders who want to ride centuries and 200Ks more comfortably;
- athletes who are trying to improve their personal bests in the local century;
- century veterans looking to see more countryside on multiday tours; and
- experienced endurance riders who are ready for the challenge of double centuries or brevets (events with specific time limits, typically 200 to 1,200 kilometers in length and sometimes longer).

The book focuses on the century and its 200-kilometer metric equivalent because they are the basic endurance rides. For many cyclists, one of these rides is the culmination of the riding season or year. Like marathon runners, cyclists may plan the entire year with a century as the big goal. Although these events are not races, participants often try to better their previous times or finish ahead of other riders.

Sport scientists have written good books on physiology and on specialized training methods, and successful coaches and cyclists have written helpful books on how to train. Our book brings together a solid foundation in sport science and years of coaching experience in a way that is useful to readers with little or no scientific background.

We both actively coach, and we know that much more than training goes into a successful ride. In the book we cover the breadth of what you need to know to eliminate the showstoppers that could keep you from finishing your chosen event. Athletic achievement involves these six success factors:

- *Planning*—self-assessment, goal setting, and season planning
- *Training*—aerobic, strength, and flexibility workouts for baseline conditioning and specific event training
- *Mental skills*—relaxation and visualization techniques and dealing with hard times during a ride
- *Nutrition*—good nutrition year round, nourishment before an event, and fuel during the ride and for recovery
- *Equipment*—bike selection and fit, clothing, tools, other accessories, and bike maintenance before and during rides
- *Technique*—safety, cycling economy, group riding, pacing during events, and dealing with problems like flat tires

We have written this book as coaches speaking to athletes in an easy-to-understand manner. We offer the same kind of instruction that we would give to a rider in one-on-one sessions. Step by step, we guide you through the process of preparing for and completing distance cycling events.

We provide 8-week and 15-week training programs for riders preparing for a first century or 200K to show you how to apply the basic principles of training—progression, overload, specificity, variation, and individuality—to achieve your goal. We help you improve your riding technique and overcome obstacles.

After mastering the century or 200K you may be ready for a new challenge. The final chapters help you choose among various options: riding several centuries in the same year, challenging yourself with a 300K or double century, doing a weekend or weeklong tour, or completing a series of brevets. We extend your knowledge of the six success factors to help you reach your goal.

We also include safety and performance sidebars that contain practical advice from experienced endurance cyclists—century and double century riders, brevet and randonnée veterans, and Race Across America winners. These sidebars address the questions that cyclists commonly ask us: What can I learn from ultraracers about dealing with fatigue? What should I eat during a training ride or event? How do I ride safely in traffic or in the rain? How do I ride in a pack? What is the best way to descend and corner?

Think of this book as your personal cycling coach and allow it to be your constant companion on your journey to becoming a better distance cyclist. Unlike many textbooks, this book features practical advice from which riders of all ability levels can learn and be inspired. Success in endurance cycling doesn't require endless training and the forfeiture of normal life. Regular riders with everyday responsibilities have completed everything from half centuries to the renowned Race Across America. This book will help you manage the delicate balance of training and daily life to ensure an enjoyable and successful ride.

Let's go for a ride—your big event is right around the corner!

CHAPTER 1

Going the Distance

The bicycle is a wonderful invention. Throughout the world, people ride bicycles for many reasons. Some use the bicycle to transport people, goods, and services. Some commute to work by bicycle, and others use it to stay healthy and fit. Cycling is also a great way to spend time with others, whether on a leisurely Saturday morning ride with friends, a family ride and picnic, or a weekend trip to a B&B with your significant other. In all its varieties, riding a bicycle is a rewarding and enjoyable activity. H.G. Wells remarked, "Every time I see an adult on a bicycle I no longer despair for the future of the human race" (Strickland, 2001, p. 18).

Bicycling is the second most popular outdoor activity in the United States according to a 2008 survey by the Outdoor Foundation. Forty-two million adults and children over the age of six went on 2.62 billion bicycle outings, averaging 62 outings per cyclist. The study investigated motivating factors behind participation in outdoor activities and concluded that the number one reason for riding is that it's fun.

The popularity of cycling has led to the establishment of countless cycling events worldwide. Participating in these events can be your gateway to fun and adventure, allowing you to explore local roads, trails, and routes that go unnoticed in an automobile. These rides are almost guaranteed to put a smile on your face.

This chapter looks at why we ride and provides an overview of the types of cycling events throughout the world.

Fitness Benefits of Cycling

Besides offering fun, cycling is an effective form of cardiovascular exercise. A strong cardiovascular system is vital for overall health and well-being, and it contributes to an enhanced quality of life. Today, heart disease is the number one killer worldwide as well as in the United States (Mayo Clinic, Heart Disease, n.d.). Regular aerobic exercise substantially reduces the risk of cardiovascular disease and improves cardiovascular function. Table 1.1 on page 2 highlights the physical benefits of cardiovascular exercise such as cycling.

TABLE 1.1 **Physical Changes Associated With Cardiovascular Exercise**

Improves cardiovascular health
Helps maintain healthy weight
Lowers blood pressure
Increases HDL (good) cholesterol
Lowers LDL cholesterol
Promotes better sleep
Reduces possibility of diabetes, can be used to manage diabetes
Decreases risk of chronic diseases
Increases immune system function

Adapted from Wilmore and Costill 1994.

Riding a bike is easier on the joints than running and other high-impact activities. Provided the bicycle is fitted properly, the activity produces virtually no impact and little strain on the musculoskeletal system. Because of this, cycling is often the first choice in rehabilitation from injuries. People with knee, ankle, or hip problems may find that cycling is a way to continue participating in sports without aggravating previous injuries.

After a long day, you can relax by going for a bike ride. The moment that you step on the pedals, your senses awaken; as time goes by, your troubles seem to disappear. Besides providing physiological benefits, cycling improves psychological health and reduces tension. Stress is prevalent today, and riders tend to be happier and less stressed than those who do not exercise. As a result, cycling can lead to better relationships with family, friends, and coworkers. Better relationships off the bike will make a difference in your training. Those close to you will have a better understanding of your cycling goals, and you'll feel less conflict when the volume of training increases. You'll be more successful, both on and off the bike, with the support of others.

Social Aspects of Cycling

Get some friends, grab your bikes, and go for a ride or join a cycling club to enjoy the company of others. Throughout the world, thousands of cycling groups offer activities ranging from casual rides for the whole family to racing on international levels. Regardless of the kinds of riding that you do, you may find a club in your area that will increase your enjoyment of the sport.

Many clubs hold regularly scheduled rides that provide opportunities to spend time with and learn from fellow riders. We look at regular club rides later in the chapter. Many clubs also host metric centuries (100 kilometers, or 62.5 miles), centuries (100 miles, or 160 kilometers) or its international equivalent, the 200K, and other rides throughout the year. Many events have become extremely popular, drawing crowds from around the country, providing great challenges, and offering a chance to meet others who love the sport. Centuries are often the focus of a training program that starts in winter and prepares the participant to complete a first century or improve on the previous year's time in a particular summer or fall event.

Besides riding with a club, you can socialize with cyclists off the bike. Most clubs hold regular meetings that often feature presentations on training, bike maintenance, and other topics as well as slide shows of trips. Many clubs take great pride in helping others both on and off the bike. Charity rides, potluck dinners, and other events hosted by a club are ways that cyclists can give back to the community.

The noncycling members of clubs are also important because without volunteers, many events would be impossible. Becoming involved with a cycling group offers camaraderie, companionship, and a chance to teach, learn, and be inspired by others.

Of course, you don't need to belong to a group to enjoy cycling. In many parts of the world, access to organized clubs is limited. If that is the case, get together with your cycling friends, order a pizza, and plan some rides on your own. Laying a map on the table and grabbing a highlighter to plan a ride are exciting. It wasn't much different than that for John Marino and Michael Shermer in 1982 when they planned the route for the first Great American Bike Race from the Santa Monica Pier in California to the Empire State Building in New York. (Marino had set the transcontinental cycling record of just over 12 days, and Shermer held the Seattle, Washington, to San Diego, California, record of 4 days 14 hours.) John Howard and Lon Haldeman also raced. (Howard had competed three times in the Summer Olympics and was four-time U.S. national road cycling champion. Haldeman had set the double transcontinental record of 24 days 2 hours 34 minutes, breaking Marino's one-way cross-country record in the process.) Haldeman won the race in 1982 and again in 1983; the race is now the Race Across America (RAAM), the world's most difficult ultra bike race.

Importance of Setting Goals

By Lon Haldeman

Long-distance cyclists tend to be goal oriented. For most riders involved in the sport, the process of setting and reaching goals is the sport. Many riders want to achieve new accomplishments just beyond their comfort zones. But it's important to be realistic about what you really want to achieve.

For most riders the perception of a long ride is a distance farther than what they have ridden before. When I was 10 years old, I pedaled my coaster brake bike 3 miles (5 km) toward the water tower of the next town. I thought I was a long-distance cyclist when I arrived there. When I mastered that distance, the next month I rode 6 miles (10 km) to the next town. Even at that age the process of setting goals and accomplishing them was one of the thrills and rewards of distance cycling for me.

This sport offers many goals for individuals. For some riders the personal challenge of testing themselves is the goal, such as finishing a century. For others, the goal is to set a new record and be the best. Other riders like the social aspect of long-distance riding while enjoying the scenery and seeing new places.

The benefits of goal setting in long-distance cycling include practical applications related to planning events, buying equipment, and making efficient training plans. For example, the training required for achieving a goal of riding 400 miles (640 km) in 24 hours is different from the training required for completing a century. By defining the goal, the type of training to reach that goal becomes clearer. Setting goals also makes all the decisions easier about what nutrition is needed and even what type of bicycle to ride.

Dreaming, goal setting, and planning can be among the most interesting aspects of long-distance cycling. These are the first steps toward a more rewarding and fun season.

Types of Participants

At the start of any long-distance cycling event you're likely to see a broad spectrum of the cycling community: spandex-clad riders tuning up their racing machines, more casual cyclists on touring bicycles, kids on trailer bikes with their parents, couples on tandems, and people on recumbent bikes. The racers are mixing their sports drinks while the weekend warriors are loading up on coffee and donuts. People from all walks of life and athletic backgrounds enjoy cycling events. Organized century and 200K rides often feature shorter options (10-, 25-, 50-mile, metric century, and so on) to appeal to various riders and to offer choices for the entire family. Experienced riders may race through the century while others cycle at a leisurely pace or do a shorter ride. Then everyone enjoys the postride festivities. Riding one of the shorter options is a useful introduction to organized events and a step toward riding longer events.

Whether riding in an organized event, on a club ride, or alone, be an ambassador for our sport. Do your best to promote the pleasure and benefits of cycling and demonstrate courtesy to others on the road.

Types of Cycling Events

If you browse websites of cycling clubs or look at cycling magazines, you'll find information about thousands of cycling events throughout the world and rides that appeal to cyclists of all levels. From charity rides to multiday tours, there are events to please any cyclist who wants to get out and have fun on a bike. Here are some of the more common types of rides.

Club Rides

Most cycling clubs host scheduled rides throughout the season. By participating in club rides you can meet other riders, learn from them, test new gear, see different routes, and explore your local area. Rides range from casual spins with stops at coffee shops or art galleries to fast pace lines that rival team time trials. To help cyclists select rides, many clubs offer ride categories based on planned speed and may also factor in terrain (see table 1.2). As you enjoy club rides, you may also bond with others.

On club rides you can learn the dynamics and etiquette of group riding, which are important skills. On these rides you can get accustomed to drafting other riders, dealing with traffic, communicating with others, and developing other skills impossible to work on while riding alone. You will need to be comfortable riding in a group to participate

TABLE 1.2 **Example of Ride Categories**

A rides: 20 mph (32 km/h) and above
B rides: 17–20 mph (27–32 km/h)
C rides: 15–17 mph (24–27 km/h)
D rides: 13–15 mph (21–24 km/h)
E rides: below 13 mph (< 21 km/h)

in most organized events, and club rides will help you become a more efficient and safer rider.

Personal Rides

Despite the benefits of club rides, they may not be available or fit your interests or schedule. If you ride alone or with friends, you have more choices about when and where to ride. Personal rides can fit into other activities such as commuting and family outings. Many riders choose some solo rides to decompress mentally.

Even if you have access to many club rides, solo rides provide an important way to improve. Every rider has weaknesses, and riding alone is the best way to work on exactly what you need to improve. Want to improve your endurance? Ride at your optimal endurance pace rather than with faster riders. Are you weak climbing? Tackle a hilly route at your sustainable pace. Want to boost your average speed? Hammer some intervals at your optimal effort. Later in the book, we talk about specific training plans and workouts. Doing some of these training rides by yourself will make you a stronger rider both physically and mentally and will help you achieve your goals.

Centuries

Ride 100 miles (160 km) on a bike (roughly the driving distance between Manhattan and Philadelphia)? For fun? You bet! Some people dread driving a car 100 miles in a single day, yet for cyclists, the century and its international equivalent, the 200K, are among

Riders beginning a ride during Fireweed, an event including rides ranging from 50 to 400 miles (80 to 640 km) held in Alaska every summer.

Courtesy of Alaska Digital Visions.

On my after-work ride tonight I saw a rider who was violating most of the safe cycling rules!

- He was riding without a helmet. If you fall off your bike, without any forward momentum, and hit your head, the consequences could be fatal. I always wear a helmet, even to ride around the block to test an adjustment on the bike.

- He was wearing dark clothes and was almost invisible in the late afternoon shadows. Wear a bright jersey or windbreaker.

- He was riding on the separate bike path rather than on the shoulder. A separate bike path is generally more dangerous than a bike lane on the side of a roadway or the shoulder. A bike lane is part of the roadway, essentially a wider shoulder marked for bicycles. A bike path is set back from the roadway several meters or more. A driver entering the street from a parking lot or cross street will look for traffic in the street, including the shoulder, but might not notice you in the separate bike path, especially if you are riding against traffic. Riding on the sidewalk is even more dangerous because pedestrians don't expect you and drivers aren't looking for you.

- After a few blocks he looked left and right and then zipped through a stop sign. Fortunately, there was no traffic, but illegal and discourteous behavior hurts the image of cyclists.

- The rider decided he wanted to turn left, so he signaled with his left arm (that's good!) and then cut clear across the road from the right edge to the left edge. From his brief signal, drivers, especially in oncoming traffic, would not have anticipated his action. To turn left, check both directions for traffic—and then check again, just to be safe. Signal and move to the left of your lane. Keep signaling, check again for traffic, and then turn left.

- Instead of turning left at the next intersection, he decided to continue to ride on the wrong side of the road against traffic. This practice is extremely dangerous. Drivers turning right onto the road from a street or parking lot would look left for oncoming cars but might not look right and see the rider.

The safest way to ride is to behave like a car. You will be more visible and more predictable to other vehicles:

- At a four-way stop with a right-turn lane, stay in the straight-ahead lane, unless you are turning right. If you move into the right-turn lane, drivers may assume that you are turning right and cut you off when you try to go straight.

- To turn left, check twice for traffic, signal, and then move to the left side of your lane. If there is a left-turn lane, move into the right side of that lane. Turn left when traffic is clear.

- When riding down a street with occasional parked cars, ride in a straight line. Don't move right into the space between parked cars and then swerve back out into the traffic lane. If you move right, a driver behind you may assume that you plan to stop rather than pull back out into the traffic flow.

- Similarly, ride in a straight line on the shoulder or bike lane. Don't swerve in and out of driveways or other spaces.

- Do not let traffic build up behind you. If several cars are waiting to pass you, stop to let them by.

- Finally, obey all traffic laws.

In sum, be visible and ride like a car. You'll be more predictable and safer, and you'll make a good impression. Drivers will have a better image of cyclists and be more courteous to all of us.

the most popular recreational cycling events. The century and 200K are to cycling what the marathon is to running, and they attract all kinds of cyclists. Participants range from first-time century riders to veterans seeking a personal best. All participate together, face the same challenges, and reap the same rewards. These rides are usually noncompetitive and may be a big cycling party. Enthusiastic volunteers run start and finish areas and rest stops, cyclists form friendly groups, and experienced riders cheer others on, all of which add to the enjoyment of the event. Many events have become incredibly popular over the years, so do your homework and plan early because some centuries fill up months in advance. For information on the most popular rides, see http://tinyurl.com/49ha5wb.

Many riders spend the entire season preparing for a particular century or 200K (or several). This book focuses primarily on these events. We provide information on training, nutrition, equipment, and riding events for new century and 200K riders and then more advanced information for experienced riders who want to ride faster or farther.

Multiday Tours

Multiday bicycle tours open up new experiences through cycling. Charity organizations host the most popular tours, and the funds raised make remarkable differences in the lives of others. These two or three day rides feature established routes, rest stops, prepared meals, and organized camping areas. Most even haul your gear from one overnight stop to the next. You can just ride and have fun! Spending several days with hundreds of riders sharing a goal of helping others is an enriching experience.

If you have time to plan or prefer to ride alone or with a small group, you can do a multiday tour almost anywhere. You can pack a change of clothes on your bike, take your credit card, and pedal down the road. You can buy groceries en route, eat in cafes, and stay in interesting hotels. Credit-card touring allows you to enjoy multiday outings and travel faster than riders who carry camping gear. Credit-card tours are an excellent way to prepare for 600-kilometer and longer events.

If you have a touring bike or bike trailer, you can load your camping gear, food, and accessories and head off for an adventure. Packed properly, bicycles can safely and comfortably carry you and your gear from one end of your country (or continent!) to the other. Throughout the world, thousands of campsites and public areas allow cyclists to enjoy traveling under their own power.

Longer Events

After the century bug has bitten, many riders look for new challenges. In addition to touring, double centuries, longer brevets, and 12- and 24-hour events offer additional challenges.

Double centuries (200 miles) and the metric equivalent, the 300K, can introduce you to the world of ultracycling. You can build on what you've learned about training, nutrition, and cycling techniques to extend your distance. If you have completed several centuries you can prepare to complete a double or 300K. The California Triple Crown encourages riders from across North America to participate in double centuries and offers a wealth of information at www.caltriplecrown.com.

Brevet (pronounced to rhyme with "say") rides are immensely popular in North America, Europe, Asia, and Australia. Participants ride a specified course and have control cards signed at specified checkpoints on scheduled dates. A "permanent" is like a brevet, but you can ride a set course following the same rules any day you want. Brevets are usually 200, 300, 400, and 600 kilometers (125, 186, 250, 375 miles), building up to very

Cyclists participating in the internationally renowned Paris-Brest-Paris 1200K brevet, much of which is ridden at night.

© Gregg Bleakney

difficult 1,000- and 1,200-kilometer (625 and 750 mile) events. The first 1,200-kilometer brevet was the venerable Paris–Brest–Paris (PBP), first held in 1891 and run every four years. Much of the tradition and culture of distance cycling is rooted in PBP. Randonneurs USA sanctions brevets in the United States (visit www.rusa.org). A list of randonneuring organizations offering brevets in other countries is in the resources section on page 243.

In 12- and 24-hour events riders strive to cover as much distance as possible in the given amount of time. These rides can be done on or off road, by relay teams or solo, and may be drafting or nondrafting. The nondrafting events require mental strength because you are working on your own during the entire race. Riders interested in ultra-racing may start with shorter durations and then step up to longer races. For example, the Texas Time Trials draws an international field that competes in 6-hour, 12-hour, 24-hour, and 500-mile (800 km) nondrafting races run simultaneously on a 26.5-mile (42.6 km) looped course (www.tt24tt.com). Participating in nondrafting races is terrific training for other ultradistance cycling events such as setting cross-state records and racing in qualifying races for the Race Across America (RAAM) or RAAM itself (www.raceacrossamerica.org).

Organizations with calendars of cycling events are listed in the resources section at the end of the book.

N ow that you have an overview of distance cycling, its events, and its participants, the next chapter will help you assess your goals and style of riding and then assist you in selecting the right type of event for you.

CHAPTER 2

Selecting Your Event

In this chapter we focus on planning, one of the six factors that contribute to cycling success listed in the introduction and developed over the course of this book. Planning includes self-assessment, goal setting, and selecting and planning the event or events in which you'd like to participate. Planning a season of cycling events can be nearly as exciting as the riding itself. Training should start on a piece of paper, not in the saddle. Riders often dust off the bike in the spring, inflate the tires, and train without a plan. Riding a bike should be fun and spontaneous, but planning will help you have a more rewarding cycling season.

Thousands of events throughout the world are available, but before picking your specific ride, grab a piece of paper and a pen. By asking yourself several questions, selecting your event from all the choices will be easier.

Self-Assessment

First, why do you like riding a bicycle? Do you get pleasure from a relaxed ride with family and friends? Do you enjoy riding as far or as fast as possible? Do you like pedaling through challenging terrain? Do you like to travel on your bike? People ride for various reasons, and identifying the types of riding that you enjoy will help you choose the event that is right for you.

What is your athletic history? If you have been active recently in an endurance sport such as running, training for and completing a cycling event will be easier than if you are taking up athletics for the first time in years. You will have an endurance base and be used to exercising regularly. If you're an experienced endurance athlete you could consider a more challenging initial cycling event.

What is your experience level as a cyclist? If you are a new rider attempting a first century, avoid (at least for the first outing) the more difficult rides. Most organizers provide information about rider support as well as difficulty including total elevation gain and climb gradients, which can help in event selection and planning. Many rides cater to new cyclists, and some events offer training and support to help you achieve your goals. Experienced riders can seek out more challenging events to add a new dimension to their preparation and training.

What seems exciting to you as a cyclist? Many cycling events focus on the experience of the journey as opposed to riding a particular distance. For example, the city of New York closes its roads to traffic for Bike New York, in which riders get a fun and unique perspective of all five boroughs of the city. Special-interest cycling events feature themes such as wine tasting, local history, recumbent riding, couples-only tandem rides, and cultural interests.

For many, helping others brings great satisfaction. Many organizations worldwide host charity rides to raise money and awareness for various causes. Your entire family can enjoy these events because they typically feature a variety of distances and offer a friendly atmosphere. By evaluating your interests and motivations, you can choose an event that offers a rewarding experience that goes beyond completing a certain number of miles or kilometers.

Where would you like to do your event? Do you want to travel to a far-off destination as part of a vacation, or would you prefer to stay close to home? Traveling with your bike opens up exciting possibilities to explore new areas and meet new people, but this choice may present logistical challenges. Staying close to home is less complicated and may allow you to train on parts of the course, which can build confidence and familiarity with the event.

Are family members, friends, or colleagues going to ride or volunteer? Get others involved! Cycling is a great way to spend time with family and friends, but be sure to consider the abilities of others. A hilly century or brevet in the summer may sound like an exciting challenge to you, but it may be too much for less experienced and younger riders. Start with easier events to facilitate success and promote participation in future events. Noncycling family and friends can help with registration, rest stops, sag (support) vehicles, and other tasks. Volunteers are the lifeblood of organized cycling events. Without them, many events would cease to exist. Thank the volunteer who handles your registration, call thanks as you ride out of a rest stop, and thank the staff at the finish.

Cycling events are a great way to enjoy the company of others and meet new friends.

Courtesy of Alaska Digital Visions.

Setting Goals

After assessing your cycling interests and experience, think about your goals as a cyclist and a person. Do you want to finish your first century or brevet? Would you like to set a personal best in a ride? Do you want to complete a certain number of rides? Some riders may spend several years planning for a major event such as completing a brevet series or a 1,200-kilometer brevet. Goal setting is important for all riders and provides valuable direction and feedback to your training.

Planning a Season—Structure and Spontaneity

By John Lee Ellis

John Lee Ellis has ridden a dozen 1,200-kilometer brevets. A past president of the UltraMarathon Cycling Association (UMCA) and vice president of Randonneurs USA (RUSA), he currently serves on the board of RUSA, organizes brevets for Colorado, and chairs the UMCA's Year-Rounder Mileage Challenge.

Like many of us, I start the year by zoning in on a few peak events I'd like to do. They give focus and color to the other riding. Underlying that, though, is a multilayered structure: several strata of riding that fill out the season:

- ▶ A long ride most weekends. I live in Boulder, Colorado, and continue the long rides most winter weekends (the other winter days are devoted to cross-country skiing).
- ▶ A progression of canyon and mountain climbs that becomes more ambitious as snow melts and fitness builds.
- ▶ A series of 200-kilometer to 600-kilometer brevets.
- ▶ Other favorite club events.

Atop this structure, like mountains jutting above the plains, are my peak events: a 1,200-kilometer brevet somewhere in the world and maybe a multiday tour!

Aside from the progression in distance and climbing through the season, the peak events don't influence the other riding much. I plan no discrete phases; I might do a little tune-up or ride a little less as an event nears. I count on the volume and quality of riding to assure a comfortable level of fitness and seasoning for the big rides.

A number of programs can motivate yearlong endurance riding. I like the RUSA R-12 (www.rusa.org/award_r12.html) and the UMCA's Year-Rounder (Y-R) Challenge (www.ultracycling.com/standings/umc.html). The R-12 recognizes doing (at least) a 200-kilometer brevet for 12 consecutive months, and the Y-R rewards doing a century or more in each calendar month. The Y-R also tracks the total volume of endurance (century or longer) rides in the year. Both are great ways to keep you motivated each month, and it's fun to watch the volume mount up during the high season.

Endurance cycling tends to involve, well, riding a lot—not just the big events but also the base miles to support them. This is either an opportunity for variety and exploration, or a recipe for repeats and the feeling of drudgery.

I go out of my way to find the new or unusual outings—after all, exploring was what got me into endurance cycling. And the rides in between take on an aura of more importance, because they're in service of the special events.

What about spontaneity? Although structure and planning are good, I try to be nimble and look for new rides, and maybe that extra big event if I can squeeze it in!

When you have defined your long-term goals, write them down and put them where you will see them regularly—on your refrigerator, in your car, in a training journal—to help you stay motivated.

Cycling becomes more rewarding when you can balance several important goals, not all of which relate to cycling. Including aspirations for family, school, work, or other aspects of your life will have a positive effect on your training. Your aims might include making changes at home, maintaining a certain grade point average, and achieving work objectives. Setting and achieving life goals will free up some of your mental resources so that you can concentrate more on your training.

Finally, remember that goals aren't etched in stone. Goal setting is an ongoing, dynamic process, and over time you should reevaluate your aspirations. Fluctuating career demands, family considerations, and other facets of life will have a direct influence on your cycling. Keep the big picture in perspective and adjust accordingly.

Finding Events

Now that you have an idea of your goals and the types of riding you enjoy, start looking for possible events. The web, with its thousands of links to cycling organizations and rides, is the best resource. (See the website associated with this book http://tinyurl.com/49ha5wb for a list of popular events.) Websites offer more information about rides than other sources and may include a map of the course, hill profiles, rest stop locations, safety considerations, a list of frequently asked questions, online registration, directions to the start, and other tips that can help you select and plan your ride. Some sites host discussion forums in which riders post questions and chat with others. Past participants can provide valuable information, including firsthand accounts of their experiences with the ride. Through networking with others you may find riding partners who become friends both on and off the bike.

Grabbing a cup of your favorite beverage and poring over your favorite cycling publication can be almost as much fun as riding, particularly in the off-season. Even in this world of online information, cycling magazines can help you locate rides. Many magazines display rides according to geographical area. They also provide information about training, cycling skills, equipment, repair tips, and the race scene as well as inspiration that will motivate you to ride. (See the resources section on page 243 for a list of cycling organizations and publications.)

Cycling clubs often publish newsletters that list rides and club activities. At club outings and meetings you can chat with others about rides and get a more personal perspective on your prospective events.

Setting Realistic Priorities

Organized rides have become extremely popular. In many parts of the world it is possible to find an event during every week of the season. When planning your season, think about how many key events you would like to take part in, how many you can realistically do, and, most important, how many you can complete to your own satisfaction. Even elite riders can't always be at 100 percent of physical and psychological performance. Setting priorities among events will give your training greater direction and help you reach your goals.

If you aspire to complete your first century or 200-kiolometer brevet, you should focus throughout the season on one ride. You can dedicate your preparation to getting the right equipment, conditioning, learning on-the-bike nutrition, practicing safe riding, improving cycling efficiency, working on pacing, and developing other skills that will help you through your first major ride. You will discover a lot about your mind and body in your first season and how they respond to the demands of training. Attempting multiple events could lead to frustration and performance setbacks.

Moderately experienced riders who have completed several centuries or double metrics may target two or three key events. Previous training and participation help provide an adequate base of conditioning and skills to handle multiple events. Feedback from the first event of the season will allow you to adjust your training schedule for later events.

If you are a veteran rider with years of experience, you might plan major rides more frequently. Riding in one event per month throughout the cycling season or completing a brevet series can be a motivating challenge.

Setting priorities for key events also allows you to select other rides for training throughout the season. You can use smaller events as tune-ups for your target event. You can ride with family, friends, or colleagues in a shorter event. You will benefit from the training and enjoy spending time with others who are important in your life.

Just as when setting overall goals, avoid having tunnel vision when deciding event priorities—do not forget your family, friends, work, school, and other key aspects of your life. If you include other significant needs in your planning, your training will be less stressful and more enjoyable, resulting in a more rewarding season. Cycling is fun, but don't dedicate your life to cycling; make cycling a part of your life.

Assessing Strengths and Weaknesses

Top bike racers achieve success by focusing their preparation on the factors that could hamper their performance. We all tend to do what we enjoy on the bike—the parts that are easy—but to improve, we need to spend time on things that are hard.

To assess your strengths and weaknesses, answer the following questions:

- What is your primary cycling goal this season or year? If you have several goals, which is most important?
- What do you need to do to achieve the goal(s)? As noted in the introduction, six factors contribute significantly to athletic success. In which of these areas do you need to improve?
  - Structured planning
  - Effective training
  - Proper equipment
  - Sound nutrition
  - Cycling skills
  - Mental techniques

If you have some experience as an endurance athlete, list your successes over the past several years and the contributing factors. Also, list your less successful events and the weaknesses that held you back. With an understanding of your strengths and weaknesses, you are ready to develop objectives to work on to meet your goals.

When I start coaching a rider, I ask myself, "What kind of rider is this? What kind of training plan will be most effective?" I consider several points:

▶ The rider's goals. Does the rider aspire to (a) finish first in a 1,200-kilometer brevet or (b) enjoy the local fall century?

▶ Are the rider's goals (a) almost exclusively related to cycling or (b) inclusive of family and work priorities?

▶ Does the rider (a) give me years of training stats or (b) guess about how much he or she has ridden?

▶ Is the person (a) new to the sport or (b) wearing shorts shiny with age?

The more someone tends toward being the first type of rider, the more she or he will benefit from a structured program; the more the person tends to be the second type of rider, the more the rider needs a loose program. These days I'm the second type, although when I was training for the Race Across America (RAAM), I was definitely in the first camp.

To improve, every rider needs goals. What kind of training plan will most effectively address those goals? My goals are to go credit-card touring with a friend and to ride the Buff Classic century (mentioned in the preface) again.

To improve, each of us should honestly assess our weaknesses. I should lose my winter fat and build power so that I can carry some gear when touring and climb comfortably during the Buff Classic.

To improve, cyclists need either specific daily and weekly objectives or a set of training principles. I don't have a specific plan, but I apply these principles:

▶ *Limit intake.* I'm not counting calories, but I am pushing away from the table before seconds.

▶ *Exercise consistently.* To improve, I need to exercise at least four days a week; three days a week is sufficient only for maintenance.

▶ *Increase slowly.* I increase the hours I work out each week so that I get fitter, but I ramp up slowly so that I don't become injured or burned out.

▶ *Train specifically.* I need leg strength, so I hit the gym. I love riding and ride for fun, but I also focus on my weaknesses.

▶ *Make cookies.* Muffy Ritz, who finished second in the RAAM three times, says that training is like making chocolate chip cookies. You need the right ingredients, but you can mix them in any order. And it's better to underbake the cookies than to overdo it. Each week I get in my strength training, intensity work, stretching, and cycling without worrying about the exact order.

To improve, riders need specific, relevant feedback. I have training journals going back to 1974. Now I pay attention to four pieces of information:

1. My mood, indicated with a doodle of a smiling face, a flat face, or a frown. My coach, Michelle Grainger, taught me to do this.

2. The hours that I work out each day, rounded to the nearest quarter hour to keep the math simple.

3. The types of activities I do each day and where I went if I did something outdoors.

4. How my clothes fit. I take satisfaction if my pants don't feel as tight!

Both the structured plan for the first type of rider and the flexible program for the second type share certain key elements:

▶ Clear goals

▶ Honest self-assessment

▶ Focused training, either from specific objectives or consciously applied training principles

▶ Feedback to gauge progress and to adjust the approach when necessary

Developing Short-Term Objectives

To develop as a cyclist, you should set big-picture goals and assess your strengths and weaknesses. Depending on your goals, personality, and motivation, you may develop a structured plan and formal objectives or you may take a relaxed, flexible approach. Imagine you are in San Francisco and that your goal is to drive to New York City. You could get out a set of maps and plot your day-by-day itinerary, or you could just head east and consult the maps occasionally. Either approach will get you to New York. The first method is probably more efficient, but the second is more relaxed and perhaps more fun.

In general, achieving high-performance goals such as winning an event, earning an age-group placing, or setting a personal best requires a more detailed strategy with specific objectives. A rider attempting to complete an event for the first time may take a less structured approach. We'll look at both methods.

Are you the kind of rider who employs the latest cycling technology? Do you track and analyze your training data with training software and spreadsheets? If so, you will likely benefit from a more structured approach to planning.

At the end of a ride, do you know approximately how many hours you were gone but have to guess when your significant other asks how far you've ridden? Do you mentally compare how you felt during this weekend's ride versus last weekend's ride and use that comparison to think about next weekend's ride? If so, you'll enjoy a flexible approach to your training rather than a systematic plan.

For performance-oriented riders the smaller, short-term objectives pave the way toward reaching the ultimate goals. Yearlong objectives can be divided into monthly objectives, weekly targets, and a specific purpose for each training ride. Initially, setting objectives may not be easy—it takes hard work. If you develop set specific objectives you will

- train more productively,
- work more effectively on weaknesses, and
- be less nervous and more focused in events.

What are your general objectives this year? Can you develop specific objectives for different phases of your preparation? Your goal, general objectives, and specific objectives might look like those shown in figure 2.1.

If you take a quantitative approach you may want to assign specific targets. For example, during baseline conditioning build up general endurance to a 2.5-hour cross-training workout, and during event training work up to a 6-hour training ride.

If you take a structured approach to preparation, set one specific objective before a ride or workout. You'll improve most effectively if you work on just one ability at a

General objectives	Baseline Conditioning Phase	Event-Specific Training Phase	
	Specific objectives	Specific objectives	Goal: Complete moderately hilly century
#1 Increase climbing power	Increase single leg strength in gym	Increase functional leg strength climbing hills	
#2 Increase endurance	Increase general endurance through cross-training	Increase cycling-specific endurance	

FIGURE 2.1 **Relationships among goals, phases, and objectives.**

time, such as increasing your endurance by riding farther than before, improving your hill climbing, or practicing riding with others.

Keeping Training Records and Journals

Whether you take a structured or flexible approach to planning and training, feedback is key. All riders need records to assess progress and plan future training. What differs is the kind of information that each finds relevant.

Keep a training log or journal keyed to your goals to track training and progress. The journal essentially becomes a personalized training manual. Everyone responds differently to training, and because you can't foresee the future, even a plan designed just for you may be imperfect. Keeping workout records takes effort, but the information you collect will help you become a better cyclist.

Training logs vary from blank notebooks in which you record information to complex software that tracks various aspects of riding. You may need to experiment to find something that works well for you. Making the entries in a timely manner and sticking

Training Plan				
Day	Date	Workouts	Time (HH:MM)	Intensity
Mon	4/4	Core Strength	0:15	N/A
Tue	4/5	Brisk Ride 0:10 warm-up 0:10 mixed intensity hard recovery 0:10 cool-down	0:30	120-152 BPM 153-160 BPM <120 BPM <120 BPM
		Stretching	0:10	
Wed	4/6	Active recovery	0:20	<120 BPM
Thur	4/7	Tempo Ride	0:40	141-152 BPM
		Stretching	0:10	
Fri	4/8	Core Strength	0:15	N/A
Sat	4/9	Long Ride	1:30	120-140BPM
		Stretching	0:20	
Sun	4/10	Active recovery	0:30	<120 BPM
		Resistance training	0:20	
Totals			5:00	

FIGURE 2.2 **Sample training log.**

with it over time will provide you with accurate information. If you find a particular log or program too complicated, switch to an easier method—keeping a simple log is better than none at all.

Review your log periodically to assess your progress. You will learn a lot about yourself and be able to make sound decisions regarding your training. For example, you may find that after a hard day at work or a poor night's sleep, you may be okay the next day but feel fatigued two days later. If you have been tracking your mood and energy levels with a log, you can recognize this pattern. Then if you have a high-intensity workout planned, you may have the foresight to postpone that effort and go for an easy ride instead.

In your log record the data relevant to your particular needs. When in doubt, start with a simple format and add more information when it becomes useful. Data can be grouped into two categories: quantitative and qualitative. Ride distance, time, average speed, average heart rate, hours slept, weight, and so forth are quantitative. Your motivation in the morning, how you felt during the workout, quality of sleep, workout ratings, other stressors in life, and any similar factors are qualitative elements that affect your cycling. Figure 2.2 illustrates a sample week in the log of a cyclist who has completed a period of baseline training, which we outline chapter 3, and is just beginning targeted

Training Actuals					Weight 170
Total time (HH:MM)	Total mi (km)	Ave pulse	Ave speed	Total climbing	Comments
0:10					
0:30	8.0	145 155 115 110	16		Tough intervals, tight, extra stretching
0:15					
0:20		N/A			Ran errands
0:30 0:10	8.0	145	16		Busy day at work; felt a little tired; back tight
0:15					
1:45 0:20	26.3				Fun club ride; need to get friends to ride a century
0:45 0:20		N/A			Hiked with family and dog
	5:20	42.3			

FIGURE 2.2 *(continued)*

Safety: You're Invisible

When you are riding, a driver might pull out right in front of you, or another rider might cut in sharply after passing. What can you do? Assume that you are invisible when you are riding and take precautionary measures.

▶ Wear bright clothing and use other bright gear to enhance your visibility. John's hydration pack has an "H" in reflective tape on the back, and he has a reflective triangle hanging from his seat bag.

▶ Get a mirror and use it. The more difficult it is for drivers to see you, the more important it is that you look for them! Glancing back frequently allows you to anticipate and avoid problems. Mirrors are available that mount on the end of the handlebar, on the helmet, or on your glasses. We prefer a mirror on the helmet because it's easy to glance in it while also looking forward. To look in a mirror on the handlebar you have to look down and back up, and having to put a mirror on your glasses or put on your cycling glasses for every ride can be inconvenient. Whatever your preference, select a mirror that you can use easily and consistently.

▶ If a vehicle is turning, watch the front wheels. You will see them turn before the car moves.

▶ At an intersection where you meet a vehicle or another rider, try to look into the person's eyes. Give a friendly wave—the motion may attract the person's attention. By establishing eye contact, you become visible.

▶ Always signal before you move. Even if you don't see any cars a less visible cyclist or jogger may be approaching.

training for a century. The intensity ratings shown in this figure are based on the use of a heart rate monitor; we discuss other ways to rate your exertion in chapter 6. Several online logs are included in the resources section of this book.

Training involves pushing yourself harder than before. If you increase the workload enough, you'll adapt and become fitter. If you do too much, you may suffer from overtraining and slip back. Some research has suggested that the best predictor of overtraining is your mood, particularly your waking mood. Are you excited about getting on your bike, or do you want to crawl back into bed? You can track your mood with a sentence or two, rate it on a +3 to −3 scale, or draw cartoon-style faces. Whichever method you choose, you may notice patterns in your mood that affect your riding.

You're probably thinking, Can we work out yet? A fair question—all we've done so far is plan for the season: set goals, select events, assess limitations, and set up a training log. It's time to start moving! In chapter 3 we talk about activities to improve fitness and prepare to tackle the main training program.

Baseline Conditioning

Now that we've discussed choosing the right type of cycling event and setting goals, let's look at what to do leading up to the event-specific physical training. You'll be more successful in cycling if you follow a baseline conditioning program that fits your personal goals, experience level, and strengths and weaknesses. Developing your personal conditioning program will take time. While you're doing that we encourage you to do something aerobic three or four days a week. Depending on the season and your interests you could ride, jog, hike, snowshoe, cross-country ski, swim, or play a team sport.

In this chapter we introduce a fictitious character named Kyle. Kyle has followed the suggestions from chapter 2.

- He has thought about his cycling experience—in the summer he's comfortable with 50-mile (80 km) club rides in moderate terrain.
- He has set his goal—to complete the club century in September.
- He has defined his weaknesses—he is dropped when the road pitches up or when the pace quickens. He can roll through 50 miles on an energy bar and a couple of bottles of sports drink, but he wants to learn what to consume to sustain him for a ride twice as long.

Substitute your name for Kyle's and think about your goals, limitations, and preparation. Kyle's aspiration is to ride a century. In chapter 6 we describe sample 8- and 15-week programs for the century. What should Kyle do to prepare to start one of these programs? A couple of months before the start of the century training program, his conditioning should include

- aerobic workouts (outdoor rides, indoor rides, and cross-training) to build endurance,
- resistance training (either at home or in a gym) to increase strength, and
- flexibility exercises to stay loose and supple.

If riding a century or 200K is your goal too, you can use these activities to become a stronger rider, avoid injuries, and have a healthy and productive life off the bike.

Muscles and Energy Systems for Cycling

Our training methods and principles are based in part on the way muscles and energy systems pedal a bicycle. Muscles are composed of muscle fibers that are either fast twitch or slow twitch. These terms refer to how fast the muscle fibers are firing, not how fast the legs are moving. Genetics plays a large role in the composition of muscle fibers within the body; some people are born with a high proportion of fast-twitch fibers, whereas others have a high percentage of slow-twitch fibers. Slow-twitch muscle fibers are fatigue resistant, whereas fast-twitch muscle fibers are more powerful but tire easily.

Long-distance cyclists, runners, triathletes, and other endurance athletes rely predominantly on slow-twitch fibers, whereas track sprinters, football and basketball players, and other power athletes depend on fast-twitch fibers. If the goal is world-class performance, then the proportion of the different muscle fiber types is important. Otherwise, whatever their genetic allotment of fast- and slow-twitch fibers, people of all shapes and sizes can enjoyably participate in cycling events.

We've invited Kyle to dinner at a restaurant to discuss training. Our order includes buffalo wings and a grilled chicken breast entree. We use these items to explain muscle fibers to Kyle.

A chicken can walk around all day because its legs have primarily slow-twitch fibers, which use fat more efficiently as a fuel source, promoting greater endurance. Metabolizing fat requires more oxygen, so slow-twitch muscles have a rich blood supply. The buffalo wings appetizer—the drumstick of a chicken—contains a vast blood supply, so the meat is dark, or red. The chicken's leg muscles are not powerful but can keep firing for a long time, courtesy of slow-twitch fibers.

Chickens can fly only for short bursts, so the chicken breast is composed primarily of fast-twitch fibers to provide the power for liftoff. These muscles can act more powerfully, but they fatigue quickly. They have a smaller blood supply, so the breast meat is light. On the other hand, a migratory bird such as a duck or a goose can fly great distances. Its breast has primarily slow-twitch fibers, so the meat from its breast is dark.

Muscle fibers require energy, which comes from the ATP molecule (adenosine triphosphate). ATP is used in every muscular action, from washing dishes to sprinting up a steep hill. The body draws on three energy systems, each of which uses ATP:

1. *ATP-CP (or phosphagen) system.* This system uses the ATP stored inside the muscles, which is immediately available for energy needs. Stored ATP will last for 5 to 20 seconds of high-intensity effort. Sprints and other all-out efforts rely on this system.

2. *Lactic acid (or glycolytic) system.* As the ATP stores become depleted, carbohydrate (either glycogen stored in the muscle or glucose in the blood) is metabolized to form lactate, which helps regenerate ATP. Lactic acid is a by-product of this process. A hard hill climb, leading a fast group, and other hard efforts use this system.

3. *Aerobic (or oxidative) system.* At moderate efforts the body metabolizes carbohydrate (in the form of glycogen or glucose) and fat for energy, a process that requires a great deal of oxygen. The fat can be either stored body fat or fat from the digestive system. Metabolizing fat requires the presence of carbohydrate—fat burns in the flame of carbohydrate. Because of the large supply of fuel, this energy system predominantly fuels distance cyclists. Half centuries, centuries, brevets, and other distance events depend primarily on aerobic energy production.

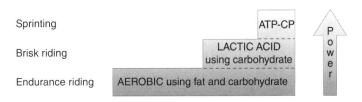

FIGURE 3.1   **The degree of involvement of each energy system depends on the amount and type of energy required.**

As illustrated in figure 3.1, you draw on each energy system as needed. Suppose you are on a long ride. As you cruise along a flat road at an easy pace, your body is deriving most of its energy aerobically. You reach a steep hill. Your heart rate and breathing increase as you tap into the lactic acid system for additional energy, while the aerobic system continues to contribute to the effort. At the top of the hill a snarling dog starts chasing you. Your ATP-CP system kicks in to help the other two systems as you sprint to get away. Once free, your heart rate lowers, the demands for the ATP-CP and lactic acid systems diminish, and your body again relies primarily on the aerobic system until the next hard effort.

Principles of Training

At dinner we ask Kyle if he has all the time in the world to prepare for his century. He laughs, "I've got a wife, two active kids, a job, and a yard." Fortunately, Kyle can draw on established principles to make training more effective and efficient. The following eight principles work together to provide a solid foundation and to reduce the possibility of overtraining and injuries:

1. *Training overload leads to adaptation.* When asked to do something it can't, the body adapts so it can handle the new workload. Of course, when asked to do too much, the body may rebel.

2. *Progressive overload.* You'll adapt best in training if you introduce the overloads progressively and follow a pattern of stress and recovery to allow improvement. Think of when you were in grade school. Each grade was more challenging than the previous one, and the breaks between sessions kept you fresh. To apply progressive overload to cycling, Kyle can increase his training volume by riding more or longer workouts. He can increase the intensity by adding some faster or hillier workouts. Along with increasing his volume and intensity, Kyle can work on skills such as cornering, climbing out of the saddle, and group riding.

3. *Individuality.* Kyle is unique and will respond in his own way to a training program. Cyclists have different mixes of fast- and slow-twitch muscles, various fitness levels, and diverse psychological needs. So, fitness programs should take into account their individual needs. The sample programs later in the book include options for tailoring training to individual circumstances.

4. *Specificity.* "Ride lots" is the advice that cycling legend Eddy Merckx gave for achieving success in cycling, and he is right—becoming a better rider requires spending time on the bike. The muscles and neurological system adapt specifically

to the demands placed on them. Kyle can play racquetball and basketball with friends, but he should cycle regularly so that his body becomes accustomed to riding.

5. *Isolation.* Although specificity is key, isolating a specific factor will produce greater fitness in that component. For example, Kyle can build greater leg strength with cycling-specific resistance exercises than he can by just riding a lot. But he'll need to translate this strength into on-the-bike power with intensity workouts later in the season.

6. *Variation.* To continue to improve, the body needs new challenges. This spring Kyle has been riding twice a week for 10 miles (15 km) on flat terrain, averaging 15 miles per hour (24 km/h), and riding a moderately hilly 25-miler (40 km) on the weekend. He's good at doing that! Kyle's goal is a century, so he needs to increase the length of his weekend rides. Because he wants to be a faster rider, after he's built his endurance he should challenge himself with a faster ride once or twice a week. One of Kyle's weaknesses is climbing, so later in the summer he should add hilly rides. Periodically changing the type of overload will help Kyle improve and prevent boredom.

7. *Reversibility.* The gains made in training are not permanent. To maintain fitness, Kyle must continue exercising. Taking days and an occasional week off for recovery are important, but if Kyle takes three or four months off after completing his first century, he will need to build back up from scratch to complete another. When training stops, the body realizes that it does not have to meet the demands of working out. Fitness declines to what is needed to meet the needs of daily activity.

8. *Recovery.* Recovery is an integral aspect of conditioning because most adaptations occur when the body is resting, not during the training sessions. Recovery is especially important after high-intensity workouts, because some microtrauma occurs in the muscles. To keep improving, the body needs time to rebuild. Kyle's work, school, family, and other obligations all draw on his physiological and psychological capacities. Toss in training stress and the overload may be too much at times. By including rest and recovery in his training program Kyle will keep progressing, rather than burning out.

Early Training

If you haven't been working out regularly, then your body needs at least two months of baseline conditioning to prepare it for an event-specific training program, whether it's an 8-week or a 15-week program. Kyle's century is six months away, and he's eager to start. He plans to do 8 weeks of preliminary conditioning and then the 15-week century training program in chapter 6.

The baseline conditioning program should include aerobic training to improve endurance, resistance workouts to increase muscle strength and muscle balance, and flexibility exercises to relieve soreness and improve comfort on the bike.

Aerobic Training

Aerobic base training provides the foundation for training, and the stronger the foundation the better it will support the demands of harder training. Think of building this aerobic base like building a house. If the foundation is not solid, the house will shift or crumble.

Aerobic base training builds the endurance necessary for a successful cycling season; it's like putting miles in the bank. In *Serious Cycling* the late Dr. Edmund Burke writes that endurance cycling is a must for all cyclists because it

- increases the potential of the muscles and liver to store carbohydrates,
- improves the respiratory system, bringing more oxygen to the circulatory system,
- boosts the pumping efficiency of the heart so it can pump more blood to the working muscles,
- helps the thermoregulatory system by increasing the blood flow to the skin,
- brings about increased neuromuscular efficiency of pedaling,
- enhances the capacity to burn fat during long rides, and
- improves the endurance of the cycling muscles by increasing the number of mitochondria, the subcellular structures in the muscles where aerobic energy is produced.

Adapted from Burke 2002.

Depending on where you live and what you enjoy, building the base could include riding outdoors, cross-training, and indoor sessions. Kyle lives in the North. Following the principle of specificity, Kyle should ride, either outdoors or on his trainer. But if weather is a problem or for variety, he also may cross-train.

Outdoor Riding

When conditions permit, Kyle spends time with friends on weekend club rides and with family members on appropriate rides. He meets new people and shares the joys of being on a bike.

The rides should be at moderate intensity and a conversational pace. If Kyle is not able to talk, preferably in complete sentences, he's riding too hard. Ultimately Kyle wants to ride faster and be a better climber. After he's built his aerobic base, he'll be fit enough to work on those areas.

Rather than just riding, he uses his base period to develop specific aspects of his cycling. On group outings he becomes more comfortable riding with others.

Kyle practices riding with a smooth pedal stroke of 80 to 90 revolutions per minute (RPM) in his middle gears. To improve his climbing and overall speed, he might be tempted to ride in higher gears, but if he rides too hard too early he risks an injury because he hasn't built his foundation yet. His muscles aren't ready for the effort.

Riding for long distances requires regular nutrition, and being able to eat and drink on the bike is more convenient than having to stop. Kyle practices eating and drinking regularly while riding safely. He uses this period to try different fuels and to get his digestive system used to processing food and drink while riding. One endurance rider we coached ate breakfast on her trainer every morning for this reason. We talk a lot more about fueling in chapter 4.

Kyle also uses this base period to test his gear. He has a new bike with clipless pedals, which handle differently. For safety's sake, he's getting used to the equipment. He also has a new heart rate monitor and cycling computer and uses these rides to become familiar with their operation and the information they provide. We discuss equipment in detail in chapter 5.

Besides riding with the club and his friends, Kyle explores new roads. His friends give him suggestions, and he uses maps, mapping software, and websites to find new routes. He plans rides to try a new restaurant, to visit a friend, and to enjoy a picnic with his family. Base training should be fun, not just grinding away at the distance.

Safety: Staying Upright!

Group riding is more fun than riding alone and can require less effort. When riding on the flats at 15 miles per hour (24 km/h) you are primarily overcoming aerodynamic drag, which increases exponentially as your speed increases. If you ride (draft) behind another rider you can cut your workload significantly. But it takes skill to ride with other riders without an accident. To stay upright in a group, observe these points:

Never allow your wheel to overlap the wheel of the cyclist in front of you.

▶ Pay attention to your riding even during a fun conversation. Don't become distracted.

▶ If you are the first rider in the group, call and point out hazards to your companions. Point at the hazard and call out, "Hole," "Gravel," or "Glass," as appropriate.

▶ For your own safety, particularly in a new group, don't assume that riders in front will call out all the obstacles. Ride slightly to the left or right of the rider ahead so you can watch the road ahead and spot potential problems.

▶ Learn to ride a straight line so you are not a risk to other riders. Always signal or call out before you move.

▶ Ride smoothly. Rather than speeding up and then hitting the brakes to stay with others, accelerate gently and when necessary soft-pedal or feather the brakes.

▶ Protect your front wheel; do not overlap your wheel with the rear wheel of a cyclist ahead of you. If you've overlapped wheels and the rider moves sideways, you'll both be in trouble.

These tips apply any time you ride with others. In chapter 6 we describe the more complex technique of riding in an organized pace line.

Weather permitting, Kyle could commute to work. He could drive to work once a week to take in clean work clothes and pick up the dirty laundry. He could take a short route to work to avoid getting too sweaty and take a longer way home. He should eat something before he starts his cycling commute and carry fruit and breakfast bars to eat at his desk. By commuting he could save on gas, help the environment, and have fun.

Recovery during base training is important. We've explained to Kyle that his body adapts while he is resting. Kyle rides outdoors when he can and does cross-training, stretching, and resistance training. We suggested that he keep track of the total time he spends each week on training and increase the volume by only about 5 to 10 percent each week. We recommended that he at least level off a bit every three or four weeks and, if he feels fatigued, cut back for a week. These planned recovery weeks in training will help Kyle recover both physically and mentally before the next increase in volume.

Cross-Training

Although getting on the bike is important, off-the-bike aerobic activities are fun and can contribute to greater overall health. Think about the mechanics of cycling. You are sitting on a saddle and bearing no weight. Your leg muscles are making circular motions using a specific set of muscles in a specific movement pattern. Your core muscles should be engaged to provide a platform against which your leg muscles push and pull. Your upper body controls the bike, but the demand on the muscles of the upper torso is limited. Cross-training involves muscles and movement patterns different from those used in cycling and will help you become fitter. In addition, doing other activities prevents boredom and offers the opportunity to work out with those who may not enjoy cycling.

When cycling, our legs move in one plane. When we skate ski, swim, in-line skate, or play team sports, we move our bodies in multiple directions. These activities use different muscles and stress cycling muscles and joints in new directions.

Finally, cross-training provides a mental and physical break from structured training. Kids don't outline their games or activities on a week-by-week basis—they play to have fun! One day they may play baseball, the next start a game of hide-and-seek, and the next go running in the woods. Kids aren't slaves to heart rate monitors, power meters, or average speed. Their objective is to enjoy themselves. We encourage Kyle to emulate kids when cross-training; heck, he should play with his kids! One day he can go for a run, on the next he can play sandlot football with the kids, and on the weekend he can take his family hiking or snowshoeing. All exercise is healthy.

Running   Running is a versatile, efficient form of cross-training. You can squeeze in a run with friends at lunch or a jog before dinner. Running develops eccentric strength, the muscle's ability to generate force while lengthening, and thus balances cycling. During the running stride, the muscles of the lower body decelerate the leg when ground contact occurs—an eccentric action. In cycling most of the power is from shortening of the muscles (during the first 180 degrees of the pedal stroke), which is concentric strength. Cycling involves little eccentric activity. Thus, cycling is less stressful on the joints and muscles and therefore is often prescribed for injured or deconditioned people.

If you decide to start running or to add volume, be conservative. Avoid pavement if possible; running on grass or trails reduces the chance of injuries. Listen to your body. If your body cannot handle the demands of running, plenty of other enjoyable activities are available.

Hiking   You can hike to enjoy the fresh air without the impacts of running, and you can share the experience with friends and family. While hiking, youngsters can learn the value of protecting our diverse yet vulnerable environment. Carrying a pack and using hiking poles can turn a simple walk into a calorie-burning adventure.

Cross-country skiing and snowshoeing   For many riders, snow may prevent consistent outdoor riding, but provide cross-country skiing and snowshoeing opportunities. Cross-country skiing engages both the upper and lower body and arguably produces the most conditioned endurance athletes. The traditional diagonal stride and the skating technique provide a low-impact, highly demanding, and enjoyable cardiovascular workout. Cycling legends Andy Hampsten, Greg LeMond, Ned Overend, and Davis Phinney all used cross-country skiing as an integral part of their base conditioning.

Cross-Training Works!

By Muffy Ritz

Cross-training means training in different ways to improve overall performance as well as combining exercises to work various parts of the body. We all know that a balanced diet is the best diet. The same can be said for a balanced training program that incorporates all the body's systems—endurance, strength, and power—by changing the routine and introducing different stressors on the body. This means getting off the bike and training in other ways.

I placed in the top five overall (men and women) in the RAAM in 1993, 1995, and 1997. In 1993 I set the long-standing women's RAAM rookie record, 9 days 16 hours 29 minutes for 2,910 miles (4,683 km) from Irvine, California, to Savannah, Georgia, or 12.49 miles per hour (20.1 km/h) including all sleep breaks and other off-the-bike time.

In every RAAM, my road bike training was minimal compared with most other riders. I trained for three to four months on the road bike to prepare. I would come into cycling season in April

Muffy Ritz competing in the American Birkebeiner, one of the longest ski races in North America.

© www.asiphoto.com

in great shape after having Nordic skied and raced all winter and hiked, mountain biked, and weight trained all fall. I was never sick of the bike when RAAM rolled around because I hadn't ridden enough to be tired of cycling!

I have also raced three times in the grueling Leadville 100 mountain bike race, placing as high as second woman one year. I owe my success to my overall fitness from combining Nordic skiing with mountain biking, road biking, strength training, and keeping fresh in every sport.

I've found that Nordic skiing is the best sport for overall conditioning. You cannot ski year-round (unless you live at the North Pole!), so you must cross-train in the off-season. Most Nordic skiers train on dry land by roller skiing, running, hiking, biking, and incorporating a strength program. Because of all their cross-training, they do extremely well in running races, road and mountain bike races, and running and hiking hill climbs. One of the top mountain bikers in the United States, Carl Swenson, was also an Olympic Nordic skier.

My advice for long-distance cyclists is to make sure your training program is balanced. Get on your feet and hike or run. Go to the gym and lift weights. Use your upper body in combination with your lower body. Get your core working and keep your back strong. Do your speed work and your long days and take at least one day off per week. You'll be fitter and have more fun!

As an alternative to skiing, if you can walk, you can snowshoe. An easy summer trail can become a strenuous cardiovascular workout. Poles help your balance and work the upper body.

Mountain biking   You can get out your mountain bike, put on low-pressure studded tires for traction and enjoy packed roads and trails. Some riders participate in multiday endurance events on MTBs that are equipped to ride in the snow.

Swimming   Swimming provides an excellent low-impact, total-body workout. Swimming improves the aerobic base, but you should complement it with activities that use the primary cycling muscles. Good swimming requires good technique to avoid overuse injuries to the shoulder. A new swimmer should invest in lessons with a swim coach.

Rowing   Like swimming, rowing provides a challenging full-body, low-impact workout. Many health clubs have rowing machines, which are less popular and therefore often more available than treadmills and elliptical machines. Rowing can expend as much energy as running, so people unable to run may benefit from an indoor rowing workout. Peter Lekisch, the first 60-year-old to finish RAAM, trained in the winter on his rowing machine and by cross-country skiing.

As with swimming, technique is important to avoid injury. About 80 percent of the force should come from the lower body and only 20 percent from the upper body. Concept 2 is an excellent resource on indoor rowing; see www.concept2.com.

In-line skating   Eric Heiden set 15 world records as a speed skater and won five gold medals in the Winter Olympics before he raced for the 7-11 professional cycling team. Besides strengthening the primary cycling muscles, skating develops the muscles on the inside and outside of the leg. In regions where snow for skate skiing is nonexistent or unpredictable, in-line skating can be a valuable and enjoyable form of cross-training. Protective gear is essential. Every year emergency rooms treat hundreds of injuries from in-line skating. Wear a helmet (a cycling one is fine), kneepads, elbow pads, and wrist guards.

Recreational team sports   Depending on the season, kids have fun playing basketball, volleyball, baseball, and other sports. We can follow their lead! Competing in team sports develops speed, power, agility, coordination, and balance, and can include family and noncycling friends. Playing team sports also reminds us of the value of teamwork. Bicycle racers compete on teams, and a club century is a team effort that involves rest stop volunteers, sag drivers, and fellow riders. Some cyclists choose to train alone, but riding with a group requires less effort because riders take turns breaking the wind. It's more fun, too.

Getting outside in the winter is a lot of fun and provides much-needed variety. The sometimes-barren landscape of autumn becomes a wonderland of possibilities to improve your fitness. But be careful to avoid frostnip and frostbite (see chapter 11).

Kyle is intrigued by the cross-training options we outlined for him. He wants to train for the century, but he also loves doing things with his family. He decides that one day each weekend they will hike, snowshoe, or shoot hoops indoors depending on the weather. What activities fit your goals and interests?

Indoor Riding

Despite the fun of cross-training, specificity is important. For overall fitness Kyle can cross-train, but he should ride his bike at least a couple of times each week. If he can't get outside on his bike, he can bring the bike inside, turn on some tunes, and pedal away! Indoor riding can be enjoyable and productive.

Training inside can be efficient if you keep the trainer set up. You can hop on the trainer as quickly as you can get ready for a run.

On the trainer you can work on specific skills, such as pedaling with a rounder stroke or learning to grab your water bottle without looking down or worrying about traffic or weather. Extra layers of cold-weather clothing can alter your positioning while riding outdoors, but riding on a trainer allows you to wear the clothing you plan to wear for a warm-weather event. If you are trying a new piece of equipment such as a shifting system or electronics, you can master it safely while riding indoors.

Many gyms offer group cycling classes that can provide a fun workout. Some instructors are avid riders and pattern the workouts like rides on roads or trails with simulated hills, headwinds, intervals, and sprints. Indoor classes are usually intense. Remember that your reason for taking a class is to improve cycling strength and endurance, not to ride to extreme fatigue. Backing off a little is fine.

Some class leaders may introduce moves on the bike that are potentially risky. Don't attempt anything on an indoor bike that you wouldn't do during an outdoor ride. Sustained out-of-the-saddle climbing, push-ups, and working with dumbbells or bands will not help you achieve your cycling goals, nor will getting off the bike to perform explosive movements.

You can organize indoor workouts with friends by setting up the bikes and trainers, putting on some music, and riding together. Riders of all abilities can train with one another because no one gets dropped! Take turns leading workouts or use one of the commercially available DVDs to coach you through specific rides.

Cooling and hydration during an indoor workout are important. Some riders set up the trainer in the cooler garage, and others mount a huge fan in front of the trainer. Be sure to drink enough, and take breaks if necessary. A towel under the bike and another on the handlebars will help protect the bike and the floor from sweat.

The key to effective indoor training is to have a plan for each session. The plan should include a 5 to 10 minute warm-up, main set, and at least a 5-minute cool-down. Here are several samples of main sets for after warming up:

- *Tempo workout.* This workout will boost average speed. Ride for 5 minutes at a pace that is a little harder than normal cruising effort and then pedal easily for 5 minutes to recover. Do two brisk efforts in the first couple of workouts, three brisk efforts the next couple of times, and then four.

- *Isolated leg workout.* This workout improves pedaling efficiency so you can go a bit faster with the same effort. Unclip the left foot and rest it on a box or stool. Select a moderate gear. Pedal for 1 minute with the right leg, then with both legs, and then 1 minute with the left leg. Concentrate on moving the pedal through the full circle. At the top of the stroke imagine kicking a soccer ball or pushing the knee toward the handlebars. At the 6 o'clock position point the toes down a bit and imagine scraping mud off the bottom of your shoe. Even pro racers don't pull the pedal up at the back of the stroke; rather, try to unweight the pedal so that the momentum from the first 180 degrees carries your foot back to the top.

- *Hill climb workout.* Simulate a series of 2- to 4-minute hill climbs with a couple of minutes of recovery after each. Vary your gearing and resistance to simulate different grades. You can make this more realistic by elevating the front wheel on a block of wood.

- *Pyramid workouts.* Pyramid workouts are a classic form of interval training. Ride 1 minute hard and 1 minute easy; then go 2 minutes hard and 2 minutes easy. Progress up to 4 or 5 minutes hard and then easy and then work your way back down to 1 minute.
- *Sport-themed workout.* Improvise! A football fan we know pedals hard every time the ball is in play and recovers during the huddles.

These are challenging workouts, so always warm up and cool down adequately to avoid injury.

Many types of indoor trainers are available. Trainers attach to the rear wheel of the bicycle and use a flywheel to provide resistance as you pedal. These units can use fans, magnets, or fluid as the source of resistance. Let's look at the advantages and disadvantages of different types of stationary trainers:

Fan trainers   Fan, or wind, trainers use a fan attached to the flywheel to provide resistance. Air is a great source of resistance. To double your speed, you'll need to exert eight times more power (for the same reason that riding in a group is easier). Wind trainers are generally the least expensive and simplest type of trainer. All you do is set your bike in the unit, tighten it onto your rear wheel, and go. To increase resistance, shift to higher gears and pedal faster. However, fan units can be loud when pedaling at high intensities. If you plan on midnight pedaling sessions while others are asleep, keep that in mind!

Magnetic trainers   These trainers use a series of magnets to provide resistance. Most have a control that you attach to your handlebars so you can increase or decrease resistance as you ride. Magnetic units are much quieter than fan trainers, but some riders feel that the resistance can be uneven around the pedal stroke. Strong riders can overpower the unit and run out of resistance.

Fluid trainers   Fluid trainers use a flywheel encased in fluid for resistance. Like a fan trainer, you use your gears and pedal faster or slower to modify resistance. They offer quiet operation and a smooth, road-like feel.

Virtual reality trainers   Virtual reality trainers offer a dynamic new world of training. How would you like to ride up L'Alpe d'Huez or practice the course of an event without leaving your home? Virtual trainers have a rear wheel stand and magnetic resistance unit, which is attached to a computer. The trainer usually comes with preprogrammed courses, includes integrated mapping and terrain software, and offers the ability to create courses. Because they are computer based, they record workout speed, cadence, heart rate, and power output. Some can scan the pedal stroke to compare the right and left legs in terms of pedaling efficiency. Virtual reality trainers let you race against previously recorded workouts, connect to other units for group rides, and even ride with others online. This fun comes with a substantial price tag, the major drawback of virtual reality trainers.

Studio bikes   You can purchase a studio bike like those used in indoor cycling classes. A dedicated studio bike is always ready to go, but it can't be adjusted to fit exactly the same as your road bike. Studio bikes generally have fixed, weighted flywheels like track or fixed-gear bikes. You can't coast, which helps you develop a smooth cadence at high RPM. They usually come with brake pads to tighten against the flywheel to increase resistance. If you try to use your legs to decelerate the flywheel, you may stress your knees, so use the brake pads and allow the wheel to lose momentum. Be sure to become comfortable with a studio bike before pushing the intensity.

Before you buy any type of trainer, try to test the specific model you're considering to see whether it fits your needs.

Rollers   Rollers have three cylindrical drums linked with a belt but nothing to stabilize the bike. You put the rear wheel on the two rear rollers, the front wheel on the front roller, and ride. Because nothing holds the bike in place, rollers are a great tool to learn balance and riding a straight line. To get started place the rollers in a doorway so your elbow will bump the doorjamb if the bike moves too far to the side. After you master them, rollers are superior for developing a smooth pedal stroke. Many riders use traditional trainers for intensity and rollers for technique. Be careful when watching TV, especially sports, while on rollers because moving your head to follow the action can cause you to ride off the side and crash!

Having been given the aerobic training suggestions included here during our evening out, Kyle calls us a few days later in a panic: "I enjoyed dinner and learned a lot about the principles of training. You gave me a smorgasbord of aerobic options—what am I supposed to chose? How much should I consume?"

We answer his question with a question: "Kyle, how big is your appetite? Realistically, about how many hours a week can you invest in baseline conditioning?"

He thinks for a moment and responds, "Well, I could probably put in three hours during the week, a few hours on the weekend doing something with the family, and ride an hour or two."

"Excellent!" we tell him. "To improve your aerobic fitness, you should do something aerobic four times a week, if possible. We'd like you to be on the bike at least twice a week, because specificity is important."

Kyle decides that each week he'll either ride the trainer before breakfast or jog for about 30 minutes during a couple of lunch hours so he's sure to get in his workouts before evenings at home. On the weekend he's excited about family fun one day, and on the other he'll go on a club ride, weather permitting, or ride the trainer.

We ask all our cyclists to determine how much time they can invest and to allocate that time according to the training guidelines and principles laid out in this chapter. We encourage you to do the same.

Resistance Training

Research has shown that resistance training can enhance muscular strength, power, and aerobic capacity. Along with building his aerobic base, Kyle should incorporate some high-volume resistance training for greater endurance as an essential step toward his goal of climbing better and riding faster.

Recent studies have suggested that core strength is important for all activities. During pedaling, the primary cycling muscles are exerting force along the upper leg, which works as a lever that has one end connected to the lower abdomen and pelvic core. If one end of the lever is anchored to a stable platform, then the quadriceps on the front of the thigh, the gluteus muscles on the hip, and the hamstrings on the rear of the leg exert more power. The stable platform is a strong abdominal core, the deeper muscles within the abdominal area and the connectors of the spine. The deeper core muscles run around the body to provide a solid platform. Resistance training for cycling includes specific exercises to work these deeper, stabilizing muscles. In contrast, sit-ups strengthen only the surface muscles on the front of the abdomen, which don't stabilize the core.

Kyle also wants to develop *specific* leg strength that can be turned into power on the bike. In addition to the following resistance exercises, he should do an isolated leg workout on the trainer once a week during baseline conditioning and then a brisk ride once a week during event-specific training as described in chapter 6. An avid racer who spends all winter on the leg press building up to 400 pounds (180 kg) may still be dropped by other riders in the spring if he or she hasn't turned those gains in general leg strength into on-the-bike power.

Any repetitive activity can result in muscle imbalances. Riders generally develop strong quadriceps but have weaker hamstrings and gluteus muscles, which may result in inefficient movement patterns. Further, the hamstrings and gluteus muscles are anchored by tendons that wrap around the knee and help to stabilize it, whereas the quadriceps are anchored along the side of the knee and don't stabilize it. Better muscle balance reduces the risk of knee injuries. You can increase strength and improve joint stability by doing specific exercises. This training concept is prehabilitation (opposite of rehabilitation), that is, recognizing the potential for injury and implementing specific exercises to prevent problems rather than trying to repair the damage afterward.

Bones, like muscles, become stronger if overloaded, and they atrophy if not used. Studies on pro racers doing the grand tours have shown osteopenia, or lower than normal bone mineral density, because of the lack of weight-bearing activity. Bicycling is non-weight bearing; tests with Olympic racers have shown that even when sprinting the force on the pedals and skeleton is less than full body weight. Gymnasts have the strongest bones, because the landings can exert impacts up to 10 times their body weight. For cyclists, occasional running or hiking will produce marginal benefits, but the overload isn't enough to stress the bones and produce significant improvement. Following the principle of increased intensity rather than increased repetitions, plyometrics or barbell squats (assuming no other physiological problems) will do more for bone strength. Resistance training also strengthens ligaments and tendons, improving overall joint integrity.

Many athletes enjoy the discipline of going to the gym, but Kyle groaned when we suggested joining a club. We said that instead he could get an inflatable exercise ball, a hard foam roller, and a few dumbbells.

If you prefer to exercise at home, buy your equipment from a fitness dealer, not a department store. Items from the latter often do not stand up to the rigors of repeated use. See the equipment section of the resources document at the back of this book for a list of online dealers.

Exercise balls can be used to perform exercises for core strength as well as muscular balance. See table 3.1 for information on selecting a ball of the right size.

Besides an exercise ball, Kyle buys a hard foam roller 3 feet (90 cm) long by 6 inches (15 cm) in diameter for doing core strength exercises and working on sore muscles.

Kyle is 5 feet, 8 inches (173 cm) tall and weighs 170 pounds (77 kg). We suggest that he visit a gym and do the recommended exercises with various dumbbells to see which sizes are appropriate for him. If you want to work out at home or use dumbbells in the

TABLE 3.1 **Exercise Balls**

Height	Ball diameter
Less than 5 ft (150 cm)	45 cm (17 in.)
5 ft–5 ft 6 in. (150–170 cm)	55 cm (21 in.)
5 ft 6 in.–6 ft 2 in. (170–190 cm)	65 cm (25 in.)
Over 6 ft 2 in. (190 cm)	75 cm (29 in.)

TABLE 3.2 **Dumbbell Weights**

Body weight	Dumbbell weight
Less than 140 lbs (64 kg)	5, 10, and 15 lbs (2, 4, and 6 kg)
140 lbs (64 kg) and up	10, 15 and 20 lbs (4, 6 and 8 kg)

gym, see table 3.2 for suggested dumbbell sizes. Adjustable weight dumbbells are also available, although more expensive.

For Kyle, we recommend at least seven exercises: two for core strength, one for overall leg strength, one for leg muscular balance, and three to tone his upper body. Doing these will take less than half an hour. If he has more time some days, he can add another leg strength exercise. We suggest exercises that work each leg (or arm) independently, because they promote better muscle balance. For each exercise we list the recommended sets and repetitions. Kyle is new to resistance training. We want his body to get accustomed to it without getting sore, so we suggested he do just one set the first week, two sets the second week, and then the full recommended number of sets starting the third week.

For a leg exercise we might specify three sets of 10 to 20 reps. Kyle will do the exercise 10 times with the left leg, rest for about 30 seconds, and then repeat 10 times with the right leg—that's one set. The first week he'll do one set of 10 reps, the second week two sets of 10 reps, and the third week three sets of 10 reps. He'll start with enough weight so that he's tired after one set of 10 reps. When he can do three sets of 10 reps, then over several weeks he'll build up until he can do three sets of 20 reps. Then he'll increase the weight, go back to three sets of 10 reps, and build up to three sets of 20 reps again.

To develop strength more effectively, Kyle performs each exercise slowly, taking about two counts to raise his body or other weight and about four counts to lower. He keeps his rests short—about 30 seconds between sets and just a minute between exercises.

Kyle decides to do the following program at home a couple of mornings before breakfast and then one weekend day. You can follow the same program or use the gym variations provided for some exercises.

Core Strength

Whether exercising at home or in the gym, start with the following roller bent-leg raise and exercise ball bridging. After you master the roller bent-leg raise, progress to the roller straight-leg raise and continue exercise ball bridging. These exercises all strengthen the core muscles: the transversus abdominis and internal obliques in the abdomen, and the multifidus in the back, as well as the gluteus muscles. A strong core improves power and reduces upper-body fatigue on the bike.

ROLLER BENT-LEG RAISE

Lie back on the roller with your spine along the roller and your head supported on the far end. Bend your knees about 90 degrees and place both feet flat on the floor. Place your hands on your belly so that only your feet are touching the floor. (You can rest hands lightly on the floor at first, if necessary, and place them on your belly as you develop better core strength and balance.) Tighten your core, using imagery if needed to guide your muscles: Imagine that you are pulling your belly button down to your anus, trying to make yourself thin enough to slip sideways through a crowd, or pulling on a tight pair of pants. Once your core muscles are engaged, lift your right foot a few inches off the floor, keeping your knee bent, then replace it, and repeat with the other leg. Do three sets of 10 to 20 repetitions. Lifting and replacing the left foot and then the right foot is one repetition.

ROLLER STRAIGHT-LEG RAISE

When you can do three sets of 20 reps of the roller bent-leg raise without your hands on the floor, then progress to the straight-leg raise. Lie on the roller with your head and back in the same starting position as for the bent-leg raise. Place your hands on your belly and keep your legs straight, with only your heels on the floor. (You can rest hands lightly on the floor at first, if necessary, and place them on your belly as you develop better core strength and balance.) Tighten your core, using imagery if needed to guide your muscles: Imagine that you are pulling your belly button down to your anus, trying to make yourself thin enough to slip sideways through a crowd, or pulling on a tight pair of pants. Once your core muscles are engaged, lift your right foot a few inches off the floor, keeping your leg straight, then replace it, and repeat with the other leg. Do three sets of 10 to 20 repetitions. Lifting and replacing the right foot and then the left foot is one repetition.

EXERCISE BALL BRIDGING

In addition to either the roller bent-leg raise or straight-leg raise do exercise ball bridging. Lie on your back with your hips on the floor, heels on the exercise ball, and your knees straight but not locked. Place your hands out to the side for balance. Balancing is easier with palms down and harder with palms up. Tighten your pelvic muscles to stabilize your core and to keep from moving sideways as you bridge. Push your heels into the exercise ball while raising your hips off the floor. Hold this position for three to five seconds and then come back to the floor. The key is keeping your core, hips, and gluteal muscles tight in the top position. Do three sets of 10 to 20 repetitions.

Leg Strength

The following leg strength exercises can be done at home. When time is short, do lunges and hamstring curls. When you have more time, add step-ups or wall squats (or both!).

LUNGES

This exercise strengthens the primary cycling muscles—the quadriceps, hamstrings, and gluteus muscles—as well as connective tissues. Standing with your feet together, step forward about 3 feet (1 meter) with your right foot. This action requires balance, so you may need to hold onto something initially. Then lower your left knee toward the floor until your right quadriceps is almost parallel with the floor. To avoid straining your right knee, keep your right knee over your ankle, not in front of your foot. From the lower position, step up and back to a standing position. Start with three sets of 10 to 20 reps with no weight in your hands. Stepping forward 10 times with your right foot and then 10 times with your left foot counts as one set. When you can do three sets of 20 reps without holding on to something for balance grab a couple of 5- or 10-pound (2 or 4 kg) dumbbells and start again with 10 reps.

HAMSTRING CURL WITH EXERCISE BALL

This exercise strengthens the hamstrings and gluteus muscles to balance the stronger quadriceps, and it works the core muscles as well. Lie on your back in the same starting position you used for bridging—heels on the exercise ball, knees straight, and hands out to your sides for balance. Tighten your core, bridge up by raising your hips and pushing your feet into the exercise ball. Then bend your knees and use your hamstring muscles to draw the exercise ball toward you. Finish one rep by pushing the ball away from your body while maintaining the bridging position. Keep your butt in the air for each full set of hamstring curls. Do three sets of 10 to 20 repetitions.

STEP-UP

Use a step or bench 12 to 16 inches (30 to 40 cm) high. Step up with your right leg and back down. Then step up with your left leg and back down. Keep your upper knee behind your toes and concentrate on having the top leg doing the work, not the bottom leg pushing off. Stepping up with both legs is one repetition. Start with three sets of 15 to 20 reps with no weight in your hands. When you can do three sets of 20 reps then use a pair of 5- or 10-pound (2 or 4 kg) dumbbells and start again with 15 reps.

WALL SQUAT WITH EXERCISE BALL

Stand with your exercise ball between your lower back and the wall (or use a soccer ball or basketball). Move your feet about 18 inches (45 cm) forward of your hips. Bend your knees and, using the ball as a roller, squat down as if you're sitting in a chair. You have positioned the ball and your feet correctly if, when you go down, your hip and knee joints form right angles (as if sitting in a chair). Squatting to this right-angle position and then standing back up is one repetition. Start with three sets of 15 to 20 reps with no weight in your hands. When you can do three sets of 20 reps then get a pair of dumbbells (totaling 20 to 40 pounds, or 8 to 16 kg) and start back at 15 reps.

If you prefer to go to a gym instead of exercising at home, start with the roller bent-leg raise or straight-leg raise and exercise ball bridging and lunges to warm up, and then do the following exercises:

MACHINE SINGLE-LEG HAMSTRING CURL

Depending on the machine either sit or lie down with your left ankle hooked over the bar. Draw the bar toward you using the hamstring muscles in your left leg. If lying down don't arch your back—use just your hamstrings. Lower the bar. Do 10 reps with one leg and then 10 with the other. Do three sets of 10 to 20 repetitions.

SINGLE-LEG PRESS ON MACHINE

This exercise can be done instead of step-ups or wall squats. Do not use the leg extension machine, which puts excess strain on the kneecap. Sit with your left knee at right angles (don't bend more) and the sole of your left foot resting on the plate. Using your hip and upper leg muscles, straighten your leg by pushing your foot away from you. Don't lock the knee. Return to flexed position. Do 15 reps with one leg and then 15 with the other. Do three sets of 15 to 20 reps.

Performing Olympic squats or using the squat machine also builds overall leg strength and develops stronger bones. But because of the risk of injury, these exercises are outside the scope of this book. Ask the instructor at your gym to teach you the proper technique.

Upper Body Strength

You can do the first three upper-body exercises at home.

EXERCISE BALL DUMBBELL MILITARY PRESS

This exercise builds overall upper-body strength and stability, which can reduce upper-body fatigue while riding. Sit on the ball and hold a 5- to 15-pound (2 to 6 kg) dumbbell in each hand with hands slightly wider than your shoulders, at the level of your ears, and with your palms facing up and forward. Tighten your core muscles so that you are stable during the exercise. Push the dumbbells smoothly toward the ceiling, being careful not to hyperextend your back, and then lower them back to the starting position. Do one set of 10 to 20 reps.

EXERCISE BALL DUMBBELL BENCH PRESS

This exercise strengthens the chest and arm muscles used to support the upper body and to control the bike. Sit on the ball with a 10- to 20-pound (4 to 8 kg) dumbbell in each hand. Then walk your feet away so that your torso forms a platform supported by your lower legs and your head and shoulders are on the ball. Raise the dumbbells straight up in the air above your chest. Lower the dumbbells to just outside your chest and push them back up while keeping the core muscles tight, so your body is flat like a table. Finish the set by tightening your abs and rolling back up to the starting position while holding the dumbbells against your belly. Do one set of 10 to 20 reps.

STANDING SINGLE-ARM ROWING

This exercise strengthens the muscles of the upper back and arms, which support the upper body, neck, and head in the cycling position. Stabilize your torso by placing your left forearm on a stable object so that your back is roughly parallel to the floor and your head is up and looking forward. Your right arm is hanging toward the floor and holding a 10- to 20-pound (4 to 8 kg) dumbbell. Raise the dumbbell straight up to your shoulder–chest joint. Keep your back and shoulder motionless; use only the muscles on your right upper back. Lower and repeat 10 times and then switch sides. Do one set of 10 to 20 reps.

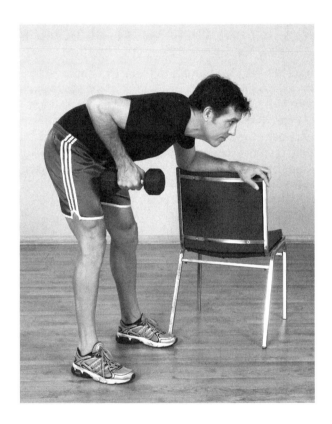

In the gym you could substitute some of the following exercises.

MILITARY PRESS

While seated on a bench or standing with feet shoulder-width apart, hold a 5- to 15-pound (2 to 6 kg) dumbbell in each hand, with hands slightly wider than your shoulders at the level of your ears and your palms facing up and forward. Push the dumbbells smoothly toward the ceiling, being careful not to hyperextend your back, and then lower them back to the starting position. (Alternatively, perform the same motion using a shoulder press machine; this version builds shoulder strength but not shoulder balance and control.) Do one set of 10 to 20 reps.

DUMBBELL OR BARBELL BENCH PRESS

This exercise can be done instead of the exercise ball dumbbell bench press, although it doesn't work the core. If you use dumbbells rather than a barbell, you'll develop more balance and control. Lie on the bench with your feet on the floor for balance. Use a pair of 10- to 20-pound (4 to 8 kg) dumbbells (or equivalent barbell). Lower them to just outside your chest and push them back up. Keep your back flat against the bench. You can also do this exercise on a chest press machine, which develops the chest muscles but not the stabilizing and balancing muscles. Do one set of 10 to 20 repetitions. On one day a week you could substitute the incline dumbbell press with less weight.

SEATED ROWING MACHINE

This exercise is an alternative to the exercise ball single-arm rowing. Sit with your chest braced against the pad, your legs straight, and your knees slightly flexed. Keep your back and shoulders flat. Pull the handles toward you. Your torso should be motionless. Use only your shoulder muscles, not your lower back, to pull the weight. Return and repeat. Do one set of 10 to 20 reps.

LAT PULL-DOWN

This exercise is a good addition to either single-arm or seated rowing. Stand and grasp the bar with a wide grip. Your hands should be about a foot (30 cm) on either side of your shoulders. Then sit down with your back arched slightly. Pull the bar down in front of your chin to your chest, not behind your neck. Keep your chest high and back and shoulders motionless; use only the muscles of your upper back. Do one set of 10 to 20 reps.

You may find it convenient to work out at home. Because the home exercises use body weight or free weights as resistance, they require more balance and control and are superior for developing core strength as well as joint stability.

If you prefer to go to a gym or health club, that's great! You can even mix up your workouts using the dumbbells and the exercise ball one day and the machines the next time. Gyms also have a variety of equipment and classes, so you can do both aerobic and strength workouts.

Whether you work out at home or in the gym, we encourage you to fit in resistance training two or three days a week. Some cyclists are concerned that resistance training will add bulk to their muscles, but these exercises use high repetitions and low resistance, which builds muscle endurance, not muscle mass.

For more information, see the training section of the resources document at the back of the book.

Plyometric Training

After you have been doing leg exercises for at least a month, you may add some plyometric exercises to your regimen. The jumping and landing in plyometrics causes muscles to stretch and contract rapidly, which can increase leg power and help develop stronger bones. Start and progress slowly to avoid injury. With plyometrics, a little goes a long way.

Start by jumping rope, which will get you accustomed to the dynamic forces involved. Jumping rope is relatively easy to learn and can be done almost anywhere.

After you are comfortable with jumping rope, try the squat jump. Squat so your knees are bent about 90 degrees and jump up as high as you can. Concentrate on landing softly to minimize stress to your joints and allow your muscles to act as shock absorbers. Immediately repeat the jump. Start with 4 to 6 repetitions and work up to 8 to 10 repetitions.

If you want to learn more plyometric exercises, find a strength and conditioning specialist who is familiar with the techniques and safety precautions.

Flexibility Training

Because Kyle has been broadening his conditioning program with resistance exercises and cross-training, he feels some tightness in his muscles. As his rides become longer, Kyle also feels stiff at times. He has a desk job, and over the long hours in front of his computer he tightens up. Stretching and self-massage before, during, or after working out can address these issues. Stretching doesn't have to be time consuming. Kyle decides to stretch and do core strength exercises most evenings while watching TV with his family. He also stretches for five minutes when he takes a break in a ride.

Static Stretching

Static stretching is holding a constant stretch for 15 to 30 seconds to enhance range of motion. The muscles and connective tissues respond better when the body is warm, so warm up before stretching or stretch after a workout. Follow the guidelines provided in table 3.3.

The following stretches target the quadriceps, hamstrings, calves, lower back, neck, and chest and can be done at rest stops as well as at home.

TABLE 3.3 **Guidelines for Static Stretching**

• Stretch to the point of mild muscle discomfort, not pain. Pain will cause the muscles to tighten rather than relax.
• Breathe slowly and with each exhalation, stretch just a little farther.
• Hold each stretch for 15 to 30 seconds.
• Do not bounce.
• Try to relax into the stretch. Some people unconsciously tighten the muscles that they are trying to stretch.

CAT

On hands and knees, slowly arch your back up and roll your head forward and chin down toward your chest. Then starting with your pelvis, slowly reverse the movement, pushing your abdomen toward the floor and finally rolling your head up and back. Repeat three times. On the bike, if you coast with the pedals at 3 and 9 o'clock and get out of the saddle, you can also roll your back—but keep looking down the road!

QUADRICEPS

Lie on your right side. Bend your left leg until you can hold your left ankle with your left hand. If you can't reach your ankle, loop a towel or exercise strap or band around your ankle and grab that. Keep your pelvis forward and gently pull up until you feel your quad stretch. Repeat with the other leg.

HAMSTRINGS

Lie on your back with your left knee bent if you are new to stretching or with your left leg straight if you are pretty flexible. Loop a strap, exercise band, or towel under the arch of your right foot. Keeping your right leg straight, raise it into the air until you feel a gentle stretch in your right hamstrings. Repeat with the other leg.

OVERHEAD

Interweave your fingers, reach overhead, and push your palms toward the sky. Stretch and imagine your spine elongating.

NECK

Stand with your head rolled forward and your chin on your chest. Put your hands on the back of your head and allow the weight of your arms to pull your head down and stretch your neck. Release and straighten your neck. Then roll your head toward your right shoulder. Wrap your right arm over top of your head and allow the weight of your arm to pull your head gently to the right and stretch your neck. To increase the stretch push your left palm toward the floor. Repeat for the left side. Never stretch your neck backward, which may strain vertebrae.

CHEST

Stand with your right elbow at shoulder height and right forearm and hand resting on a wall or door jamb. Rotate your torso slowly to the left until you feel a gentle stretch in your chest. Repeat for the left side.

The following stretches are best done at home or at the gym:

BACK ROTATION

Lie on your back with your right leg extended along the floor. Bend your left leg and place your left foot on the floor on the right side of your right knee. Extend your left arm and place your left hand on the floor behind you. Place your right hand on your left knee and pull your left knee toward the floor on the right, rotating your trunk to the right. Repeat to the right side.

HIP FLEXOR

Hook an exercise band or towel over your left foot, bend your left knee and lie on your stomach with your left knee on the floor and right leg straight. Pull on the band lifting your left knee off the floor until you feel a gentle stretch. Repeat with the other leg.

ACHILLES TENDON AND GASTROCNEMIUS

Stand with your right foot near a wall and your right knee bent, and with your left leg straight and your left foot several feet (a meter or so) away from the wall. Place your hands on the wall and slowly lean toward the wall to stretch the left Achilles tendon and gastrocnemius muscle of the calf. Repeat with the right leg.

SOLEUS

Stand with your right foot near a wall and your right knee bent, and with your left leg bent about 20 degrees at the knee and your left foot several feet (a meter or so) away from the wall. With your hands on the wall, slowly lean toward the wall to stretch the left soleus muscle. Repeat with the right leg.

GROIN

Sit with your knees bent about 90 degrees and your feet flat on the floor. Lower each knee out to the side, drawing the soles of your feet together. To increase the stretch either lean forward or use your butt muscles to try to pull your knees down closer to the floor.

PIRIFORMIS AND GLUTEUS MEDIUS

Lie on your back on the floor with the right knee bent and your right foot flat on floor. Bend the left knee out to the side and rest the left ankle on the right knee. Curl up, grab the back of the right thigh, and pull it gently toward your chest. If you can't reach behind your right thigh, hold a towel or band looped behind your thigh. You'll feel a gentle stretch in the left gluteus muscle. Reverse position to stretch the right gluteus muscle.

Dynamic Stretching

Dynamic stretching uses specific movements to prepare the muscles and nervous system for activity. Dynamic stretching should be done *before* an activity and thus differs from static stretching. Some recent studies suggest that performing static stretches before an activity may reduce power because the stretches have a numbing effect on the nervous system. In contrast, dynamic flexibility exercises take the muscles and joints through a full range of motion (ROM) that primes the neuromuscular system for subsequent activity. Follow the guidelines provided in table 3.4.

TABLE 3.4 Guidelines for Dynamic Stretching

• Perform 5 to 10 repetitions of each exercise.
• Progressively increase ROM with each repetition.
• Move smoothly without bouncing.
• Don't sacrifice form for additional ROM.

HIP ROLLS

Start by lying face up on the floor with your arms extended out to your sides (to act as stabilizers), your knees bent, and your feet flat on the floor. Then rock your bent legs slowly side to side, keeping your shoulders, torso, and feet in contact with the floor for several repetitions. You should feel this stretch in your lower back and lateral core muscles.

INCHWORM

Starting from a push-up position, walk your feet forward using short ankle steps toward your hands, keeping your legs straight (envision a moving inchworm). When you can no longer keep your legs straight (your ROM will improve as you work on this movement), pause for a second or two, and then walk your hands back out to the push-up position. Repeat several times. You should feel this progressively stretch your hamstrings as you walk your feet toward your hands. You also get a core workout because you are in the push-up position at the start.

LUNGE WALK

This exercise is virtually identical to the lunge strengthening exercise. From a standing position, take a big step forward with your right leg, keeping your foot pointing directly ahead. Then drop down into a lunge, keeping your right knee directly over your ankle until your right thigh is almost parallel with the floor. Rather than stepping back to a standing position, push off the floor and lunge forward with your left foot. Repeat for 5 to 10 steps forward with each leg. This stretch targets the entire leg and hip musculature and prepares the body both for riding and for lower-leg strength exercises.

SUMO SQUAT

From a standing position, bend at your waist and grab your big toes. Keeping your arms straight and inside your knees, drop your hips down as far as comfortable between your ankles and lift your chest (imagine what a sumo wrestler looks like). Then stand back up and repeat several times.

We suggest you try these dynamic stretches. Those familiar with yoga will find that the sun salutation is a great form of dynamic stretching.

We encourage you to find time to stretch most days. You can stretch while watching TV, after a ride while listening to music, or anywhere you can fit it in. Consistently doing just a few minutes of flexibility work will help you feel better and perform at your best.

Yoga and Pilates classes can add an enjoyable social element to your flexibility exercises. Find a class suitable for your level. If you are new to yoga or Pilates, start with a beginner's class. If you have any health or orthopedic concerns, let the instructor know beforehand. No classes in your area? Get a video to coach you through some sessions.

Self-Massage

Kyle knows that the pros get a massage after every stage and that massage helps recovery, but he has neither time nor money for regular massage. He can use the same foam roller for self-massage that he uses for core exercises. Imagine that Kyle's muscles are dough and the foam roller is a rolling pin. When he has a particularly sore spot Kyle uses the roller to roll out those muscles. On the weekends when he has time, he uses the foam roller as part of his recovery program, even if he's not hurting,

We recommend this general technique:

- Practice good posture and engage your core muscles.
- Lie or sit with the foam roller under the tender spot and most of your body weight on the roller.
- Wait about a minute and then roll back and forth along the tender spot.
- If you feel any pain in a particular area, rest that area on the roller for a minute to stimulate the muscle to relax further.
- Experiment over several sessions to find the exact position that works best. By varying your body position, you can control the amount of body weight you put on the affected body part and roller.

As needed, Kyle uses this general technique with the pillar of pain, as it's affectionately known by many athletes. These specific roller massages target particular muscle groups:

ILIOTIBIAL BAND (ITB)

The ITB runs along the outside of the thigh from the top of the hipbone to slightly below the knee. To massage the right ITB, lie with your right leg straight and the right hip on the roller. Roll back and forth from just below your hip joint to your knee. You can vary the pressure by keeping the lower part of the leg on which you are working off the floor, by keeping your other leg off the floor, or by supporting your upper-body weight with just your hands.

HAMSTRINGS

Lie with your hamstrings on the roll and your feet crossed to increase leverage. Roll forward and back on both hamstrings. To emphasize one leg individually, cross your legs and roll on each leg independently.

QUADRICEPS

Balance on your elbows, face down, with your quadriceps on the foam roller. Roll up and down, massaging both quadriceps. You can also work one of your quadriceps by shifting your weight to one side.

LOWER BACK

Assume a sit-up or a crunch position with the foam roller under your lower back and at 90 degrees to your spine. Extend your legs and place your hands on the floor behind you for balance. Resting on the roller, roll up and down it, keeping good posture and maintaining a tight core. To add pressure, keep your hands folded across your chest or behind your head if your neck is sensitive (you can also support your neck with a towel).

PIRIFORMIS AND GLUTEUS MEDIUS

This technique takes some practice. The piriformis muscle is located deep within the gluteus region of the hip. To massage the right piriformis sit with the back of the right hip on the foam roller. Then cross the ankle of your opposite leg over the right knee. As with the other movements, roll back and forth on the back of your right hip to work the gluteus and piriformis muscle.

UPPER BACK

Lie with the foam roll under your upper back beneath your shoulder blades at a right angle to your spine. Use your hands to support your head. Bend your knees and place your feet flat on the floor to support part of your body weight. Roll up and back to target the upper back muscles.

Program Integration

In the beginning of the chapter, we described Kyle's goals: boosting his average speed, climbing better, and completing a century. You have your own goals. By following a simple baseline conditioning strategy, you can accomplish several things:

- Lay your aerobic base with riding (both indoor and outdoor) and cross-training.
- Increase your strength through a resistance-training program to develop more power and reduce the risk of injuries.
- Improve your flexibility to enhance your comfort on the bike, which will lead to greater endurance and efficiency.

What should you do during baseline conditioning? Remember the concept of individuality discussed earlier? We've described Kyle's program, but what works for him may or may not work for you. Think about what you'd like to include in your baseline strategy. At the start, your plan might look something like this:

Monday	20 minutes of stretching and core strength exercises while watching TV
Tuesday	30 minutes on the trainer and 30 minutes of lower and upper body resistance training
Wednesday	20 minutes of stretching and core exercises
Thursday	Racquetball with friends and 30 minutes of lower and upper body resistance training
Friday	A yoga class or 20 minutes of stretching and core exercises
Saturday	A 60-minute club ride and 20 minutes of stretching and core exercises after riding
Sunday	Outdoor fun with the family: hiking, snowshoeing, riding, or maybe a game of catch with the kids; lower-body resistance training if time permits

Depending on your mix of activities, your time commitment will vary, but you shouldn't need much more than seven hours. Keeping a simple training log will help you track progress and keep you motivated. About 50 percent of people quit working out within the first three months. In your log you can outline your baseline program, the planned activities for each week, and your actual accomplishments.

Training progresses to longer workouts toward the end of the baseline conditioning. Yours might look like this:

Monday	Day off
Tuesday	A 45-minute ride and 20 minutes of stretching and core exercises
Wednesday	30 minutes of resistance training and 20 minutes of stretching and core exercises
Thursday	Basketball with friends
Friday	A 45-minute easy ride and 20 minutes of stretching and core exercises
Saturday	A 2-hour group ride and 20 minutes of stretching and core exercises
Sunday:	More outdoor fun with the family and 30 minutes of resistance training

This set of activities will take only about an hour more per week than what you did at the start of baseline conditioning.

You can incorporate your training activities in a variety of ways. Experiment to find something that works for you. A baseline conditioning program with aerobic, resistance, and flexibility training will pave the way toward a successful and enjoyable cycling season. These workouts and exercises will also help you become a healthier person overall. Enjoy your training—meet other riders, participate in various activities, and above all have fun! In the next chapter we'll look at nutrition to support the demands of your training and allow you to perform at your best.

CHAPTER 4

Fueling the Distance Cyclist

What do a race car, fighter jet, speedboat, and long-distance bicycle have in common? Besides the heart-pounding thrill of operating them, they all rely on finely tuned engines that need adequate supplies of fuel to perform. We're not just talking about optimal levels of performance—an F-22 fighter jet with no fuel in its tanks is just a $340 million heap of metal and electronics sitting helplessly on the tarmac. It may look impressive, but without fuel it is useless. For long-distance cyclists, no matter how much we spend on lightweight, aerodynamic equipment, without fuel to power our engines, our performance will be severely limited.

Kyle knows that one of his limitations on the bike is nutrition. He does club rides with just an energy bar and a couple of bottles of a sports drink. He understands that he needs to eat more, but how much more and what should he eat? Kyle currently weighs 170 pounds (77 kg) and averages 15 miles per hour (24 km/h) on level ground on his training rides. He burns about 750 calories per hour on his bike, not counting hills, headwinds, or other conditions, which affect his caloric expenditure. If he averages that speed during his century, he'll burn over 5,000 calories during his almost seven hours of riding. To train effectively, Kyle needs to replenish the calories spent on training and day-to-day activities.

In this chapter we start with the basics of a well-rounded nutrition plan to support both performance on the bike and everyday health and provide options to suit individual needs and preferences. Eating for athletic performance is not very different from eating for a healthy lifestyle, but active people need more fuel than those who are sedentary. We also talk about eating and drinking on training rides to maintain energy. Finally, we suggest shopping and eating-out options to help you make healthy choices. Good nutrition does not have to be complex or expensive. By following some simple guidelines, you can make the best choices to stay strong and healthy both on and off the bike.

We do not tell you specifically what or how to eat. Many eating styles can provide adequate nutrition. Different cultures, religions, and personal beliefs make it impossible to outline specific recommendations for everyone. The training concept of individuality applies to nutrition as well. Use the material that we provide to outline a plan that will work for you.

General Nutrition Guidelines

Whatever your approach to eating, nutrition should

- help you perform at your best,
- promote optimal body composition, and
- support good health and reduce the chances of life-threatening and chronic diseases such as heart disease, cancer, and diabetes.

Where should you start? Keeping a simple food journal for a week or so of what and when you eat will give you a good idea of your current eating habits. Reviewing this record will help you identify any issues that you may want to address. For example, do you eat a good breakfast every day or are you famished by midmorning? Do you go for hours without eating? If so, drastic changes in your blood sugar can occur, which will affect your energy level and performance. If you haven't eaten regularly and healthfully you may feel sluggish when you ride.

By looking at your nutrition and training logs side by side, you can obtain useful information that will help your riding. You can assess whether you are getting enough daily calories to support your volume of training and determine whether you are recovering adequately after demanding workouts or need to increase your intake of postride calories. Like a training log, a food journal does not have to be complex. Simply write down what you are eating and drinking throughout the day for a week and calculate the number of calories per item. By analyzing your total consumption, mix of nutrients, and eating patterns, you can get a good idea of what, if anything, you need to change. See table 4.1 for an example of a simple food journal page.

When you have some data, you can use one of the several food pyramids to evaluate the adequacy of your diet. Food pyramids provide a graphical representation of the proportions of basic food groups: grains, vegetables, fruits, lean meat and beans, milk, and oils. The Mediterranean diet pyramid, the Swiss food pyramid, and MyPyramid each provide models of healthy eating.

Mediterranean Diet Pyramid

The Mediterranean diet pyramid represents 50 years of nutrition research in an area of the world that has one of the lowest rates of chronic diseases and some of the highest adult life expectancies. This diet includes several notable features:

- An abundance of food from plant sources including fruits and vegetables, potatoes, breads and grains, beans, nuts, and seeds
- Minimal processed foods, emphasizing locally grown foods
- Olive oil as the principal fat
- Daily consumption of low to moderate amounts of cheese and yogurt
- Modest amounts of fish and poultry as the primary protein
- Fresh fruit as the typical dessert
- Red meat a few times per month
- Restrained consumption of red wine
- Regular physical activity at a level that promotes a healthy weight, fitness, and well-being

See the Mediterranean diet pyramid at www.oldwayspt.org/mediterranean-diet-pyramid.

TABLE 4.1 **Food Journal**

Food or drink	Amount consumed	Calories
Breakfast		
Oatmeal	1 cup	300
Raisins	½ cup	260
Brown sugar	1 tbsp	15
Yogurt non-fat	6 oz	75
Coffee, black	2 cups	5
Snack		
Banana	1 medium	105
Lunch		
Chicken breast	4 oz	190
Brown rice	½ cups	110
Steamed broccoli	½ cups	20
Snack		
Almonds	¼ cup	155
Dinner		
Salmon filet	4 oz	245
Spinach salad	1 ½ cups	15
Couscous	1 cup	175
Red wine	4 oz	100
Snack		
Air popped popcorn	3 cups	90
	Total	1,860

Swiss Food Pyramid

The Swiss Society for Nutrition developed the Swiss food pyramid to cover the daily energy and nutrition needs for healthy adults exercising five hours or more per week. In addition, it provides guidelines on how to adjust your nutrient intake for each additional hour of daily exercise. The Swiss food pyramid recommends the following each day:

- Drinking one to two liters of fluid per day, preferably unsweetened
- Eating several servings of fruits and vegetables one of which should be raw
- Eating several servings of grain products (two of which are whole grain, if possible) and legumes
- Alternate eating one serving of meat, fish, eggs, cheese, or plant proteins each day, as well as three servings of milk or dairy products, preferably low-fat varieties
- Using one serving a day of plant-based oils for cold dishes, one portion for cooking, and if needed, one portion of butter or spread

- Consuming sweets, salty snacks, sweetened drinks, and alcoholic beverages in moderation and as part of a meal, noting that alcoholic beverages or low-sodium drinks may delay recovery after exercise

For athletes the Swiss food pyramid recommends the following increases in daily intake for each additional hour of exercise beyond five hours per week:

- 400 to 800 ml of sports drink
- 1 serving of grain products
- 1/2 serving of oils

See the Swiss food pyramid at www.sge-ssn.ch/fileadmin/pdf/100-ernaehrungsthemen/10-gesundes_essen_trinken/Food_Pyramid.pdf

MyPyramid

The U.S. Department of Agriculture's MyPyramid incorporates the latest nutrition research and like the Swiss food pyramid provides adjustments for the physically active. MyPramid recommends each day:

- Eating several servings of grains, at least half of which are whole grain
- Eating several servings of vegetables including more dark green and orange vegetables
- Eating a variety of fruit and limiting the amount of fruit juices for caloric reasons
- Eating several servings of low-fat or fat-free dairy products
- Going lean on protein with more fish, beans, nuts, and seeds
- Using oils from vegetables and nuts and limiting solid fats like butter and lard

See My Pyramid at http://foodpyramid.com/wp-content/uploads/2009/09/MyPyramid2.jpg

Daily Caloric Expenditure

You can use these pyramids and guidelines to start evaluating the composition of your diet. The next step is to estimate the number of daily calories that you need. To do that you first need to figure out your basal metabolic rate (BMR). The BMR represents the number of calories needed to support your bodily functions only; it does not take into account any activity at all. Kyle weighs 170 pounds (77 kg). To estimate his BMR, he multiplies his weight by 10; his BMR is 1,700 calories per day. (Multiply by 22 if you're using your weight in kilograms.) This figure is just an estimate because without laboratory equipment it is impossible to be exact.

Then add the additional calories needed to support daily living activities:

Add 30 to 40 percent of BMR if lightly active (mostly sitting, desk work).

Add 50 percent of BMR if moderately active (some walking or standing, household chores, moving often).

Add 60 to 70 percent of BMR if active (moving a lot, performing physical labor, and so on).

Because Kyle spends most of his day sitting at his desk at work, he estimates that his daily activities require 35 percent multiplied by 1,700, or about 600 calories per day.

The next step is to add the calories to support training. To keep it simple, we assume that Kyle does all his training on the bike. You can use table 4.2 to determine the approximate number of calories burned while cycling. If you're also cross-training, your calorie expenditure will vary.

If Kyle rides for an hour at 15 miles per hour (24 km/h), he uses 4.5 calories multiplied by 170 pounds, or about 750 calories per hour. At the end of his baseline conditioning and start of his specific century training, Kyle is working out eight hours per week. He needs to add about 850 daily calories to fuel his exercise $[(8/7) \times 750]$. Kyle has the following daily fuel requirement:

Basal metabolism	1,700
Activities of daily living	600
Working out	850
Total calories	3,150

TABLE 4.2 Approximate Number of Calories Needed While Riding

Speed	Description	Cal × lb⁻¹ × h⁻¹	Cal × kg⁻¹ × h⁻¹
11 mph (18 km/h)	Leisure, slow, light effort	2.5	6
13 mph (21 km/h)	Leisure, moderate effort	3.5	8
15 mph (24 km/h)	Racing or leisure, fast vigorous effort	4.5	10
16–19 mph (26–31 km/h)	Racing, not drafting, fast	5.5	12
>19 mph (31 km/h)	Racing, drafting, very fast	5.5	12
>20 mph (32 km/h)	Racing, not drafting, very fast	7.5	16

Reprinted, by permission, from N. Clark and J. Hegmann, 2005, *The cyclists food guide* (West Newton, MA: Sport Nutrition) 138.

Kyle is concerned about his weight, which affects his climbing, one of his weaknesses. If you want to lose weight to improve your performance, you shouldn't cut your calories too much while training. Because you will be working hard, your body needs sufficient calories (think fuel). Consuming too few calories will cause your performance to suffer and increase the chances of fatigue and illness. As a rule, don't cut daily calories by more than 20 percent. This means that Kyle could restrict his calories by up to 600 calories per day.

When attempting to lose weight, weigh yourself regularly to ensure that you are not chronically dehydrating your body or tapping into lean muscle tissue for energy. Aim to lose about .5 to 1 pound (.25 to .5 kg) per week. To lose 1 pound per week, you would need to consume 3,500 calories less than you burn over the course of the week, or 500 less per day.

Use figure 4.1 to get an idea of how many calories you need:

FIGURE 4.1 DAILY CALORIE WORKSHEET

1. Estimate your basal metabolic rate using your body weight:

body weight (pounds) × 10 or body weight (kilograms) × 22 _____

2. Add calories for activities of daily living:

30 to 40% of BMR if lightly active

50% of BMR if moderately active

60 to 70% of BMR if very active _____

3. Add calories for riding:

from table 4.2 _____

4. Approximate calories required for the day:

add all three numbers _____

Total calories

When riding a century or more, you may be mostly resting when not on the bike. If so use 10-20% of BMR for calories for activities of daily living.

Based on Clark 2008.

Components of a Healthy Diet

Eating an appropriate number of calories is a start, but taking in the right types of calories is also important. Foods are composed of three macronutrients (nutrients required in significant amounts): carbohydrate, protein, and fat. Of these macronutrients, carbohydrate and fat provide the energy to support muscular activity. Protein can be used for fuel, but it is not as efficient as the metabolism of carbohydrate and fat for energy. Protein, however, is essential for building and repairing tissues. Carbohydrate, protein, and fat are all important for both athletic performance and a healthy life.

Carbohydrate

Carbohydrate supplies muscle and liver glycogen, which provide energy for physical movement as well as for the nervous system. Carbohydrate also regulates the metabolism of fat and protein. Three-quarters of your glycogen is stored in your skeletal muscles, and the other quarter is stored in your liver. But these supplies are limited. They can provide enough energy for only 60 to 90 minutes of hard exercise, so you must replenish glycogen regularly to fuel your workouts. Fortunately, with training, your body will store 20 to 50 percent more glycogen than the body of an untrained person. Consuming adequate carbohydrate will ensure that you keep your fuel tank topped off. Foods with high carbohydrate content include

- grains such as bread, cereal, rice, pasta, and potato,
- fruits,
- vegetables, and
- sports drinks.

Carbohydrate should make up 60 percent of your total daily calories. One gram of carbohydrate contains four calories.

Fat

Dietary fat is an essential nutrient. Fat is necessary for the vitamins A, D, E, and K to perform their jobs to keep you healthy. Moderate consumption of fat can slow the rate of digestion, thus enhancing nutrient absorption and helping you feel full. Before and during events, too much fat will slow gastric emptying and may result in an upset stomach.

Let's face it—fat tastes good! But most of the population consumes much more fat—especially saturated fat—than they need, resulting in cardiovascular disease and other health complications. The basic unit of fat is the fatty acid, which is used for energy. Fatty acids come in two forms: saturated and unsaturated. Saturated fat can raise cholesterol levels and is linked to numerous diseases. Foods containing high amounts of saturated fat include beef, butter, coconut oil, and palm kernel oil. Unsaturated fat is divided into monounsaturated fat and polyunsaturated fat and in general is healthier than saturated fat.

Unsaturated fat does not have the same effect on cholesterol as saturated fat does, and some studies have shown that unsaturated fat can lower cholesterol. Nuts, fish oils, avocados, and seeds are good sources of healthy unsaturated fat. Fish oils found in salmon, mackerel, and tuna contain omega-3 fatty acids, which are critical for cardiovascular health and neural function. For good health, look at the types of fat that you consume and make adjustments accordingly. Fat should constitute 25 percent of your daily calories, preferably from nuts, seeds, fish, and other healthy oils. A gram of fat contains nine calories.

Through repeated, moderately paced endurance workouts, the body becomes more efficient at using fat as a fuel source during exercise, sparing the precious stores of glycogen. You will be able to ride longer and still have enough energy to tackle the hills or ride in a fast group. Note that training your body to use fat more efficiently and spare glycogen happens only when exercising at moderate intensity, not when riding harder. Kyle wants to lose weight, and riding at a moderate, fat-burning pace won't cause him to lose weight per se. Nor will eating more fat stimulate his body to burn additional fat. To lose weight, Kyle simply needs to burn more calories than he consumes.

Protein

Protein serves a vital role in the body by supporting the growth, maintenance, and repair of tissues. Proteins are composed of 20 amino acids, which are classified as essential or nonessential. The 9 essential amino acids must be obtained through diet, because the body cannot manufacture them, whereas the remaining 11 can be synthesized by the body.

Complete protein contains all the essential amino acids. Examples are meat, fish, poultry, eggs, and milk. Protein from vegetable and grain sources is incomplete protein

Food for Thought—The Glycemic Index

You may be familiar with the terms simple carbohydrate and complex carbohydrate. Simple carbohydrate (fruits and sweets) contains sugar, and complex carbohydrate (potatoes, breads, and so forth) contains starch. Some athletes think that complex carbohydrate is the preferred food to provide long-lasting energy to the body. Recently, nutritionists have been looking beyond simple versus complex and are using the *glycemic index* (GI) of foods. The glycemic index refers to how high and how quickly a particular food raises blood sugar. White bread or glucose is the reference food, and it has a value of 100. Foods with a high GI raise blood sugar rapidly and can cause the body to rely on glucose for energy rather than burn fat. Diets with a high percentage of high-GI foods may be linked to obesity, heart disease, and diabetes. Foods with a low GI raise blood sugar more slowly. These foods can help manage hunger and assist with weight management. Low-GI foods also tend to be less processed.

Have you ever been hungry almost immediately after eating candy? That happens because candies have a high GI and send your blood sugar level through the roof. Then your blood sugar crashes, and you crave more sugar, resulting in an unhealthy rollercoaster effect. Instead of reaching for a candy bar the next time you are hungry, try a handful of nuts or trail mix. The lower GI may help you avoid those drastic swings in blood sugar.

Don't avoid high-GI foods completely. A mashed potato has a GI of 83; however, the potato also contains many essential minerals. Cyclists can eat a variety of foods with higher and lower GI values both during a ride to sustain energy and after riding to start replenishing glycogen stores. See table 4.3 for the glycemic index values of some common foods.

Experiment to learn how your body responds to different foods. The glycemic index is not an exact science, and GI is one of several factors that you should consider when choosing foods. The website www.glycemicindex.com is an excellent resource.

TABLE 4.3 Approximate GI Values of Various Foods

Food	Examples (GI in parentheses)
Bakery products	Bran muffin (85) to cake-type doughnut (108)
Breads	Hamburger bun (87) to bagel (103)
Cereals	All-bran (60) to cornflakes (116)
Grains	Barley (36) to instant rice (98)
Fruit	Cherries (32) to banana (75)
Legumes	Kidney beans (39) to pinto beans (55)
Vegetables	Peas (68) to baked potato (121)
Snack foods	Peanuts (21) to rice cakes (117)

Data from NSCA 2008.

because it does not supply all the essential amino acids. Vegetarians, in particular vegans, need to plan their protein intake carefully. When eating incomplete protein, combine foods so that you get all the essential amino acids. Consume grains along with legumes and beans, for example, or combine legumes and seeds.

In recent years several popular diets have overemphasized the importance of protein. Protein is not a wonder nutrient. Eating more of it will not make you stronger and faster. Increased power and speed come through proper training and recovery supported by balanced nutrition. Protein should constitute 15 percent of your total calorie intake to support your training and daily life. One gram of protein contains four calories.

Micronutrients

Besides carbohydrate, protein, and fat, your body needs two types of micronutrients, nutrients required in small amounts to support various metabolic functions: vitamins and minerals. Many myths about vitamins and minerals exist, so let's review the basics.

Vitamins are organic compounds needed in small amounts to act as catalysts in specific biochemical processes to maintain health. For example, thiamin (B_1), riboflavin (B_2), and niacin (B_3) are necessary for the production of energy. We don't burn these vitamins (i.e., use them for energy); rather, the vitamins facilitate the process of using fat and carbohydrate for fuel. Vitamin D regulates how the body uses calcium and phosphorus, which are essential for strong bones and teeth. Vitamin A helps us see in dim light.

The vitamins C and E, beta-carotene, and the mineral selenium serve as antioxidants, which help protect the body from free radicals. The more you exercise, the more you generate free radicals, which are one of the causes of muscle inflammation. Free radicals are also a contributing factor in heart disease, some cancers, and cataracts. Taking antioxidant supplements won't protect you from disease, but eating a diet rich in these vitamins (mainly fresh fruits and vegetables) can reduce the effects of free radicals.

Minerals are inorganic substances that also perform specific functions in the body. Examples are iron, which helps with the transport of oxygen; calcium for bone structure; sodium and potassium for water balance within the body; magnesium, which is necessary for muscular contraction; and chromium, which aids with glucose metabolism (Clark, 1990; Clark & Hegmann, 2005, p. 44). But if you are sensitive to salt, overconsumption of sodium can lead to high blood pressure, which in turn can lead to heart disease, stroke, kidney disease, and congestive heart failure (Mayo Clinic, *Sodium*, n.d.).

Our bodies cannot produce these vitamins and minerals, so we must ingest them in sufficient quantities. The National Academy of Science has established the Reference Daily Intake or Recommended Daily Intake (RDI) for vitamins and minerals as well as carbohydrate, protein, fiber, and fat. The RDI is the daily dietary intake level that is sufficient to meet the nutrient requirement of nearly all (97 to 98 percent) healthy people. The RDI determines the Daily Value (DV), which is printed on food labels in the United States, Canada, and Australia. The Daily Values are recommended daily targets and in some cases, such as sodium and saturated fat, are recommended upper limits because of health risks associated with overconsumption.

Supplements

Walk into a health food store and you'll see hundreds of products claiming to do everything—cure ailments, improve your energy level, and detoxify your body. Nutritional supplements are a multibillion-dollar industry that is loosely regulated by federal safety agencies. Few of the products are supported by scientific studies. If you are eating a balanced diet with plenty of wholesome foods and have no known nutrition deficiencies, you probably do not need supplements. Obtaining nutrients from food is much better than relying on a pill or a powder because foods contain a variety of nutrients that are absorbed better in the form of food. People at risk for developing nutrient deficiencies, such as pregnant women and people with chronic diseases, may want to add a supplement to their diets. If you are eating less because you are dieting or are a senior who naturally consumes less, you are also getting fewer micronutrients. Vegetarians are also at risk for developing deficiencies. If you are concerned, consult with a registered dietitian (RD) or physician for specific recommendations about supplementing your diet.

Daily Diet

You now have a general understanding of the three food pyramids and the various food groups and how they relate to both physical performance and overall health. You have your food journal with your current consumption and caloric intake as well as an estimate of your caloric requirement. With this information you can decide what changes to make in your diet to support both your training and overall health.

Some people train better with detailed plans and others train more effectively following general principles. Similarly, some people like daily nutritional plans and others use the basic recommendations of one of the pyramids.

If you would like a daily plan, visit MyPyramid's website (www.mypramid.gov), which includes an interactive feature that provides a recommended caloric and nutrient intake and a menu planner based on height, weight, sex, and activity level. You can enter your daily nutrition and exercise to see how they match up against the recommendations, and you can get tips for healthy eating and food preparation. The site also has information on nutrition for children. Childhood obesity is nearing epidemic proportions, and teaching kids about the value of good nutrition will make our world a healthier and happier place. This online service is free and easy to use.

As with training, John prefers a more general approach. He follows the principles of the Mediterranean and Swiss food pyramids. In doing so, he

- eats fish twice a week,
- steams, grills, or bakes food rather than frying,
- uses spices, mustard, and salsa rather than sauces for flavoring,
- uses a small plate so he can have a full plate without eating too much, and
- covers the plate primarily with carbs and limits his protein to about the size of a deck of cards.

The following sections describe typical breakfast, lunch, dinner, and snack choices for a cyclist. Like training plans, food plans should be tailored to each person. You can adapt these examples to suit your particular plan for eating. Exact calories are not provided because they vary from producer to producer. Read the nutrition label on each food to get accurate data.

Breakfast

Breakfast is the most important meal of the day. A good breakfast helps fuel your body and mind for the day. Breakfast at home could include fortified cold cereal or cooked cereal (preferably old-fashioned, not instant) with fruit, low-fat or nonfat milk, and brown sugar.

You could add a multigrain bagel or slice of whole-wheat toast, perhaps with peanut butter for added protein, and a glass of fruit juice. Or choose low-fat or nonfat yogurt mixed with more fruit.

For a more traditional breakfast, have one or two eggs (poached, boiled, or scrambled without using butter) and a whole-grain bagel with peanut butter.

If you're in a hurry, you could make a peanut butter and jelly sandwich on whole-wheat bread, take along some breakfast bars and fruit, or grab some leftovers from the night before. Your day will go better if you eat some healthy foods in the morning, even if they aren't traditional breakfast foods, rather than skip breakfast.

Snack

Eating something small and nutritious between meals helps stabilize blood sugar. Many people go too long between meals and then become extremely hungry. Think grazing rather than gorging. You can keep healthy snacks in a backpack, desk drawer, or your car to help prevent raids of the candy machine. To help keep your blood sugar stable, eat one or two of these snacks midmorning: a bag of pretzels, a piece of fruit, a bag of raisins, a few carrot and celery sticks, a breakfast bar, or a sports bar.

Lunch

When at home, try a sandwich of canned fish on whole-wheat bread with spinach, tomato, and mustard. Lunch is a great time to eat your veggies. Along with the sandwich have a salad of mixed greens, fresh vegetables, and low-fat or vinaigrette dressing. Then have fruit for dessert. Or you could skip the sandwich and add a bit of cooked pasta and fish from last night's dinner to the salad.

If fast food is the only option, go for a salad with low-fat or vinaigrette dressing. Be careful about dressings and other ingredients that need refrigeration—they should be *on ice*, not just in cold water. Improperly refrigerated salad ingredients are a leading source of food poisoning, which will definitely ruin your day! Instead of a salad, you could have a slice of cheese pizza with vegetable toppings, a sandwich with lots of veggies, or a bean burrito and rice. Soft drinks offer plenty of sugar but no micronutrients. Choose low- or nonfat milk, fruit juice, or plain water instead.

You could also prepare a bag lunch, such as turkey on whole wheat with greens and mustard (skip the mayonnaise), fresh vegetables in a sandwich bag, a piece of fruit, and a can of vegetable or fruit juice.

Preworkout Snack

Kyle chooses to get up early to work out, so his evenings are free with his family. He doesn't want to exercise on a full stomach, so he has a container of fruit yogurt as soon as he gets up. After he trains he makes a breakfast to eat while commuting to work. When he can commute by bike he eats a snack before leaving home and packs breakfast to eat at his desk.

If you train after work, eat an energy-rich snack about an hour before exercising so you have fuel for training. For example, you could eat an energy bar or fig cookies, a banana, or a nutritional drink such as Ensure. After exercising hard, another snack will stabilize your blood sugar so that you are not too tired while fixing dinner with your family.

Dinner

At the end of a long day including a hard workout, you can finally relax over a healthy dinner with your family.

While you are preparing dinner you could serve vegetable sticks with several mustards for seasoning. You could make whole-wheat pasta with green onions, grated carrots, tomato sauce, salsa (for added flavor), and lean beef, and add a salad with a low-fat or vinaigrette dressing. Or you could fix brown rice, steamed vegetables, and poultry or fish. You could enjoy berries or melon for dessert, depending on what is in season, or perhaps fat-free frozen yogurt.

These are just examples of what you could eat throughout the day. Developing your personal nutrition strategy may take some trial and error. Eating is pleasurable, so enjoy the process of figuring out foods that fit your nutrition requirements, palate, social and cultural norms, and personal beliefs. Include your training schedule in your eating strategy. Be sure to have a generous snack before a workout and some carbohydrate right after you finish to restore your blood glucose. If you are trying to lose weight, don't skip a meal because doing so will trigger pangs of hunger. Instead, cut back on the portions at each meal. Have fun planning and eating healthy foods. On the bike and off, your body will thank you!

Safety: Drink Just Enough

Perhaps you've seen pro racers drift back to the team car to get drinks during the Tour de France. The pros know that not drinking enough may limit their performance, but drinking too much can be dangerous as well. Drinking well beyond thirst, particularly in hot conditions, can dilute your blood sodium, a condition known as hyponatremia. Extreme hyponatremia can cause the brain to swell, a potentially fatal condition. If you start to develop puffiness around your sock lines or gloves, then you're retaining fluid and should stop drinking until you start urinating. If you develop a frontal lobe headache or start to become confused, then the hyponatremia is serious and you should seek medical attention.

▶ Electrolyte sports drinks contain some carbohydrates and sodium, but they don't contain enough sodium to keep your blood sodium in balance. Because the sodium in sports drinks is dilute compared with normal blood, drinking them will not prevent hyponatremia if you drink too much.

▶ Consuming additional sodium will not prevent hyponatremia if you overdrink.

How much should you drink? Drink to satisfy your thirst, but don't drink more (Hew-Butler et al., 2008).

Nutrition During Rides

High-performance fighter jets have only enough fuel for relatively short missions. If they have to fly long distances, they need to refuel in midair. Our bodies are the same. We have enough glycogen stored within our bodies for hard training rides of 60 to 90 minutes. For longer brisk rides we need to keep our bodies fueled to avoid fatigue or even worse—hitting the wall (using up muscle glycogen) or bonking (running out of liver glycogen to power the brain). Eating and drinking adequately every hour while riding will help prevent fatigue.

You've heard the maxim that you should drink before you are thirsty and eat before you are hungry. Your body provides good feedback about how much fluid you need, and you should drink to satisfy thirst. Drinking much more may be dangerous. How much fluid you need depends on your body size, weather, and the intensity of your riding. Thus, we can't give you quantitative guidelines on how much to drink while you are riding. Drink to satisfy thirst.

On the other hand, eating before you are hungry is good advice. Your body is slow to send messages to the brain about low glycogen. By the time you feel hungry, you may be low on fuel. To stay on top of your nutrition you should eat a carbohydrate-rich snack every hour. The American College of Sports Medicine recommends consuming 25 to 60 grams, or 100 to 240 calories, which is sufficient for several hours of exercise, per hour after the first hour of exercise (ACSM, 2007). Based on more recent research (Jeukendrup, 2010) we recommend for longer rides that you consume a mix of carbohydrates totaling 60 to 90 grams, or 240 to 360 calories, every hour plus a little protein and fat. If you're Kyle's size (170 pounds, or 77 kg), eat at the upper end of these ranges. You can consume less if you're smaller. Figure out your personal caloric target while riding. The key to staving off fatigue is to eat enough every hour.

While you are riding, experiment to figure out the kinds and amounts of foods that taste good to you and sit well while riding. Some people prefer energy bars and sports drinks, whereas others like fruit, cookies, pretzels, crackers, bagels with peanut butter, breakfast bars, or other foods. Commercial bars, gels, and drinks have no performance advantage, but they may be more convenient. For riders on a budget, many common store foods offer quality nutrition at a reasonable price. The key is to select items that provide enough calories primarily from carbohydrate. Table 6.2 on page 126 offers specific examples.

After you have learned what to eat, practice eating regularly during your training rides. Figure out where to carry your drinks and food so that they are accessible. You could carry fluids in a hydration pack with the nipple conveniently near your mouth if you are comfortable with the weight on your back. Or you could carry bottles on the bike and learn to ride a straight line while grabbing a bottle and drinking. For snacks you could get a small handlebar bag or a bento bag that fits on the top tube behind the stem or carry them in jersey pockets. We offer more suggestions on how to carry fuel in the next chapter on equipment. If you are taking portions of common store food you can store them in sandwich bags with folding tops, which are easy to open one-handed. Whatever your system, practice eating regularly and drinking to satisfy thirst.

As part of your preparation for events, learn what kinds of foods and fluids will be available. Most rides will have fruit, bagels, cookies, water, and some form of sports drink at rest stops. If possible, check the event's website or talk to the organizers to find out what they will have. Test their offerings in training. Don't experiment with unfamiliar foods or drinks during your event.

In chapters 6 and 7 we provide more information about nutrition and hydration on the bike.

Shopping Tips

Good nutrition starts at the store. Supermarkets contain thousands of food products. Some are healthy, and others are not. By following these suggestions, you can stock your refrigerator, freezer, and cupboards with nutritious food.

- *Have a plan.* Make a list of healthy, staple foods that you eat regularly to use as a template while shopping.
- *Avoid shopping while hungry.* You'll probably buy more than you need, especially higher calorie items.
- *Use a small cart.* Limiting the size of your cart can help reduce the temptation of adding unnecessary extras.
- *Focus on the perimeter of the store.* You will find the healthiest and freshest items along the perimeter: fresh produce, meat and seafood, dairy products, and fresh baked goods.
- *Buy less-processed foods.* The skin and shells of raw food contain micronutrients, which are removed when the food is processed too much. For example, whole-wheat flour is healthier than white flour, multigrain bread is better than white bread, and brown rice is more nutritious than white rice.
- *Read the labels.* Start by reading the ingredients (at the bottom of the label), which are listed in terms of proportion; the food contains more of the first ingredient than the second, more of the second than the third, and so on. Are the main ingredients healthy, or are they polysyllabic words that you've never heard of? Then check the serving size and consider whether you'll eat just one serving. The labels provide information per serving on total calories and calories from fat; the amount of total fat, saturated fat, cholesterol, carbohydrate, and protein; the percentage of Daily Values (DV) for these nutrients; and the percentage of DV for sodium, potassium, vitamins A and C, calcium, and iron. From time to time comparison shop. For example, the fat content of granola can vary from 3.5 to 10 grams per serving. The macronutrients are listed in grams; use table 4.4 to convert the number of grams to calories.
- *Buy ingredients instead of cans.* Prepared food is made out of more-processed ingredients and may contain additives that aren't the healthiest. For example, one serving (1/4 cup) of prepared alfredo spaghetti sauce could contain as much as 4.5 grams of saturated fat (23 percent of the DV) and 450 milligrams of sodium (19 percent of the DV). Sodium in canned soup ranges from 600 to 900 milligrams (25 to 37 percent of the DV).

TABLE 4.4 **Macronutrient Calories**

Nutrient	Calories per gram
Carbohydrate	4
Protein	4
Fat	9

Eating Store Food

By Jenny L. Hegmann

You can eat a wholesome, low-fat sports diet anywhere, whether you shop at home before a ride or on the road. Supermarkets, village groceries, minimarts, and corner delis offer a variety of healthy choices that can keep you fueled while riding. Choose primarily high-carbohydrate foods and limit your consumption of greasy foods and excess protein, which fill your belly but don't provide the glucose that your working muscles and brain need. Foods from these groups offer the most nutrients:

▶ The grain group provides carbohydrate. Choose low-fat granola bars, breakfast bars, fig cookies, an individual pita pocket roll, a bagel or baguette from the sandwich counter, crackers, pretzels, and single-serving cereal (plain or with milk).

▶ The meat and bean group supplies protein, carbohydrate (beans, lentils, and nuts), and healthy fat (fish and nuts). Try pop-top canned lentil or bean soups, baked beans, nuts, single-serve canned tuna, a boiled egg, or a lean turkey or ham sandwich.

▶ Fruit gives you carbohydrate, vitamin C, and potassium. Select 100 percent fruit juices, all fresh fruits, canned fruit cocktail, or dried fruit such as raisins, apricots, or dates.

▶ Milk provides protein, calcium, and carbohydrate. Choose low-fat or fat-free chocolate, strawberry, or white milk; part-skim cheeses; and low-fat or fat-free sweetened yogurts.

▶ Vegetables have carbohydrate, vitamins C and A, and sodium (if canned). Eat fresh vegetables, tomato or vegetable juice, and vegetable soup.

▶ Among combination foods, try a turkey or ham sandwich (hold the mayo) with less meat and more bread; peanut butter on a bagel, bread, or baguette; a veggie or cheese pizza slice (discard excess cheese); broth-type (not creamy) soup with bread or crackers; and gorp (good old raisins and peanuts).

▶ Among sugary treats, choose those with little fat such as soft drinks, sweetened tea or coffee, fat-free cookies, gumdrops, hard candies, peppermint patties, skittles, licorice, and honey and jam or jelly on bagels.

A helpful tip is to use a coffee cup for a cereal bowl. Whatever you choose, eat tried-and-true foods and drinks that have worked well for you in training. Save unfamiliar stuff for trial (and error!) in the off-season.

Restaurant Meals

As part of balancing his life Kyle takes his family out to dinner on the weekend. Healthy eating doesn't preclude you from enjoying meals at your favorite restaurants. Dining should be a pleasurable social experience. Recently, more restaurants have become aware of customers' nutrition concerns and offer healthier choices. Here are some tips for restaurant dining:

• *Plan your full meal.* Do you want an appetizer, main course, and dessert? If so, select them so that together they fit within your overall nutrition plan for dinner.

• *Ask for doggie bags.* As you order, plan to take some food home. You could even ask the wait staff to place half of the main course in a to-go container before serving you. You won't be tempted to overeat, and you'll have an additional meal for later in the week.

- *Stay away from fried foods.* Grilled or baked choices generally have much less fat than fried items.
- *Remove the skin of poultry.* Removing the skin of chicken or turkey will reduce the amount of fat.
- *Watch the sides.* Side dishes can add a lot of calories. Request steamed vegetables or rice in place of a side dish with a rich sauce or have a baked potato garnished with scallions.
- *Watch for hidden fat.* Think before you add salad dressing, sour cream, or butter.
- *Don't drink your calories.* Calories add up quickly with alcoholic beverages and soft drinks.
- *Express your concerns.* Restaurants are usually willing to cater to specific requests. Don't be afraid to ask!
- *Enjoy the meal.* Try to make reasonably healthy choices but don't spend so much energy worrying about your diet that you don't enjoy the time out.

Kyle is confident that by following some basic nutrition guidelines, he can improve his riding performance and maintain a healthy lifestyle. Here is his nutrition plan to support his daily needs and prepare for his upcoming century:

- 2,600 total calories, 500 less than he is burning so that he'll lose weight
- 60 percent of his total calories from carbohydrate to support his energy needs
- 25 percent of his total calories from fat, also a source of energy
- 15 percent of his total calories from protein to help maintain and repair his muscles

While on training rides, Kyle follows our nutrition recommendations:

- Experiment to learn what works and what doesn't, incorporating the information in a training and nutrition log.
- Eat on scheduled intervals to develop good habits.
- Drink just enough to satisfy thirst.
- Learn how to get, unwrap, and consume food and drink while watching the road.

You should now understand the principles of good nutrition, know your daily caloric expenditure, and have a basic food plan to take in the right food groups. You've also learned about nutrition during rides and can practice your plan during your workouts. Keeping a simple food journal for a few weeks will help you monitor what you are consuming and learn about any interaction with your training.

CHAPTER 5

Gearing Up for the Long Haul

Bikes have become sophisticated machines. They are designed for various purposes, from road racing to off-road riding to loaded touring. Selecting the right bike and setting it up to fit will make worlds of difference in your comfort, performance, and enjoyment of endurance cycling. Besides a bike, you will need some accessories to enhance safety and functionality on the road. Finally, you should perform some preventive maintenance to keep the bike running smoothly. You need not be an expert mechanic, but every bike owner should take care of some basic upkeep and be prepared to deal with common problems on the road.

Type of Bike

Kyle's sister Erika sees the positive effect of cycling on Kyle's life. By riding and eating better, he's lost weight, has more energy, is happier overall, and has better relationships with his wife and kids. Erika decides to follow in her brother's footsteps. But in a bike shop she is confused by all the choices. We tell her that buying a new bike is a serious investment and that she should treat the process like buying a car. A bit of homework will help her select a bike that will provide her years of enjoyment. We talk about key considerations that Erika should think about before she goes to the bike shop.

   If you are looking for a new bike or want to upgrade your current bike, write down the answers the following questions so you can discuss your options at the bike shop.

- *Do you have bike fit concerns*? A bike that fits is the most important factor in comfort and performance. If you are particularly tall or short, a woman, or have orthopedic issues such as back trouble, a standard frame design may not fit you correctly. The bike should fit the rider, not vice versa. You can modify bike fit by selecting the right components, but you need to start with a frame of the right size and shape. We describe proper bike fit in detail later in this chapter. Many bike manufacturers have frames and components specifically designed for women. Women tend to have shorter torsos relative to their legs, and these frames fit women's body proportions better than generic frames do. Women's bikes usually come with smaller handlebars, crank sets, and brake levers to make riding more comfortable. Erika is 5 feet, 4 inches (163 cm) tall and should look at frames made for women.

- *How much do you want to spend?* Plan to spend close to US$1,000 for a durable entry-level bike that can withstand the demands of training for and riding centuries. Check out the websites of various manufacturers. The difference between the entry-level bikes and the top models is often the component groups. In many cases, the frames are virtually identical. If you are on a budget, you could get one of the lower-end bikes and then upgrade the components as you can afford them, although components bought later are significantly more expensive than if purchased on the original bike. Also, look for last year's models. You may save some money when dealers clear their inventories for the next year's models. There is no ceiling on price if you opt for a custom-designed frame with top-of-the-line components.

- *At what level do you want to perform?* If you want to get in shape and complete a few centuries a year, almost any standard road bike will do the job. Consider entry-level road bikes, often referred to as sport, fitness, or comfort bikes (see figure 5.1), which are suited for everything from

FIGURE 5.1 **Sport bike.**

commuting to centuries. On the other hand, if you aspire to fast times and may race one day, a racing bike with lighter components may suit you better. Improving your century or brevet times requires more training, and riding greater distances generally puts more stress on the components. Higher performance bikes usually feature better components and lighter frames. Lighter components cost considerably more and are less important than other considerations for most riders.

- *In the future might you ride longer brevets or multiday tours?* Events of 300 kilometers, 200 miles and longer, and tours require many hours or days on the bike, so cycling efficiency and comfort are essential. Racing bikes are the most efficient and suitable for many riders doing longer events. A touring bike, however, which is designed a bit differently from a racing bike, is generally more comfortable because the rider sits more upright. These bikes are more stable than a racing bike with a load of gear. The choices range from those designed to carry a very large seat pack and handlebar bag, suitable for rides up to a 1,200-kilometer randonnée, to those with attachments to carry all the gear needed for a self-supported camping trip. You could comfortably ride a century, 200 kilometers, or longer on most touring bikes, although they are heavier and less efficient.

- *How reliable must the bike be?* Road and touring bikes by reputable manufacturers are all quite reliable. Although problems will be infrequent, some components and wheels designed for lightness and higher performance will have more breakdowns than those with more robust designs. Repair of these equipment problems may require a bike mechanic. If you don't want to risk an equipment failure that may prevent you from finishing an event or are considering self-supported rides, pay attention to the reliability of components and the ease of repairing them.

Frame and Components

Now that you understand the kind of bike you want, consider the following factors to narrow your choices. We discuss the geometry and design of the frame first because these aspects, not the materials used in construction, generally have the greatest influence on riding characteristics, handling, and comfort.

- *What kind of frame geometry is best?* Frame geometry relates to your planned type of riding and performance. If you want to hustle through centuries or participate in local races, a frame designed for racing (see figure 5.2) will work best. A manufacturer designs racing bike geometry to put you into the optimal position for speed. This type of design allows you to accelerate faster, corner more quickly, and be more aerodynamic, but the bike may transmit more road shock, be harder to handle, and require a more bent-over position.

FIGURE 5.2 **Racing bike.**

A touring frame (figure 5.3) is designed with less steep angles (a more relaxed geometry) so the ride is smoother and the steering easier. Because of the geometry, however, the frame isn't as stiff, so you can't accelerate as fast or climb quite as easily. These frames allow a more upright position, because speed and aerodynamics aren't as important as they are in

FIGURE 5.3 **Touring bike.**

racing. However, these frames aren't slow; Pete Penseyres used a frame with touring geometry and aero bars to set the long-standing solo RAAM average speed record in 1986.

Sport bikes generally fall in between the geometries of racing and touring bikes and for many riders offer the best of both worlds.

- *What frame material is best?* Frames are made of steel, aluminum, titanium, carbon fiber, or combinations (for example, an aluminum frame with a carbon fiber fork). Riders often debate the best frame material, but what counts is the frame material in combination with the design. Research various bikes, talk to other riders, and try out as many as you can. Many shops and manufacturers offer extended trials or rentals to allow you time to get a feel for a particular bike. Lon Haldeman sums it up best when he says, "I have ridden many different frame materials on RAAM and couldn't tell the difference on a dark night." Haldeman recommends picking a bike that feels comfortable at the end of a century ride. If you can't take a prospective bike for a long ride, take a long ride so you're tired and then test ride the new bike.

- *What gearing is right?* Will you be riding on the plains with no wind or in the hills? Will you be doing centuries and shorter races or longer rides during which cumulative fatigue becomes more of a factor? Your type of riding will determine your choice of gearing. Bikes have either two or three chain rings attached to the cranks and pedals, which are then attached to cogs on the rear wheel. Racing bikes come with double chain rings, which are lighter, and they have a fairly narrow range of cogs in the rear. Touring and mountain bikes have triple chain rings and a wider range of cogs. Triples provide lower gears and a wider range of gearing, but they are heavier. Compact double chain rings are a good compromise between racing double chain rings and touring triples. Compacts have fewer teeth than conventional double rings and provide lower gearing at lower weight, although not as low as triples. If you will be riding in sustained windy conditions, in hilly terrain, in rides of 300 kilometers, 200 miles, or longer, or are a fairly new rider, consider getting a wider set of gears. A fully loaded touring bike can be extremely heavy, so you may need extra-low gearing to tackle the climbs.

- *What grade of components do you need?* The component groups include the derailleurs, cranks, pedals, brakes, shift and brake levers, and wheel hubs. Shimano, Campagnolo, and SRAM manufacture component groups for road bikes. Each offers groups ranging from recreation level to race grade. Most road bikes today are sold with combined brake and shift levers that allow you to shift while your hands are on the brake hoods near the brake levers. Shimano's levers are called STI (Shimano Total Integration), Campagnolo has Ergo-Levers, and SRAM features the Double Tap system. Over the years these systems have proved reliable in many races and events, but the mechanism is complicated. If a combined brake and shift lever fails, repair on the road is almost impossible. If you will be riding in an area where you won't have ready access to a bike shop, consider bar-end shifters or even downtube shift levers, which you can usually repair without a bike shop. The choice of components usually involves a trade-off between high performance and reliability. Centuries, brevets, tours, and other cycling events typically do not have the same demands as racing. Pick components that match your type of riding.

- *What model of wheels is best?* In most bike shops you'll find many bikes equipped with lightweight wheels that accelerate faster in sprints and have fewer spokes and deep rim sections that cut through the wind. Aerodynamic drag matters at racing speeds, but is less important when riding endurance events. The same trade-off exists between high performance and reliability. Wheels with fewer than 28 spokes are usually not safe to ride if a spoke breaks. They are often built with unique spokes that may be difficult to repair outside a specialized bike shop. Standard 32-spoke wheels are stronger, easier to maintain, and can be ridden with one broken spoke. Moreover, a spoke can be replaced in virtually any bike shop. Rims with deep profiles are tricky to handle in crosswinds and require special tubes with longer valve stems, which aren't available in every bike shop. If you are a bigger rider or plan to carry gear, note that most racing wheels have weight limits. If you will be racing and understand the limitations, a specialty wheel set (figure 5.4a) may be right for you. Otherwise, conventional 32-spoke wheels (figure 5.4b) may be better. If you can afford it, you could get a pair of each.

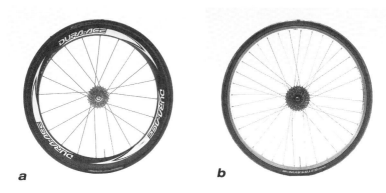

FIGURE 5.4   **(a)** Aerodynamic wheels accelerate faster but are less durable than **(b)** conventional wheels.

- *How easy is it to maintain the bike*? Sooner or later, bike components will malfunction. When this happens, can you fix it yourself or will you need to take it to a bike shop? Many parts of the sophisticated components (dual control levers, sealed cartridge bearing units, aerodynamic wheels, carbon components) may require special tools and knowledge to fix. Many shops offer free 30-day tune-ups after the purchase of a bike as well as discounted repairs on the bikes they sell. Establish a solid relationship with a shop and its mechanics, whether you'll be relying on them for parts and advice while you do your own maintenance or asking them to take care of the bike for you.

We've laid out many points to consider. Take your notes to the bike shop so that you get a bike that meets your needs. If necessary, ask them to customize your bike. Often components and wheels can be substituted, different stems and handlebars can be mounted, a different saddle can be put on, and other changes can be made to make it your personal bike. You will be spending your money, so be sure that you are satisfied with your investment.

Bike Fit

Erika has picked out a road bike that is within her budget and will suit her riding needs. Now she has to have the bike fitted to her to provide comfort and efficiency and to minimize the chance of injuries. Nearly every bike shop will offer this service to customers who buy a new bike. Shops vary in their expertise; some just rely on formulae, whereas others are trained to size the bike and components to the individual. Whether you are getting a new bike or starting your training program on your current bike, we strongly recommend that you have the bike fit evaluated, if possible, by a trained technician. A proper fit will improve the efficiency of your pedaling so you will use less energy to maintain the same speed or expend the same energy and go faster. Further, a good fit will increase your comfort and thereby reduce off-the-bike time and cut your century time.

Coach John's Stable of Bikes

I've been enjoying endurance cycling for 35 years and have a large stable of mounts, even though I've retired a few. My favorite mount is a 12-year-old titanium frame with conventional geometry, which fits me well. I've outfitted it to serve my riding. I enjoy unsupported centuries and minimally supported brevets and 1,200-kilometer randonnées. The bike has a 20-year-old leather saddle and a seat bag large enough to carry my tools, rain gear, and extra food. I changed the stem to a slightly shorter one, which points up a bit so I don't have to bend as far to reach the handlebars. The titanium frame, conventional geometry, leather saddle, and higher bars provide a comfortable ride. A half-dozen years ago I took mercy on my knees and put on a triple chain ring. After years of using integrated shifting and brake levers, and breaking cables at inconvenient times, I switched to bar-end shifters, which I can repair on the road. I have robust 32-spoke wheels. I once popped a spoke just 50 miles (80 km) into an unsupported double century, but I trued the wheel and kept riding. I've swapped out my racing pedals for mountain bike pedals; it's much easier to walk into the minimart in MTB shoes!

I also ride a 30-year old steel frame, which was a top racing frame when I bought it. I've changed it to a single-speed and put on MTB pedals and wider cyclo-cross tires. I run errands on it and train in the winter on snowy roads. For variety, I've ridden a few centuries on it.

I still ride my custom steel touring bike, also 30 years old. It has relaxed geometry and is extremely comfortable, although a bit heavy. I've ridden the 1,200-kilometer Paris–Brest–Paris twice on this fine steed.

On my trainer I have my old carbon-fiber racing frame. The fit mimics the titanium bike. It's always ready—and the frame is impervious to my sweat!

I particularly enjoy riding somewhere for lunch and back with a friend on my tandem. Tandems are slower on the hills, but we make good time on the flats and motor on the downhills! I like the social aspect of riding a tandem. I've ridden several 200-kilometer brevets and a 12-hour race on my tandem. Tandems are more complex mechanically, and you need to know a bit about working on the bike. But they are a great choice for riders of different strengths, can be quite fast, and are a lot of fun!

Recumbents are similar to tandems. A 'bent is slower on the hills but more aerodynamic than a traditional bike and is good on the flats and fast on the downhills. I have a friend who has ridden all of California's toughest double centuries on his 'bent. He's loaned me his bike, and I've found it quite comfortable, especially on the butt.

When I was doing ultraraces I also had a beam bike (see photo). The saddle is mounted on a beam, which absorbs the road shock, and makes a big difference on centuries and longer rides.

I loved to run trails. Now my knees can't handle it, so I have a mountain bike, another versatile mount. I've coached a number of riders who've ridden centuries on MTBs. MTBs are heavier than road bikes but are robust and comfortable. Put bar ends on the handlebars for another hand position, add high-pressure smooth tires, and you're ready to ride.

Over 35 years I've learned that it's really about the rider, not the mount. Get a good road bike frame that fits you correctly, and then over time you can adapt it to your particular riding style, or chose a different type of mount that suits your needs better. There's no one right bike.

If you tune your engine with good nutrition and effective training, you can ride the bike of your choice in endurance events.

Beam bikes dampen road shock.

Courtesy of AIRO-Series, Inc.

The bike should be fit to you; do not try to fit yourself to the bike! Use these guidelines to assess your fit with the help of a friend or a bike shop technician. Before going to the bike shop, write down the key points to help dial in the right position.

- *Injury history*. Have you had any overuse or traumatic injuries in the past? Knee, hip, lower back, shoulder, neck, wrist, or hand injuries can influence positioning on the bike. Leg-length discrepancies are not uncommon and should be addressed while setting up your bike.
- *Chronic pains*. Discomfort in the neck and shoulders, hands, crotch, or feet often can be ameliorated with a better bike fit.
- *Other activities*. Do you run, hike, lift weights, or play other sports? Different sports may affect your flexibility or injury potential, which could influence your bike fit. For example, runners may develop knee conditions that warrant a change in saddle height or cleat position.
- *Flexibility*. Can you easily touch your toes with a flat back? If not, you may need a more upright position for comfort.
- *Core strength*. If you have been doing the core and flexibility exercises from chapter 3, then your core can support your upper body and you can ride with more bend at the waist without putting too much pressure on your hands.
- *Cycling history*. Is this your first road bike? If you've been riding an MTB, how easily can you adjust to the more bent forward position on a road bike? If you are currently riding a road bike and getting a new bike, take your old bike in so you can compare your new setup to your older bike.
- *Cycling goals*. Do you want to try racing in addition to long-distance events? If so, aerodynamics and responsiveness may be as important as comfort.

Body Geometry

Erika is buying a stock woman's frame, not a custom frame. She can adjust her position over the bike, but not the bike itself. Here we offer general recommendations. Everyone has a different anatomy, riding style, and other considerations that need to be taken into account.

Leg Geometry

Power comes from the legs, and bike setup starts with adjusting the saddle and pedal positions to your legs. Because you will be moving several points of contact, changing one dimension may change other dimensions, which will need to be rechecked.

Put your bike on the trainer and pedal for at least five minutes until you are warmed up and settled into a reasonably comfortable position. Then check the following:

Saddle height   Saddles can be adjusted up and down, moved fore and aft, and tilted up and down. The height is a tradeoff between power and knee stress. If you have no problems with knee pain, adjust the saddle height so that there is a 30- to 35-degree bend in your knee when your foot is in its normal position at the bottom of the pedal stroke (see figure 5.5 on page 80). If you have any knee pain, a slightly higher position (around 25 degrees) may provide more comfort. Don't just eyeball the adjustment—have a knowledgeable coach or therapist use a goniometer to measure your knee angle. A goniometer is a protractor-like device used in the medical field to measure joint angles and range of motion; you can also improvise one with a protractor and sheet of cardboard.

Saddle fore and aft Next adjust the front-to-back position. With the cranks at the 3 o'clock and 9 o'clock positions, drop a plumb bob (a weight tied to a string; see figure 5.6) from the kneecap of your forward leg. Adjust the saddle forward or backward so that the plumb bob lines up with the end of the crank arm. Moving the saddle farther forward will improve power but increase stress on the knees.

When you move the saddle forward or backward, you also change the effective saddle height, so recheck your knee angle with the goniometer. To see if the saddle is too high, pull your jersey up and have a friend stand behind you and watch the top of your shorts. If the shorts line is rocking up and down, so are your buttocks, and the saddle is too high.

FIGURE 5.5 **Use a goniometer to adjust saddle height.**

The steps just described will give you a neutral position and may be adjusted slightly depending on individual concerns or riding style.

Saddle tilt Start with a level saddle, which you can check with a carpenter's level laid from the rear of the saddle to the nose. Then experiment a bit with the saddle tilt; you may prefer a slight nose-up or nose-down position, but avoid extreme angles. Tilting the nose too far up will put excess pressure on your groin, and tilting it too far down will cause you to slide forward constantly, putting unnecessary pressure on your hands, wrists, and shoulders.

FIGURE 5.6 **Measure saddle fore-aft position using a plumb-bob setup.**

Feet and Cleats

"The toe bone's connected to the heel bone . . . the heel bone's connected to the foot bone . . . the foot bone's connected to the ankle bone . . ." Our bodies are kinetic chains—all our joints are interrelated. Therefore, the cleat position may vary on each foot. An improperly adjusted cleat may cause problems not only in your foot and ankle but also in your knee and hip. Cleats can be adjusted fore or aft, rotated, and moved closer to or away from the cranks.

Cleats fore and aft Start with the cleats set so that the ball of each foot is over the pedal axle and each foot is parallel to the respective crank. The heels should be neither in nor out.

Have someone observe you carefully from the rear. Is the left hip dropping down, while the other hip is stable? If so, your left leg may be shorter and you may be prone to tendon injuries or saddle sores on the left side! If you suspect a leg length discrepancy, have a medical professional measure the length of both legs to determine the possible cause and extent of any discrepancy.

If the leg length discrepancy isn't too large, you can compensate by moving the left cleat forward slightly and the right cleat backward a bit. If you adjust the cleats fore and aft, check the saddle height again with the goniometer. If the leg length difference is more than 6 millimeters, you should shim the cleat on the shorter leg. Put a shim between the sole of the shoe and the cleat. The thickness of the shim should be one-half of the discrepancy in leg length. You can make a shim out of a material that is hard enough to resist compression but soft enough to mold to the serrated top of the cleat.

Cleats in and out Next, the person should watch your knees from the front as you pedal to see whether your cleats are aligned with your kneecaps. Are your kneecaps tracking straight up and down over your second toes? Are one or both knees kicking out to the side? If so, the foot under the misaligned knee should move outward so that it's under where your knee naturally aligns. First, move the cleat toward the inside of the shoe, effectively moving your foot outward. If the knee and foot still don't track, you can insert a thin washer between the pedal and crank where the pedal screws into the crank.

Are one or both knees brushing the top tube? If so, insert a thin wedge-shaped shim between the cleat and the shoe, with the wedge toward the inside (crank side) of the shoe. This adjustment will tilt your foot slightly outward so that your knee goes up and down straighter.

If you ride with traditional clips and straps but without cleats, you don't have cleats to adjust, but you should pay attention to how your feet normally rest on the pedals.

Handlebars and Stem

To fit your body size, flexibility, and riding style, you can select different handlebars and change their position by adjusting the stem reach (length) and angle (height).

Handlebar width and depth The width of drop-style bars should be about the same as your shoulder width. With wider bars you have a more open posture and somewhat easier breathing but a bit more wind drag. Racers may use narrower bars, but for riding long-distance events, comfort is key. Bars also vary in how far forward and how deep the drops extend. Bars with deeper drops are more aerodynamic but less comfortable in that position. Some come with more ergonomic shapes. Erika is a small rider with small hands, so she gets a narrower bar with smaller and shallower drops so she can easily reach the brakes.

Stem The stem connects the handlebars to the top of the fork. Pedal on your bike on the trainer and rest your hands on the brake hoods; your torso should form about a 45-degree angle from the top tube (see figure 5.7 on page 82). When your hands are in the drops, the angle should be closer to 30 degrees. The top of the handlebars is usually 2 to 4 inches (5 to 10 cm) below the seat. Handlebars that are lower or farther away may be more aerodynamic but can cause discomfort in the lower back. If you are less flexible, then a stem with less reach or one that angles up instead of down may be more comfortable. Ride the bike a bit on your trainer, and while pedaling experiment with various hand positions between the brake hoods and the top of the handlebars to find the most comfortable spot. Then if possible get a stem that puts your brake hoods at the sweet spot.

Brake hoods To start, position the brakes on the bars so that a straightedge placed along the bottom of the handlebars touches the bottom of the brake levers. You can then move the hoods up or down on the bars for a better feel, and you can adjust them indepen-

FIGURE 5.7 **Check your torso angle with a goniometer.**

dently to increase comfort. Women and riders with smaller hands may need smaller levers. Whatever position you chose, make sure that you can quickly grab the brakes while in the drops.

Documentation and Reassessment

When you are happy with your setup, document everything. Bolts can loosen, you may decide to dismantle your bike, or you may want to switch some components. Use table 5.1 to record your measurements.

You can make marks on your bike, but markings and tape can wear off, particularly if you travel a lot with your bike. You can also record everything by taking photos of your measurements and reference points.

Get your fit reassessed every few years—it's not etched in stone. Your flexibility may improve, your riding style and goals may change, or you may develop chronic problems. Bear in mind that if you adjust one element, you may have to adjust another. For example, changing the saddle position will influence handlebar reach and foot placement.

Be sure to keep stretching. Maintaining flexibility will make you more comfortable on the bike and will become more important as you start riding longer distances. If a certain area of your body is getting tight, spend extra time on stretches and self-massage in that region. If that doesn't help, have your bike fit rechecked.

Andy Pruitt, director of the Boulder Center for Sports Medicine in Boulder, Colorado, and one of the foremost authorities on bike fitting, says that bike fit is a marriage between the body, which is slightly adaptable, and the bike, which is slightly adjustable. Take the necessary time to get a proper fitting. A well-fitted bike will balance comfort, power, and efficiency while minimizing the stress on your body, making the time that you spend on the road more enjoyable.

TABLE 5.1 **Bike Fit Record**

Area	Measurement	Date
Saddle height from the bottom bracket center up the down tube to the top of the saddle		
Stem length from the center bolt over the headset to the center of the bars		
Stem height from the top of the stem to the top of the headset		
Stem angle up or down in degrees from horizontal		
Distance between the center of the tops of the handlebars nearest the stem and the top of the headset		
Distance between the tip of the saddle and the center of the tops of the handlebars		
Distance between the tip of the saddle and top of the top tube, that is, saddle angle		
Left cleat position fore and aft relative to the ball of your foot (widest part of your shoes)		
Left cleat distance out from the cranks		
Left cleat rotational angle in or out in degrees (parallel to the crank is neutral)		
Right cleat position fore and aft relative to the ball of your foot (widest part of your shoes)		
Right cleat distance out from the cranks		
Right cleat rotational angle in or out in degrees (parallel to the crank is neutral)		
Other equipment, such as aerobars		
Other		

From J. Hughes and D. Kehlenbach, 2011, *Distance Cycling* (Champaign, IL: Human Kinetics).

Points of Contact and Increasing Comfort on the Bike

Erika has purchased her road bike and spent an afternoon at the bike shop getting it fitted to her. After a few rides, however, she has a bit of discomfort, particularly in her hands, and her saddle doesn't seem to be quite right.

Bike fit is a start toward comfort, but the bike may need some changes, especially in the points of contact. Points of contact refer to where you come in contact with the bike—butt, feet, and hands. As your rides become longer you may notice points of contact that you'd like to improve.

Three general factors influence comfort at the points of contact:

1. *Bike geometry.* On a racing bike with a straight fork and radially spoked wheels, you will feel the road bumps more than you will on a touring bike with a raked fork and wheels laced with crossed spokes.

2. *Tire size and pressure.* Twenty-millimeter racing tires pumped as hard as possible will transmit more road shock than will 28-millimeter tires inflated to 110 pounds per square inch (750 kilopascals).

3. *Conditioning.* As you become fitter, points of contact will be less of an issue. With stronger legs you'll apply more power to the pedals rather than just sitting on the saddle spinning. With a stronger core less weight will rest on your hands. With improved flexibility you'll be able to adjust your position frequently during rides.

Butt

The next time you are on a group ride, look at the various saddles. Each rider has a unique anatomy and a personal riding style, so each may need a different saddle. In selecting a saddle you should consider several points.

Shape The width of the saddle should fit the width of your ischial tuberosities, or sitz bones, to prevent pain on these pressure points. In recent years gender-specific saddles with anatomical cutouts have become popular. If you suffer from groin pressure or pain while riding, one of these saddles may help. Do some research and select one designed by an anatomical and cycling expert.

Padding Some saddles have a thin layer of foam under the cover, just enough to soften the pressure on the sitz bones, which may help. On a saddle with too much cushioning, your sitz bones displace the cushy material, increasing pressure to your crotch.

Surface A saddle should be smooth enough so that you can slide easily to shift your position; friction increases the risk of saddle sores. Many long-distance riders swear by a leather saddle. Leather saddles, like others, come in various models and widths. Get one whose dimensions fit your sitz bones. If you try a leather saddle, allow plenty of time to break it in and follow the manufacturer's guidelines for break-in and care. When it's broken in, you'll have a custom saddle conforming to the shape of your buttocks.

Saddles, like butts, are personal! If possible, test seats with different shapes and materials (see figure 5.8) on multihour rides; what feels good around the parking lot may be painful after 50 miles (80 km)! Don't worry about weight. A comfortable saddle, even if it is heavier, will allow you to train more and climb better.

Comfort in the saddle is only partly a result of the seat itself; it's also a function of how fit you are. As you become stronger, more power and weight will go into your pedal stroke and less will rest on your buttocks. A bike saddle is not really something that you sit on—you straddle it.

a   b   c

FIGURE 5.8   *(a)* Composite saddle lightly padded with gel, wide rear higher than nose, *(b)* wider saddle with cutout to relieve pressure on groin, and *(c)* leather saddle with flat top.

Feet

Shoes vary not only by size and shape but also by type of riding and pedal system. Several considerations are important.

Stiffness   Cycling-specific shoes have stiff soles to improve power transfer to the pedals. Road cycling shoes are very light and have rigid soles. Mountain bike shoes are a little more flexible, and the soles allow walking when necessary. Touring shoes have softer soles that are also made for walking. If you pedal with running shoes or other types of shoes, you expend energy compressing the shoes' material before the force reaches the pedal. In events lasting many hours or days, this adds up.

Cleat system   With clipless pedals, the shoe attaches to the pedal with a cleat system similar to a ski binding. You step into the pedal and engage the cleat. To remove your foot, you twist the foot outward to disengage the cleat. Some cyclists choose traditional toe clips and straps to keep the shoes positioned on the pedals. Ann Wooldridge used toe clips when she set the women's age-50-and-older North American transcontinental record in 2009.

Float   Cleats can be either fixed or rotational. Fixed cleats lock your feet into one position, whereas rotational or floating cleats allow some foot movement. Rotational cleats are more forgiving on positioning and reduce stress on your knees. Some designs allow more rotation than others. Cleats with too much float may cause knee problems because you have to use muscles and ligaments to maintain the alignment of your feet.

Design   Road cycling shoes usually have cleats that are exposed on the bottom of the shoe. Consequently, walking is difficult, especially on wet or uneven surfaces. Mountain bike and touring shoes generally have recessed cleats, so walking is easier.

Size   A shoe should have a roomy toe box and plenty of ventilation. European cycling shoes tend to be somewhat narrower than American shoes. If you use orthotics, make sure that the shoes can accommodate them. As you pedal for hours your feet will swell at least slightly. Buy shoes that are large enough that you can loosen the straps or laces to reduce pressure on the nerves, which causes a sensation of burning or hot feet. Also check that the closure system doesn't put any uncomfortable pressure on the top of your foot. Shop for shoes in the evening because your feet swell during the day.

If you are training for fast events, you may prefer lighter, stiffer road shoes, whereas if you also plan rides during which you will be walking around, a shoe with a recessed cleat and a less rigid sole will be better. Even for fast centuries and 200Ks, comfort is important. Penseyres wore touring shoes while setting his solo RAAM average speed record.

Whatever pedal and cleat system you choose (see figure 5.9), practice getting in and out of the pedals before you head out on your training rides.

a   **b**   **c**

FIGURE 5.9   *(a)* Speed play road pedals, *(b)* traditional pedals with clips and straps, and *(c)* SPD mountain bike pedals with recessed cleats.

Hands

When riding distance events, you want to increase the comfort of your hands by reducing pressure and decreasing vibration from the road. Considerations include several points.

Core strength   Your hands should rest lightly on the handlebars, as if you were typing. You will need a strong core to do this so continue doing the core strength exercises from chapter 3.

Safety   Cycling gloves make it easier to hold the handlebars, increase your control, protect your skin from blisters, and shield your hands from abrasions if you crash. You can also wipe away sweat and the inevitable runny nose.

Debris   If you ride through glass or other debris, you can carefully place a gloved hand on the rotating tire to prevent an object from becoming embedded into the tire. Put your hand in front of the brake so that the rotating tire won't drag it into the brake. Be sure to keep your eyes on the road.

Padding   A lightly padded glove can increase comfort and help prevent pressure on the nerves that causes numbness. Too much padding in a glove will compress the nerves and cause problems. You can also use gel-filled bar wrap or add some neoprene (the materials used in a wetsuit) under the bar wrap in specific places to make the handlebars more comfortable.

Shape   If you still have hand problems, consider different handlebars.

Clothing

Cycling-specific clothing helps with the points of contact as well as the weather that you will inevitably encounter, including hot sunshine, rain, wind, snow, and possibly all of these in one ride! To start, you need several pairs of shorts, a couple of jerseys, knee and arm warmers, a windbreaker or vest, and perhaps a rain jacket. Cycling clothes are functional and comfortable, and can increase safety on the road. In addition, they can be a fun way to express yourself to your fellow riders.

Helmets

Wear it. Despite skill and caution, accidents happen. A helmet has saved John's life three times. Wear your helmet every time you get on your bike, even if you are just taking it down the street for a test ride. You could sustain a devastating head injury from a stationary fall; it does not take a high-speed accident to cause an injury. Riders without helmets are 14 times more likely to die in a crash than helmeted riders are. Encourage other riders to wear helmets and set a good example for kids—you might save their lives.

A helmet should meet the standards of the United States Consumer Product Safety Commission, or comparable standards. Check the label. The helmet must fit properly. Helmets are not hats, so adjust yours for a snug, level, and stable fit (see figure 5.10).

FIGURE 5.10   **Proper helmet fit.**

Your helmet should be snug, level, and stable so it stays in place even if you shake your head violently or hit the helmet hard with your hand.

Heads come in many shapes and sizes, so a particular helmet may not fit your head. Whatever helmet you choose, adjust it properly.

Proper Fit

Adjust the fit pads or ring so that the helmet sits low on your head. You can remove the pads for the top of the head or use the thinnest ones so the helmet sits lower. Then adjust the pads or ring so the helmet is snug all the way around. The helmet should be level, and its front should be just above your eyes or glasses. When you look up the front rim should be barely visible. When your helmet fits properly, if you walk into a wall it should hit the wall before your head does.

Then adjust the straps so that the Y of the side straps meets just below your ear. The chin strap should be snug enough against the chin so that when you open your mouth very wide, you feel the helmet pull down a little bit on your head. Test the fit by shaking your head. Then try pushing up on each of the four sides—the helmet shouldn't move up more than an inch (2.5 cm).

Finally, check for strap creep. If you can move the side buckle under your ear with your hand, it won't stay adjusted. Sometimes the buckle on the chin straps loosens with use. You can solve this problem with zip ties, rubber bands, or a half-dozen stitches with heavy thread.

If you change your headgear with the seasons, perhaps from a headband to a winter hat, readjust your helmet so that it is snug, level, and stable.

Periodic Inspection

Inspect your helmet periodically to see whether it needs repair or replacement. Look at the main elements of the helmet:

- *Outside shell.* The exterior plastic of a helmet holds it together in a crash. Look for cracks or abrasions on the exterior surface that show evidence of an impact, even from dropping the helmet. If the shell color has faded, the plastic has probably become brittle, and you should replace the helmet.

- *Liner.* Take out the fitting pads if possible and inspect the foam liner carefully for any signs of cracks or compressed foam. If you discover any cracked or crushed foam, replace the helmet.

- *Straps and buckle.* Wash out any accumulated salt and then inspect. Replace the helmet if the straps are worn or faded, if the stitching is beginning to fail, or if the buckles have missing parts.

- *Rear stabilizer.* The rear stabilizer does not hold the helmet on the head, but it provides some stability for comfort. Inspect it for structural integrity and check that the adjustment is working.

Replacement

In general, if you ride thousands of miles a year, then replace your helmet every five years or so. If you ride less you probably can get more time out of it. Designs improve, however, and you may wish to replace a functional helmet with a lighter, better-ventilated one. More specifically, replace your helmet in the following circumstances:

- You can't adjust the fit properly.
- You find a problem that warrants replacement while inspecting it.
- You crashed in it.
- You dropped it hard enough to crack the foam.
- It's from before 1984, when helmet standards were set by the American National Standards Institute, or it has an exterior of foam or cloth instead of plastic.
- It doesn't have a Consumer Product Safety Commission (CPSC), American Society for Testing and Materials (ASTM), or Snell sticker inside.

For more information consult the Bicycle Helmet Safety Institute (www.bhsi.org).

Glasses

Wearing glasses while riding protects your eyes from UV radiation, dust, wind, bugs, and flying debris. UV radiation causes cataracts. Dust and wind irritate and dry the eyes. A bug hitting your eye is at least an irritant and may cause injury, as could debris. Cycling glasses come with wraparound interchangeable lenses, which provide excellent protection. You can use dark lenses during the day and clear or lightly tinted lens to protect the eyes in rain or other periods of reduced visibility. Regular glasses can also be used for cycling, although they don't offer side protection. Whether you use regular or cycling glasses, check the UV screening and impact resistance.

Shorts

Along with proper bike fit and the correct saddle, good shorts will help you enjoy cycling. Bike shorts are made of a tight fabric that helps minimize friction between you and the saddle, which is one of the primary causes of saddle sores.

Shorts have an absorbent chamois to help wick away moisture from your body. The chamois is not designed as a cushion and will not make up for shorts that don't fit or the wrong saddle. A thicker chamois isn't better; it will tend to stick out where the shorts' material doesn't hold it in place. If you put Vaseline on your crotch, this will eliminate friction between the shorts and your skin, another cause of saddle sores.

Some shorts have antibacterial chamois to help guard against infections because infected pores and hair follicles are another major type of saddle sores. Changing out of your shorts as soon as you finish a ride and washing your crotch will help to prevent infection.

Shorts come in two styles. Racing shorts are designed to fit when a rider is bent forward. They have a lower rise front and rear. Touring shorts are designed for a more upright position and have a higher rise. Some types are also available as bib shorts with suspender-type supports that hold the shorts in place more securely, which can also help minimize friction.

Shorts are constructed with multiple panels to fit your body while it is in various riding positions. More expensive shorts will have six or eight panels, but the number of panels doesn't guarantee a good fit. As with saddles, no one design of shorts will fit everybody because we all have different anatomies.

When trying on shorts, hop on a bike to see how they fit while in a riding position. If you can't sit on a bike, bend forward to simulate being on a bike.

Clean shorts are important. Buy several pair so you have a pair to wear while another pair is drying. If you will be touring, get shorts with quick-drying chamois. You may want to have several pair of shorts from different manufacturers. Each manufacturer has a specific cut and stitching pattern, and wearing different styles on different days may increase comfort.

Good shorts are expensive, but they are a sound investment in comfort. If you wash your shorts regularly in a mild detergent they will last many seasons.

Jerseys

Cycling jerseys are made out of a breathable fabric with a front ventilation zipper. They are shaped to reduce wind resistance while riding and usually have pockets in the back to hold food, maps, a windbreaker, and other items that you want handy. You can find jerseys to represent your favorite cycling team, your club, your alma mater, or virtually anything else that you wish to express. Pick jerseys with bright colors for maximum visibility. In cool, damp climates wool is a good choice because it retains its insulating value when wet.

Arm and Leg Warmers

Arm warmers are made of the same fabric as jerseys. By wearing a pair you can turn a short-sleeve jersey into a long-sleeve one. Similarly, knee warmers are made of the same material as your shorts and can extend shorts into knickers, ending below the knee. Leg warmers provide full leg covering. The knee has poor circulation. If your knees get cold, blood won't reach them and they may become injured. You can avoid this by wearing knee or leg warmers until temperatures exceed 60 °F (16 °C). When it warms up, you can take off your warmers and stow them in a jersey pocket. In colder conditions tights provide an extra layer of insulation for the upper legs and hips. Some companies make tights with windproof or rainproof fronts.

Windbreakers and Rain Jackets

Cycling is not limited to fair weather. Sooner or later the skies will open up or the wind will start howling. You want proper equipment because cycling events are usually held rain or shine. A windbreaker and warmers will help keep you comfortable on a windy day with showers, and a rain jacket will make rides in the rain more tolerable. Many fabrics are waterproof or breathable, although a compromise usually exists between the two. When shopping for a jacket, look for these features:

- Wind-blocking fabric
- A shape that fits your body contours rather than catches the wind
- A longer tail to cover your backside while riding
- A reflective or highly visible color to increase your visibility when it's raining and drivers may not expect cyclists to be out
- Zippers in the armpits to increase ventilation
- Zippered sleeves to convert your jacket into a vest
- A design that folds and stows easily

Socks

Lightweight, breathable socks will keep your feet cooler in the summer, and medium-weight fabrics will help keep them warmer in the winter. Don't ride with thick socks in cooler weather because they may make your shoes too tight and reduce circulation.

Riding in Everyday Clothes

Remember riding as a kid? You didn't wear cycling clothes. You just hopped on your bike! Sometimes we get caught up with clothing and forget how easily the bike can be used for short trips. In the United States most trips by automobile are within 6 miles (10 km) of home, so going by bike will not slow you down much. Use your bike to shop, take a trip to the post office, swing by a coffee shop, or visit a friend. Don't bother changing into riding gear—just don't forget your helmet.

Whatever your potential choices of apparel are, try them out in combination before buying. For example, would your new raincoat fit over your hydration pack or your jersey if it has full pockets? Try to test them on a bike—can you reach your water bottle while wearing an aerodynamic windbreaker?

Accessories

Even if you are just running errands, besides your helmet, you need a few other essentials on your bike. For longer rides, you may want to bring along some additional accessories.

On-the-Road Essentials

You should not leave home without these items, which fit into a small seat pack, a jersey, or your hydration pack. Safety should be your primary concern, and you should always carry the following items:

- Driver's license or other form of identification.
- Health card with a list of medications taken, allergies, emergency contact information, and other pertinent health information. This item must be readily accessible. If you are hurt, emergency personnel shouldn't have to waste time looking through your gear for your information. Commercially available wristbands or dog tags are also available.
- Money.
- Car and house keys.

Rather than having to remember these essentials each time, make copies and keep them in your seat pack or hydration pack—whatever always goes with you. Most riders also carry a cell phone, although cell coverage isn't always available. Some people choose not to carry a phone so they aren't tempted to quit rides when the going gets tough.

Besides carrying these essentials, for safety's sake always let someone know where you are going, what route you are taking, and when you'll be returning. If you deviate from the plan, let your contact know and tell him or her when you've arrived.

You should also carry these basic repair items so you can deal with minor mechanical problems:

- Pump or CO_2 inflation system.
- Spare tube or tubes.
- Patch kit.
- Tire boot to put inside the tire if it is damaged such that the tube could bulge out. A few inches (cm) of duct tape works well and is handy for other fixes.
- Tire levers.
- Allen wrenches and a couple of small screwdrivers or a multitool.
- Chain tool with spare chain pin.
- Spoke wrench.

- Fiberax cable emergency spoke. If you are doing longer brevets or touring, consider carrying a few spare spokes. The front wheel, drive side of the rear wheel, and offside of the rear wheel each use spokes of different lengths.
- Spare brake and derailleur cables. If you are touring, consider taking a pair of spare brake pads.

Even if you don't know how to fix a broken chain, true a wheel, or replace a cable, you may find another rider who can help.

Hydration Systems

As noted in chapter 4, drinking to satisfy thirst is important to keep you riding well. You can use a hydration pack, bottles, or a combination, each of which has pros and cons as noted in table 5.2.

Consider carrying a hydration pack in addition to bottles so that you can have several kinds of fluids. For example, you could carry a smaller hydration pack with water and use your bottles for a sports drink. But be careful not to load yourself down with more fluid than you need.

Regularly clean your bottles or pack bladder, because residual moisture will quickly cause mold growth.

TABLE 5.2   **Hydration Packs Versus Bottles**

Hydration packs	Bottles
More carrying capacity: 50–100 fluid ounces (2–3 L)	Less carrying capacity than a hydration pack: 16-24 fluid ounces per bottle
Handy to sip from and more aerodynamic than bottles	Require riding one-handed to get the bottle and drink
Allow for frequent sips, which are easier to absorb	Easy to squirt yourself to cool off
Difficult to gauge how much you are drinking	Easy to monitor consumption
Require sucking, which is hard to do when cycling hard or riding at altitude	Easy to squeeze fluid into your mouth when breathing hard
Added weight on shoulders and back	Can carry more than one type of drink

Food Carriers

If your food is accessible you'll be more likely to eat frequently and keep well fueled. Traditionally, cyclists have used jersey pockets to carry snacks, but they can be awkward to reach, particularly the middle one. If you are doing self-supported rides of more than a few hours, you can stop at minimarts to resupply or you may bring supplies from home. Even on an organized event you may prefer your food to what the organizers offer, particularly if you have dietary restrictions. Here are some options for carrying enough food for the day:

- *Larger seat bag.* A bag large enough to carry your emergency kit, warmers, and food can be secured under the seat, and you can move food to your pockets at stops.
- *Larger hydration pack.* Some packs include pockets to stow provisions, but you will have to carry more weight on your shoulders and back.
- *Bento bag.* This small bag fits on the top tube behind the stem and can hold a half-dozen energy or granola bars or the equivalent.
- *Small handlebar bag.* A small handlebar bag can be suspended between the brake hoods and won't restrict your hand positions.
- *Aerobar bag.* Some models of aerobars accommodate a small bag.

As you select your food carrier and food, remember that adding much weight to the bike will change the handling characteristics. This issue should not be significant with touring or sport frames, but it could be a problem with racing designs that have a straighter fork, particularly if you add much weight over the front wheels in a handlebar or aerobar bag.

Cycling Computers

A cycling computer provides feedback during your ride and data for your logbook. Basic computers give you elapsed time and distance, current and average speed, and clock time. The more intricate models offer cadence, feet or meters climbed, heart rate, interval split times, and other features. Some computers include integrated GPS receivers with interactive map displays and allow you to upload and download routes and ride details to and from your computer. Whichever model you choose, learn the features in a safe area. The open road is a dangerous place to be fiddling with your computer.

Heart Rate Monitors and Power Meters

Successful conditioning is the result of the right combinations of ride durations and intensities. The numbers from your cycle computer aren't the best way to judge the intensity and progression of your training. As an example, a 20-mile (32 km) ride through hilly terrain will be significantly different from a flat 20-mile ride. You can gauge intensity with a heart rate monitor, a power meter, or perceived exertion (see chapter 6).

Heart Rate Monitors

A heart rate monitor measures how fast your heart is beating, an indicator of how hard your body is working. However, a number of factors can influence heart rate, including stress, hydration level, air temperature, humidity level, and core temperature.

Helpful heart rate monitor features include zone alarms that warn if you are above or below your targeted intensity, records of average heart rate, and logs of how much time you spent in the various training zones. We will talk about how to use heart rate information for training in the next chapter.

Power Meters

Power meters measure how much force, or power, you apply to the pedals when you are riding.

To move forward, you use both the cardiovascular system and the muscular system. For years coaches and athletes measured the heart rate to assess the effect of training on the cardiovascular system. But heart rate tells only one side of the story—how fast your heart is beating. A power meter allows you to look at the training response of the muscular system and interpret it along with the numbers from your heart rate monitor.

Both power meters and sophisticated heart rate monitors record data during the ride, which you can then download and analyze. You can see how your body responds to specific training stimuli, so you can calibrate future workouts more accurately. Data from a power meter or heart rate monitor can also be e-mailed to a coach for analysis and planning.

A basic heart rate monitor currently costs around US$70 and a sophisticated one costs around $US270. A heart rate monitor with GPS costs around $350. Power Tap, the most popular power meter, is built into the rear wheel; a unit built to a conventional spoke rear wheel costs around US$1,200, and one built to an aero wheel can cost over US$2,000.

Whether you need a heart rate monitor or power meter depends on the type of feedback that works for you. In general, the higher your goals are, the more you need accurate feedback. You should also consider your willingness to learn how to use the equipment and software and how to interpret the data. John coaches successful riders using perceived exertion, heart rate monitors, or power meters for information. Pick the type of feedback that works for you.

Maintenance

You've invested a lot in your bike. Through basic maintenance you can keep it running smoothly for many years. This preventive maintenance doesn't replace regular shop visits; what we describe is primarily to prevent most roadside emergencies.

Washing Your Bike

A clean bike will ride more smoothly, shift better, be easier to maintain, and last longer. Regularly washing your bike allows you to spot potential problems in the components or frame. Don't wash your bike after every ride—once a week is enough. To wash the frame, lean the bike against the garage door, hang it from a hook in a rafter, or clamp it in a bike repair stand. Rinse it off with a low-pressure hose. Avoid using a high-pressure hose, which can force water into bearings, causing premature wear. Wash the frame with soapy water. A large sponge or rags work well, and an old toothbrush is handy for tight places. Spend a little extra time scrubbing any grime off the wheel rims to improve braking. Rinse thoroughly. While doing all of this, try to avoid spraying the drive train.

The chain and some derailleur wheels are lubricated internally. Cleaning them is difficult without washing away the lubricant. John replaces his chain every 1,500 miles (2,500 km), but he doesn't clean the chain unless it gets soaked in the rain or snow and picks up a lot of dirt. In this case, he wipes down the chain with a dry rag to remove most of the grit and then puts on some chain lube. Each time he replaces the chain, he scrubs the chain rings and cassette cogs. He disassembles the derailleurs including the rear derailleur wheels and then cleans, lubes, reassembles, and adjusts them.

Dan cleans his drive train weekly. He sprays degreaser on the chain and lets it penetrate for about 10 minutes. He then wipes it down with a clean rag, using a stiff brush if it's particularly dirty, and applies a penetrating chain lube.

Both approaches work; it's your choice, depending on how much time you have and how fastidious you are.

Finally, dry the bike and inspect the frame, components, and cables for cracks, wear, or other problems.

Dealing With Flats

Flat tires are a fact of life in cycling. You can reduce the incidence of flats by riding with relatively new tires and new (not patched) tubes that are properly inflated. Replacing your tires and tubes right before an important event is cheap insurance to minimize punctures. Wider tires (25 and 28 millimeters) are less prone to pinch flats than narrower tires. Several heavier, puncture-resistant tires are on the market, but no tire will be invulnerable.

Because a flat inevitably happens at a bad time, practice changing a flat at home. To make dealing with a flat easier, always mount your tires with the manufacturer's label by the valve stem on the left (non-drive-train) side of each wheel. Here's how to fix a flat:

1. Open the brake a bit with the built-in release and remove the wheel that has the flat tire.
2. If the tire isn't completely flat, let the rest of the air out.
3. Using tire levers, lift the bead of the tire over the left (non-drive-train) side of the rim, starting opposite the valve stem and working toward the valve.
4. Pull out the tube, keeping it oriented relative to the tire to help find the hole.
5. Carefully run your fingers inside the tire to locate what caused the flat. This object is sharp, so go slowly. If you don't find anything, run your hand over the outside. Then visually inspect the tire inside and out. If you find something, pull it out. If you are prone to thorns in your area, carry a pair of tweezers to pull them out. If you still haven't found the hole, partially inflate the tube and rotate it near your ear, listening for the puncture. You can confirm the location by rubbing a bit of saliva on the spot to see whether it bubbles. Then orient the tube to the tire—this is why you mounted the tire with the label in a specific place—and look for the tiny offender. Search thoroughly for the cause; you don't want to replace the tube, inflate the tire, and have it go flat again!
6. If you have no spare tube, patch the tube according to the directions in your patch kit.
7. If you have a cut through which the tube might protrude even a little, put a boot on the inside of the tire over the cut. A piece of duct tape works well, as does folded currency or a strong energy bar wrapper.
8. Inflate the spare or patched tube with three or four strokes of your pump, or blow into it. Put the tube back into the tire starting with the valve stem and working symmetrically away from the stem.

9. After you have the tube in, reseat the tire on the bead of the rim. Start opposite the valve stem and work symmetrically toward the valve. If you keep the tube slightly inflated, it will be less likely to be pinched under the bead. Do not use tire levers to remount the tire. Use the heels of your hands to roll the tire back on to the rim.

10. Pump up the tube with three or four more strokes and then check the bead all the way around the rim on both sides to be sure that it is seated correctly and that the bead isn't pinching the tube.

11. Inflate the tire so it passes the "ping" test. Snap your fingernail briskly against the tire. The sound should be a "ping" rather than a "thunk."

12. Replace the wheel and tighten the brake release. To be sure that the wheel is centered, apply the brake and then tighten the quick release.

Basic Repairs

Take the time to learn how to perform basic bike repairs. You should know how to

- adjust the front and rear derailleurs,
- adjust the action of the brakes and center them, and
- deal with a broken spoke.

If you are planning unsupported day rides, longer brevets, or tours, you should also know how to

- fix a broken chain,
- replace a brake pad, and
- replace a broken shift or brake cable.

To learn how to make these adjustments and repairs, refer to a repair manual or check with your local shop. You may be able to attend a repair clinic. Hands-on experience with a good mechanic is the best way to learn.

Preride Check-Up

We've all done it. Fifteen minutes into a ride you realize that you forgot your spare tubes or pump. What do you do? Go back and get them or continue the ride hoping that nothing goes wrong? Posting a preride checklist by your bike and reviewing it before each ride will prevent problems. Before your ride, check the following:

- Be sure that you have your on-the-road essentials listed earlier.
- Check your tires:
  - Air pressure—correct air pressure minimizes the chances of flats caused when the tube gets pinched against the rim. You can use a gauge or the "ping" test.
  - Condition—make sure that they are clean and have no cuts.
- Check your wheels:
  - Trueness—spin the wheels. They should not wobble.
  - Quick releases—they should be secure but not too tight.

- Check the brakes and shifting.
- Inspect your helmet.
- Have sufficient fluids and food for the ride or money to buy en route.

Rest Stop Check-Up

During a ride, at every stop make it a habit to do the following:

- Spin each wheel slowly against your gloved hand to clean the tires and inspect them for cuts. Also, check that the wheels are still in true and that the brakes are centered and not rubbing.
- Check the tire pressure using the "ping" test.
- Squeeze the brakes to make sure that the cables aren't wearing and stretching.

Monthly Bike Check-Up

Every month go through all the preride checks and do the following:

Check the tightness of

- crank arms,
- pedals,
- chain ring bolts,
- seat post bolt and seat mounting bolts,
- brake pads, brake mounting, and brake cable connection bolts,
- front and rear derailleur mounting and cable connection bolts,
- shifting and brake lever mountings,
- bolts or screws of bottle cages and other accessories,
- stem bolts, and
- shoes and cleats for loose screws or bolts.

Test the

- adjustment of the brake and derailleur cables,
- headset for easy movement without excessive play,
- hubs for spinning without too much play, and
- bottom bracket for smooth rotation without excessive play.

Lubricate the

- brake, derailleur, and pedal pivot points, and
- cables where they enter the housings (check for fraying and rusting as well, and replace as necessary).

Check your seat pack for

- excessive wear and firm attachment and
- the contents of your repair kit.

Annual Check-Up

Just as we get an annual health check-up, you should have your bike thoroughly checked once a year. If you are proficient with maintenance, you could do this yourself. If you have a shop take care of the annual maintenance, get this done at the end of your season. Bike shops are often swamped at the start of the new season. Then you can test everything during the off-season to make sure that your bike runs smoothly. An annual overhaul should include the following:

- Strip the frame of all parts, clean it, and wax it to protect the finish.
- Check the tires and rim tape and replace if needed.
- Check the wheels for trueness and loose spokes.
- Repack all nonsealed bearings.
- Replace the chain and cassette or freewheel.
- Replace the brake pads.
- Inspect all cables and replace as necessary. Shifting cables, especially for integrated shifting and braking systems, have a finite life. Replace them before each season to avoid a catastrophic failure on the road.
- Put on new handlebar tape.
- Inspect cleats for wear and replace as necessary.
- If you are using toe straps, inspect for wear and replace as necessary.
- Inspect bottle cages, seat pack, hydration pack, bladder, and so on for wear and replace as necessary.
- Lubricate your frame and floor pumps.
- Go through your clothes. Are they ready for another season? Do you need a new item that you didn't have this season?

Selecting the proper equipment for distance cycling will help you enjoy training and improve your safety. Researching and buying gear can be a lot of fun, but remember to keep things simple and functional. Don't get carried away accumulating the latest gadgets. To become a better cyclist, Eddy Merckx advises: "Don't buy upgrades; ride up grades." Buy the best bike that you can within your budget, learn how to take care of it, and get out and ride it! In the next chapter, we'll look at how to progress from the baseline conditioning rides to in-season training to get ready for the big event.

CHAPTER 6

Preparing Your Body to Go the Distance

The century (100 miles) and 200-kilometer (124 miles) single-day events are among the most popular distance cycling events and are stepping-stones to longer rides. Completing a century or 200-kilometer ride may seem impossible, but with the right preparation your ride will be a successful, enjoyable experience that you will remember for years. Your finishing time will vary depending on your conditioning, the terrain, the weather, and your time off the bike at stops, but you should figure around 8 hours to complete your first 100-mile ride and 10 hours for your first 200-kilometer ride. In this chapter we use the term century to cover both distances.

Having looked at assessment and planning, baseline conditioning, nutrition, and equipment in earlier chapters as they relate to successfully completing a century or 200K, in this chapter we focus on specific training for this type of event.

Kyle has completed the baseline conditioning phase and followed the recommendations from the previous chapters. He is comfortable doing a 90-minute ride on the weekends and two shorter rides of 30 and 45 minutes during the week. You should be at about the same point. You are used to time in the saddle and are familiar with your bike and its operation. Riding safely and efficiently should be habitual, so you can now focus more on training and nutrition.

The training programs in this chapter follow the training principles of progressive overload, individuality, specificity, variation, and recovery (see pages 21–22 in chapter 3) to help you improve and reach your goals.

Developing Your Training Schedule

Effective training for a distance cycling event follows a systematic plan. We present two examples: an 8-week program and a 15-week program. Erika wants to ride a century in July, and Kyle plans one in September. Erika has been running regularly and will use the 8-week program. Kyle has followed our baseline conditioning program, and, because he has more lead time, he'll use the 15-week program. Use one of the sample programs to develop your personal plan, taking into account your fitness level, calendar, and target event.

Both programs use five distinct workouts. The first four of these train the aerobic, lactic acid, and ATP-CP energy systems (see chapter 3, page 20), and the fifth targets core strength, flexibility, and muscular strength.

For each type of workout we provide shorter and longer options following the principle of individuality. Choose the option that fits your fitness level and available time. We define workouts in terms of training time as opposed to distance. A 40-mile (65 km) ride in the hills is different from one in flat terrain, and a flat ride on a windy day is a different workout than a ride on a calm day. So, train by time.

Here are the workouts:

1. *Long.* An endurance ride of 2:00 to 2:30 (8-week program) or 1:30 to 2:30 (15-week program) in the first week increasing to 5:15 to 6:30 in both programs. By doing these rides at your anticipated pace for the century, you train your aerobic metabolism, build endurance, and gain experience with pacing, nutrition, and other skills.

2. *Tempo.* A midweek tempo ride beginning at 40 to 60 minutes and building to 60 to 90 minutes in both programs. By riding once a week a little faster than your century pace, you improve the upper range of your aerobic system and increase the cruising pace that you can hold in the century.

3. *Brisk.* In both programs a brisk midweek ride of 30 to 40 minutes that includes 10 to 15 minutes of mixed intensity, increasing to 60 to 90 minutes including 20 to 30 minutes of mixed intensity. The mixed intensity is a combination of hard riding and recovery. The hard efforts work the lactic acid and ATP-CP energy systems and improve your power to climb hills and ride with a faster group.

4. *Recovery.* One or two active recovery rides of 20 to 30 minutes each using the low end of your aerobic metabolism, increasing to 40 to 60 minutes in both programs. You could run errands on your bike.

5. *Supplementary.* Core strength, flexibility, and resistance maintenance training. Depending on your choices these would total 50 minutes to 2:40 each week in both programs.

Details on each type of workout are provided in the Maximizing Your Training section beginning on page 116. Whether you follow the 8- or 15-week program, choose either the shorter or longer endurance ride, depending on your current fitness and schedule, and stay with that one through the program. The long ride should not be too much of your weekly volume. Therefore, if you plan the longer endurance ride then you should also do the longer tempo, brisk, and recovery rides. If you plan the shorter endurance ride you *may* include longer tempo, brisk, and recovery rides in your training if you have time. You'll improve your fitness faster but don't overdo it. Because the brisk ride is harder than the tempo ride, try to have two easy days (off or active recovery) before the brisk ride, although doing so may not be possible every week.

Long rides build your endurance and sense of pacing.

Courtesy of Alaska Digital Visions.

Both programs will help prepare you for your event. The 15-week program starts with 3:00 to 5:10 of riding the first week, slightly less than the 8-week program, and builds more slowly. Both programs ramp up to the same peak week of 7:55 to 11:00 of riding before the century.

Midway through both programs we include an easier week with less riding. This recovery week allows you to recover physically and mentally from the weeks of hard work before you ramp up to the peak week. Adaptations from training occur while your body is resting: "Stress plus rest equals success." You may feel great approaching the recovery week and be tempted to skip it, but don't. Your body will thank you later.

To help you recover fully for your event, both programs include a taper during the final week of training and the week before the event. During the taper you ride enough to maintain your fitness while significantly reducing the volume so that you are fresh. Right before your big event you can't get stronger, but you can run yourself down. Don't try to make up for lost training.

8-Week Century Training Program

If you are an active club rider or have been involved in another endurance sport, the 8-week program beginning on page 102 might be right for you.

8-WEEK CENTURY PROGRAM

WEEK 1

Riding:

Long ride of 2:00–2:30
Midweek tempo ride of 40–60 minutes
Midweek brisk ride of 30–40 minutes including 10–15 minutes of mixed intensity
Active recovery of 20–30 minutes
Second active recovery of 20–30 minutes (optional)
Total riding time: 3:30–5:10

Supplementary training:

Two core strength-training sessions of 10–20 minutes
Three stretching sessions of 10–20 minutes
One or two resistance-training maintenance sessions of 20–30 minutes (optional)

WEEK 2

Riding:

Long ride of 2:30–3:15
Midweek tempo ride of 50–75 minutes
Midweek brisk ride of 40–60 minutes including 10–15 minutes of mixed intensity
Active recovery of 30–40 minutes
Second active recovery of 20–30 minutes (optional)
Total riding time: 4:30–6:40

Supplementary training:

Two core strength-training sessions of 10–20 minutes
Three stretching sessions of 10–20 minutes
One or two resistance-training maintenance sessions of 20–30 minutes (optional)

WEEK 3

Riding:

Long ride of 3:00–4:00
Midweek tempo ride of 60–90 minutes
Midweek brisk ride of 40–60 minutes including 15–20 minutes of mixed intensity
Active recovery of 30–40 minutes
Second active recovery of 20–30 minutes (optional)
Total riding time: 5:10–7:40

Supplementary training:

Two core strength-training sessions of 10–20 minutes
Three stretching sessions of 10–20 minutes
One or two resistance-training maintenance sessions of 20–30 minutes (optional)

WEEK 4—RECOVERY

Riding:

Long ride of 1:30–2:30
Midweek tempo ride of 30–40 minutes
Active recovery of 20–30 minutes
Active recovery of 20–30 minutes
Total riding time: 2:20–4:10

Supplementary training:

Two core strength-training sessions of 10–20 minutes
Three stretching sessions of 10–20 minutes
No resistance training

WEEK 5

Riding:

Long ride of 3:30–4:30
Midweek tempo ride of 60–90 minutes
Midweek brisk ride of 60–90 minutes including 15–20 minutes of mixed intensity
Active recovery of 40–60 minutes
Second active recovery of 20–30 minutes (optional)
Total riding time: 6:10–9:00

Supplementary training:

Two core strength-training sessions of 10–20 minutes
Three stretching sessions of 10–20 minutes
One or two resistance-training maintenance sessions of 20–30 minutes (optional)

WEEK 6

Riding:

Long ride of 4:30–5:30
Midweek tempo ride of 60–90 minutes
Midweek brisk ride of 60–90 minutes including 20–30 minutes of mixed intensity
Active recovery of 40–60 minutes
Second active recovery of 20–30 minutes (optional)
Total riding time: 7:10–10:00

Supplementary training:

Two core strength-training sessions of 10–20 minutes
Three stretching sessions of 10–20 minutes
One or two resistance-training maintenance sessions of 20–30 minutes (optional)

(continued)

WEEK 7—PEAK

Riding:

Long ride of 5:15–6:30
Midweek tempo ride of 60–90 minutes
Midweek brisk ride of 60–90 minutes including 20–30 minutes of mixed intensity
Active recovery of 40–60 minutes
Second active recovery of 20–30 minutes (optional)
Total riding time: 7:55–11:00

Supplementary training:

Two core strength-training sessions of 10–20 minutes
Three stretching sessions of 10–20 minutes
One or two resistance-training maintenance sessions of 20–30 minutes (optional)

WEEK 8—TAPER

Riding:

Long ride of 2:30–3:30
Midweek tempo ride of 60–90 minutes
Midweek brisk ride of 60–90 minutes including 15–20 minutes of mixed intensity
Active recovery of 40–60 minutes
Second active recovery of 20–30 minutes (optional)
Total riding time: 5:10–8:00

Supplementary training:

Two core strength-training sessions of 10–20 minutes
Three stretching sessions of 10–20 minutes
No resistance training

CENTURY WEEK

Riding:

Long ride—century or 200 kilometers
Midweek tempo ride of 30–40 minutes
Active recovery of 20–30 minutes
Active recovery of 20–30 minutes

Supplementary training:

Two core strength-training sessions of 10–20 minutes
Three stretching sessions of 10–20 minutes
No resistance training

We start the training week on Monday so that the long ride can be on either Saturday or Sunday, depending on your schedule as well as factors such as weather.

After reviewing the 8-week program, Erika maps out her ride schedule (see figure 6.1) so that she can balance it with the other parts of her life. Given her running experience, Erika is confident that she can do the longer endurance rides, so she includes the longer midweek tempo, brisk, and recovery rides. Because the brisk ride is the harder midweek ride she puts it on Tuesday when possible so that she has two easy days after the weekend ride. She plans to run errands on her bike on Wednesday, and instead of the tempo workout she'll run one day a week at the same level of effort. She has a day off before the long ride and an active recovery ride after the long ride. If she misses her weekly brisk ride or run, she might be tempted to make it up on Friday, because that's a day off. That change would work only if she can take Saturday off and move her long ride to Sunday because she should be well rested for her long ride. Given other obligations she changes the workout order in weeks 5 and 6 while maintaining the pattern of rest and recovery days. Erika will do her core and flexibility workouts throughout the week as time permits. She'll try to fit in one or two resistance-training maintenance sessions after her workouts on Tuesday or Thursday so that her days off and active recovery days

FIGURE 6.1 ERIKA'S SAMPLE 8-WEEK RIDE SCHEDULE

	M	Tu	W	Th	F	Sa	Su
Week 1	Off	0:40 B/Rd, 0:20 Res/M	0:30 Act/R	0:60 Run, 0:20 Res/M	Off	2:30 L/Rd	0:30 Act/R
Week 2	Off	B/Rd, Res/M	Act/R	Run, Res/M	Off	L/Rd	Act/R
Week 3	Off	B/Rd, Res/M	Act/R	Run, Res/M	Off	L/Rd	Act/R
Week 4 Recovery	Off	Act/R	Off	Run	Off	L/Rd	Act/R
Week 5	Run, Res/M	Off	Act/R	B/Rd, Res/M	Off	L/Rd	Act/R
Week 6	Run, Res/M	Off	Act/R	B/Rd, Res/M	Off	L/Rd	Act/R
Week 7 Peak	Off	B/Rd, Res/M	Act/R	Run, Res/M	Off	L/Rd	Act/R
Week 8 Taper	Off	B/Rd	Act/R	Run	Off	L/Rd	Act/R
Century Week	Off	Act/R	T/Rd	Act/R	Off	Century!	

Abbreviations for types of workouts: Brisk Ride = B/Rd; Active Recovery = Act/R; Long Ride = L/Rd; Resistance Maintenance = Res/M; Tempo Ride = T/Rd.

allow full recovery. During some weeks, however, she might do a resistance-training workout along with the active recovery ride on Sunday if she isn't too tired from her long ride. A full day off follows on Monday.

If you plan an 8-week program, use figure 6.2 to create your own workout schedule. Put in each workout type as well as the amount of time for each activity. Spread the various rides throughout the week to provide two easy days before the brisk ride and include easy days before and after your weekly long ride. If you participate in another sport, you may incorporate it into your weekly schedule. Cross-training helps you become a stronger athlete and healthier person. But because you are training for a cycling event, you should ride at least four days a week including your active recovery sessions. Also, plan your core strength and stretching workouts, which may float during the week or be on specific days, and consider whether and when to fit in the optional resistance-maintenance workouts. We recommend a recovery week in week 4, but you could move that to week 5 if it fits your calendar better. After you have created your plan, share it with those close to you so that they can see that you have plenty of time in your schedule for them, too!

FIGURE 6.2 8-WEEK RIDE SCHEDULE PLANNING FORM

	M	Tu	W	Th	F	Sa	Su
Week 1							
Week 2							
Week 3							
Week 4 Recovery							
Week 5							
Week 6							
Week 7 Peak							
Week 8 Taper							
Century Week							

Staying With a Training Program

By Julie Gazmararian

Gazmararian has completed many brevets and twice qualified for the Race Across America. She is a member of Atlanta-based Sorella Cycling, which fosters a supportive environment for cycling for fitness, recreation, and racing for women of all ages and abilities. She is a professor at Rollins School of Public Health at Emory University, Atlanta, and a mother of two boys.

1. *Set goals.* Make your goals realistic and achievable. Set both short-term (e.g., complete this weekend's ride) and intermediate goals (e.g., build to a 50- to 60-mile [80 to 100 km] ride) that will lead to your long-term goal (e.g., a century). Your goals will help you focus your training plan.

2. *Share your goals with others.* Telling other people about your goals will help you stick to them (or have others help you stick with them). Tell your significant other, kids, or coworkers what your goal is for the current week.

3. *Develop a cycling support group.* Find a group of people or a club and support each other by showing up to ride and bugging each other if you or they don't show up!

4. *Stick with a consistent schedule.* For example, plan to ride Tuesday and Thursday before work, Saturday with the club, and Sunday for coffee with your significant other.

5. *Have a training partner.* Find a good training partner who has a pace and goals similar to yours. Work together to set and achieve your goals.

6. *Establish cycling rides as a routine.* Be consistent and block out time to ride so that it becomes part of your daily and weekly routine. Mark your planned rides and events on your calendar and make them a priority.

7. *Keep a log.* Record your training sessions (both planned for the week and what you actually did). Writing these down will help you stay on track and help you assess good and not-so-good training sessions (e.g., overtraining).

8. *Reward yourself.* Acknowledge your training milestones and training consistency, such as the first time you go a certain distance, achieve a faster pace, or do four rides in a week! Don't get too hung up on volume, but feel good when you do a bit more this week than last.

9. *Take time off.* More is not better. Taking time off is critical so that your body can rest and recover and so that you rejuvenate mentally and are excited about your next training ride or event.

10. *Plan a new route.* Seeing new scenery and exploring new roads are mentally refreshing. Cycling on new roads with different terrain is good training (e.g., hilly route, flat and fast route).

11. *Be flexible.* Events or weather may interfere with your training plans. Learn to make adjustments and not to take it too seriously if you miss a training ride.

12. *Keep it fun.* You are more likely to stick to a training program if you have fun.

15-Week Century Training Program

If you're fairly new to working out or have more time to prepare for your event, then the 15-week program beginning on page 108 is a better choice. The longer program allows more time for you to adapt physically and mentally to working out, and you can add a second recovery week if necessary.

15-WEEK CENTURY PROGRAM

WEEK 1

Riding:

Long ride of 1:30–2:30
Midweek tempo ride of 40–60 minutes
Midweek brisk ride of 30–40 minutes including 10–15 minutes of mixed intensity
Active recovery of 20–30 minutes
Second active recovery of 20–30 minutes (optional)
Total riding time: 3:00–5:10

Supplementary training:

Two core strength-training sessions of 10–20 minutes
Three stretching sessions of 10–20 minutes
One or two resistance-training maintenance sessions of 20–30 minutes (optional)

WEEK 2

Riding:

Long ride of 2:00–3:00
Midweek tempo ride of 40–60 minutes
Midweek brisk ride of 30–40 minutes including 10–15 minutes of mixed intensity
Active recovery of 20–30 minutes
Second active recovery of 20–30 minutes (optional)
Total riding time: 3:30–5:40

Supplementary training:

Two core strength-training sessions of 10–20 minutes
Three stretching sessions of 10–20 minutes
One or two resistance-training maintenance sessions of 20–30 minutes (optional)

WEEK 3

Riding:

Long ride of 2:00–3:00
Midweek tempo ride of 50–75 minutes
Midweek brisk ride of 40–60 minutes including 10–15 minutes of mixed intensity
Active recovery of 30–40 minutes
Second active recovery of 20–30 minutes (optional)
Total riding time: 4:00–6:25

Supplementary training:

Two core strength-training sessions of 10–20 minutes
Three stretching sessions of 10–20 minutes
One or two resistance-training maintenance sessions of 20–30 minutes (optional)

WEEK 4

Riding:

Long ride of 2:30–3:30
Midweek tempo ride of 50–75 minutes
Midweek brisk ride of 40–60 minutes including 15–20 minutes of mixed intensity
Active recovery of 30–40 minutes
Second active recovery of 20–30 minutes (optional)
Total riding time: 4:30–6:55

Supplementary training:

Two core strength-training sessions of 10–20 minutes
Three stretching sessions of 10–20 minutes
One or two resistance-training maintenance sessions of 20–30 minutes (optional)

WEEK 5

Riding:

Long ride of 3:00–4:00
Midweek tempo ride of 60–90 minutes
Midweek brisk ride of 40–60 minutes including 15–20 minutes of mixed intensity
Active recovery of 30–40 minutes
Second active recovery of 20–30 minutes (optional)
Total riding time: 5:10–7:40

Supplementary training:

Two core strength-training sessions of 10–20 minutes
Three stretching sessions of 10–20 minutes
One or two resistance-training maintenance sessions of 20–30 minutes (optional)

WEEK 6

Riding:

Long ride of 3:30–4:30
Midweek tempo ride of 60–90 minutes
Midweek brisk ride of 40–60 minutes including 15–20 minutes of mixed intensity
Active recovery of 40–60 minutes
Second active recovery of 20–30 minutes (optional)
Total riding time: 5:50–8:30

Supplementary training:

Two core strength-training sessions of 10–20 minutes
Three stretching sessions of 10–20 minutes
One or two resistance-training maintenance sessions of 20–30 minutes (optional)

(continued)

WEEK 7

Riding:

Long ride of 3:30–4:30
Midweek tempo ride of 60–90 minutes
Midweek brisk ride of 60–90 minutes including 20–30 minutes of mixed intensity
Active recovery of 40–60 minutes
Second active recovery of 20–30 minutes (optional)
Total riding time: 6:10–9:00

Supplementary training:

Two core strength-training sessions of 10–20 minutes
Three stretching sessions of 10–20 minutes
One or two resistance-training maintenance sessions of 20–30 minutes (optional)

WEEK 8—RECOVERY

Riding:

Long ride of 1:00–2:00
Midweek tempo ride of 30–40 minutes
Active recovery of 20–30 minutes
Active recovery of 20–30 minutes
Total riding time: 2:10–3:40

Supplementary training:

Two core strength-training sessions of 10–20 minutes
Three stretching sessions of 10–20 minutes
No resistance training

WEEK 9

Riding:

Long ride of 2:30–3:30
Midweek tempo ride of 50–75 minutes
Midweek brisk ride of 40–60 minutes including 10–15 minutes of mixed intensity
Active recovery of 30–40 minutes
Second active recovery of 20–30 minutes (optional)
Total riding time: 4:30–6:55

Supplementary training:

Two core strength-training sessions of 10–20 minutes
Three stretching sessions of 10–20 minutes
One or two resistance-training maintenance sessions of 20–30 minutes (optional)

WEEK 10

Riding:

Long ride of 3:00–4:00
Midweek tempo ride of 60–90 minutes
Midweek brisk ride of 40–60 minutes including 10–15 minutes of mixed intensity
Active recovery of 40–60 minutes
Second active recovery of 20–30 minutes (optional)
Total riding time: 5:20–8:00

Supplementary training:

Two core strength-training sessions of 10–20 minutes
Three stretching sessions of 10–20 minutes
One or two resistance-training maintenance sessions of 20–30 minutes (optional)

WEEK 11

Riding:

Long ride of 3:30–4:30
Midweek tempo ride of 60–90 minutes
Midweek brisk ride of 60–90 minutes including 15–20 minutes of mixed intensity
Active recovery of 40–60 minutes
Second active recovery of 20–30 minutes (optional)
Total riding time: 6:10–9:00

Supplementary training:

Two core strength-training sessions of 10–20 minutes
Three stretching sessions of 10–20 minutes
One or two resistance-training maintenance sessions of 20–30 minutes (optional)

WEEK 12

Riding:

Long ride of 4:00–5:00
Midweek tempo ride of 60–90 minutes
Midweek brisk ride of 60–90 minutes including 15–20 minutes of mixed intensity
Active recovery of 40–60 minutes
Second active recovery of 20–30 minutes (optional)
Total riding time: 6:40–9:30

Supplementary training:

Two core strength-training sessions of 10–20 minutes
Three stretching sessions of 10–20 minutes
One or two resistance-training maintenance sessions of 20–30 minutes (optional)

WEEK 13

Riding:

Long ride of 4:30–5:30
Midweek tempo ride of 60–90 minutes
Midweek brisk ride of 60–90 minutes including 20–30 minutes of mixed intensity
Active recovery of 40–60 minutes
Second active recovery of 20–30 minutes (optional)
Total riding time: 7:10–10:00

Supplementary training:

Two core strength-training sessions of 10–20 minutes
Three stretching sessions of 10–20 minutes
One or two resistance-training maintenance sessions of 20–30 minutes (optional)

(continued)

15-Week Century Program *(continued)*

WEEK 14—PEAK

Riding:

Long ride of 5:15–6:30
Midweek tempo ride of 60–90 minutes
Midweek brisk ride of 60–90 minutes including 20–30 minutes of mixed intensity
Active recovery of 40–60 minutes
Second active recovery of 20–30 minutes (optional)
Total riding time: 7:55–11:00

Supplementary training:

Two core strength-training sessions of 10–20 minutes
Three stretching sessions of 10–20 minutes
One or two resistance-training maintenance sessions of 20–30 minutes (optional)

WEEK 15—TAPER

Riding:

Long ride of 2:30–3:30
Midweek tempo ride of 60–90 minutes
Midweek brisk ride of 60–90 minutes including 15–20 minutes of mixed intensity
Active recovery of 40–60 minutes
Second active recovery of 20–30 minutes (optional)
Total riding time: 5:10–8:00

Supplementary training:

Two core strength-training sessions of 10–20 minutes
Three stretching sessions of 10–20 minutes
No resistance training

CENTURY WEEK

Riding:

Long ride—century or 200-kilometer
Midweek tempo ride of 30–40 minutes
Active recovery of 20–30 minutes
Active recovery of 20–30 minutes

Supplementary training:

Two core strength-training sessions of 10–20 minutes
Three stretching sessions of 10–20 minutes
No resistance training

After reviewing the sample 15-week program Kyle decides to train conservatively, so he plans the shorter weekend rides (see figure 6.3). He puts his brisk ride on Tuesday most weeks so that he has two days to recover from the weekend, and he does his easier

---

FIGURE 6.3 **KYLE'S 15-WEEK RIDE SCHEDULE**

	M	Tu	W	Th	F	Sa	Su
Week 1	0:15 Core	0:30 B/Rd 0:10 Flex	0:20 Act/R	0:40 T/Rd, 0:10 Flex	0:15 Core	1:30 L/Rd, 0:20 Flex	0:30 Act/R, 0:20 Res/M
Week 2	Core	B/Rd, Flex	Act/R	T/Rd, Flex	Core	L/Rd, Flex	Act/R, Res/M
Week 3	Core	B/Rd, Flex	Act/R	T/Rd, Flex	Core	L/Rd, Flex	Act/R, Res/M
Week 4	Core	B/Rd, Flex	Act/R	T/Rd, Flex	Core	Wedding Act/R	L/Rd, Flex
Week 5	Core	T/Rd, Flex	Act/R	B/Rd, Flex	Core	L/Rd, Flex	Act/R, Res/M
Week 6	Core	B/Rd, Flex	Act/R	T/Rd, Flex	Core	L/Rd, Flex	Act/R, Res/M
Week 7	Core	B/Rd, Flex	Act/R	T/Rd, Flex	Core	L/Rd, Flex	Act/R, Res/M
Week 8 Recovery	Core	T/Rd, Flex	Off	Act/R	Core	M/Rd, Flex	Act/R
Week 9	Core	B/Rd, Flex	Act/R	T/Rd, Flex	Core	L/Rd, Flex	Act/R, Res/M
Week 10	Core	B/Rd, Flex	Act/R	T/Rd, Flex	Core	L/Rd, Flex	Act/R
Week 11	Core	T/Rd, Flex	Act/R	B/Rd, Flex	Core	L/Rd, Flex	Act/R, Res/M
Week 12	Core	B/Rd, Flex	Act/R	T/Rd, Flex	Core	L/Rd, Flex	Act/R, Res/M
Week 13	Core	B/Rd, Flex	Act/R	T/Rd, Flex	Core	L/Rd, Flex	Act/R, Res/M
Week 14 Peak	Core	B/Rd, Flex	Act/R	T/Rd, Flex	Core	L/Rd, Flex	Act/R, Res/M
Week 15 Taper	Core	B/Rd, Flex	Act/R	T/Rd, Flex	Core	M/Rd, Flex	Act/R
Century Week	Act/R, Core	Flex	T/Rd, Flex	Act/R, Flex	Off	Century	

Abbreviations for types of workouts: Brisk Ride = B/Rd; Active Recovery = Act/R; Long Ride = L/Rd; Moderate Ride = M/Rd; Resistance Maintenance = Res/M; Stretching = Flex; Tempo Ride = T/Rd.

tempo workout on Thursday. He schedules the shorter midweek rides but will fit in the longer ones when possible. He includes a short active recovery ride on Wednesday and a longer outing with his family on Sunday, perhaps hiking. He likes organization, so he also includes his core strength, stretching, and resistance-maintenance workouts in his training plan. His core workouts are on Monday and Friday, his days off from riding. He stretches Tuesday, Thursday, and longer on Saturday to help him recover from riding those days. He wants plenty of recovery, so he plans just one resistance-training maintenance workout, which is on Sunday, and he'll skip it if he is too tired from his long ride. Like Erika, Kyle includes an easy day in his schedule before and after the weekend. Kyle won't do any resistance-maintenance training during his recovery week or during his taper. A regular weekly rhythm is easier to maintain, but Kyle moves the long ride to Sunday in week 4 so that he can go to a wedding on Saturday. Then, to allow more recovery before the brisk ride in week 5, he moves it to Thursday.

If you plan to do a 15-week program use figures 6.3 and 6.4 to create your own workout calendar. Start by noting any important nonriding events so that you can adjust the schedule as necessary. For each week put down the daily workouts and durations, which you can then enter in your training journal. Include a recovery week about halfway through the schedule and to share the plan with those close to you.

You can modify either program to train for a 200K. In general, your longest training ride should be two-thirds to three-fourths of the duration of your planned event for all but the extreme long-distance events. Thus, to prepare for a 10-hour 200K, you should build up to a long ride of 6:40 to 7:30. You could add an additional week to the program between the peak week and the taper week and do your longest ride then. Or you could keep the same 8- or 15-week format and ramp up a bit more quickly the duration of the long, tempo, brisk, and recovery rides. If you take the latter approach keep the buildup smooth, avoiding a big week-to-week jump.

Safety: Anticipate

A car turns right in front of you. The rider ahead of you hits the brakes. An animal darts into the road. Any of these can put a sudden end to your ride, your training program, and your planned century.

Fighter pilots learn to scan the sky and their instruments. If you scan rather than ride with a fixed focus, you are more likely to notice changes in your environment, differences that could be extremely important. You might notice that a car's front wheels are starting to turn to the right even before you can see the car turn. You might see a pothole just ahead of the rider in front of you. You would observe the hole in the farm fence and the unchained dog.

Use your eyes and ears. Even while looking ahead, listen for what may be coming up behind you. John was coaching at a camp in Arizona several years ago where a woman sustained a crushed pelvis after being hit by a truck. She had made a U-turn in front of the truck, which she had not heard because of the wind.

Don't just listen. Look in your mirror and then double-check by looking over your shoulder.

Practice your safe riding skills so that when a problem appears you act safely rather than react instinctively.

▶ Awareness leads to anticipation.

▶ Anticipation leads to preparedness.

▶ Preparedness leads to safety.

FIGURE 6.4 15-WEEK RIDE SCHEDULE PLANNING FORM

	M	Tu	W	Th	F	Sa	Su
Week 1							
Week 2							
Week 3							
Week 4							
Week 5							
Week 6							
Week 7							
Week 8 Recovery							
Week 9							
Week 10							
Week 11							
Week 12							
Week 13							
Week 14 Peak							
Week 15 Taper							
Century Week							

From J. Hughes and D. Kehlenbach, 2011, *Distance Cycling* (Champaign, IL: Human Kinetics).

Maximizing Your Training

Now that you've created your plan, here's how you should do each of the types of workouts to get the most training benefit. Each type of workout should be done at a different level of effort, which is explained in the next section, Monitoring Training Effort (see pages 118–122)

Weekly Long Ride

Progressively longer rides build your endurance by training your aerobic energy system to metabolize fat (thus sparing glycogen). These workouts improve your cardiovascular efficiency, develop muscle endurance, improve pedaling economy, accustom your digestive system to working while riding, and get your body accustomed to spending more time on the bike. By riding longer each week, you also gain the confidence needed to complete your century.

Remember to ride either the shorter or longer ones consistently as you train. The times for the weekly long ride include an allowance for short breaks (such as stopping at a minimart for a snack) but exclude longer stops (such as lunch).

Here are some tips for your long rides:

- *Have one or more specific objectives for each ride.* At a minimum, your objective is to complete a ride of a certain number of hours. You might also plan to sample a sports drink, or test a new saddle or shorts.
- *Pace yourself.* You should be able to talk during the entire ride including the climbs. Avoid riding partners who go too fast. If you ride at a conversational pace you will train your body to metabolize fat, which won't occur if you ride too hard. You can also use heart rate, power, or perceived exertion to pace yourself (see pages 118–122).
- *Eat and drink!* Eat regularly to keep your body fueled and drink to satisfy thirst while on the bike.
- *Identify your problem areas.* Use these rides to determine what works and what doesn't. How does your bike feel after several hours? Do you have the right gears? How is your saddle? Are you getting sufficient fuel? Do you prefer commercial energy products or regular foods (see the options listed in table 6.2 on page 126)? Use your long rides to identify and address your individual concerns.
- *Simulate your event as much as possible.* If your event includes a lot of hills, train in the hills. No hills? Alternate riding into a headwind and with a tailwind. If your event will probably be windy, ride in windy conditions to get used to them.
- *Planning for a personal record?* Ride your long ride that way. Practice holding a steady pace, and minimizing your time off the bike.
- *Riding a leisurely century?* Don't be in a rush. Break your training ride into sections and stop at a minimart after each, but don't stop too long. Ten minutes off the bike is enough to recharge without getting stiff.
- *Keep records.* You've developed your training program and a specific objective for each ride. Put these in your training journal and then log the data. Remember to include both objective (ride time, distance, average speed, etc.) and subjective (how you felt, motivation, and energy levels, etc.) notes. By reviewing your data, you can make any necessary changes to your program.

Tempo Ride

The weekly tempo ride also trains the aerobic energy system, in this case to metabolize glycogen. This workout is shorter and slightly more intense than the weekend jaunt. You should go harder during these rides but should still be able to talk. If you can sing, it's too easy. If you can only blurt out one or two words, it's too hard. If you can say a complete sentence, that's about right. The ride should feel challenging, but not all out. Remember that if you ride longer endurance workouts, you should also do the longer tempo ride. But if you do the shorter weekend rides, you may do longer tempo rides some weeks.

Brisk Ride

The brisk weekly ride trains the lactic acid and ATP-CP energy systems. By training these systems you will be able to ride harder before you accumulate significant amounts of lactic acid. Over time you will become a stronger rider, increase your climbing power, and boost your average speed during the longer rides.

You can perform more work during brief periods than you can during a continuous effort, and the higher workload produces greater adaptations and fitness. These challenging rides include a segment of mixed-intensity training. For example, in both programs the first brisk workout is a 30- to 40-minute ride with 10 to 15 minutes of mixed intensity. This period includes both hard riding and recovery—it is not 10 to 15 minutes of straight intensity! We discuss Intensity Workouts on pages 122–125.

If you ride the longer weekend rides, then also do the longer brisk rides. If you do the shorter weekend rides, you may do both longer tempo and brisk rides during the week. If you chose the shorter brisk rides, then do the shorter mixed-intensity segments.

Following the principle of individuality, if your training is going well with either the 8- or 15-week program, after the recovery week you could substitute a second brisk ride for the midweek tempo ride.

Active Recovery Rides

You train hard throughout the week, and riding one or two easy outings helps you recover faster. These rides are just as important as the others. Some amateur athletes make the mistake of not including easy days. They assume that if a little bit of hard training is good, more will be better. Intense workouts are like prescription medication; in the proper doses it works wonders, but taking too much can be harmful.

For a recovery workout, ride at digestion pace—the way that you'd ride after eating a big lunch. For recovery you could run errands on your bike or take an easy spin with your family. Pack a lunch, forget all the cycling electronics, and just go for a ride. You could also walk the dog, swim, or hike with your kids. Fit in active recovery at least once each week and twice if possible. The active recovery outings help remove waste products from your muscles so that you have more energy for your other rides.

Supplementary Workouts

Maintaining your core strength and flexibility helps you on the bike. These workouts don't have to be time consuming. You could do core exercises and stretching while relaxing with the family in the evening. Perhaps you can fit in resistance-maintenance training once or twice a week on either riding or nonriding days. If you do resistance training on a riding day, cycle first while your legs are fresh and then do the resistance training. The exercises are illustrated in chapter 3.

Core exercises	*Sets and repetitions*
Exercise ball bridging	One or two sets of 15–20 repetitions
Exercise ball hamstring curls	One or two sets of 10–15 repetitions
Roller straight-leg raises	One or two sets of 15–20 repetitions

As you progress through your program, notice which muscle groups are prone to tightness and spend some time stretching them, using the static and dynamic stretches in chapter 3.

Resistance-maintenance training doesn't take a lot of time. Choose a lower-body exercise and two upper-body exercises—one pulling and one pushing.

Resistance-maintenance training components

- *Lower body.* Pick an exercise that involves a center-of-gravity (COG) change, which helps maintain balance and coordination. Lunges, exercise ball wall squats, and step-ups are good COG exercises.
- *Upper-body pushing.* Exercises include exercise ball dumbbell chest presses, push-ups, and dumbbell overhead presses.
- *Upper-body pulling.* Exercises include single-arm dumbbell rows, lat pull-downs, and seated rows.

One or two sets of 10 to 15 repetitions of each exercise once or twice a week are plenty for maintaining fitness. For more about supplementary exercises see the resources section at the end of the book.

Monitoring Training Effort

To improve you need the right mix of volume (how much and how often you work out), intensity (how hard you work out), and recovery (allowing the body to rebuild and get stronger). You now have a schedule of how much to ride each week and how to progress. How do you know whether you are riding too hard or too easy each day? You can use heart rate, power output, or perceived exertion to monitor your intensity.

Heart Rate

Kyle is an engineer and likes data, so he gets a heart rate monitor, which consists of a transmitter that is worn around the chest and relays information to a receiver worn either on the wrist or mounted on the handlebars. To use the heart rate monitor, Kyle first needs to establish his training zones.

Training zones are related to your current fitness level and to the energy systems described in chapter 3. The key benchmark is the heart rate at which the muscles start to produce significant amounts of lactic acid. This point is called the lactate threshold (LT).

When you are getting enough oxygen to metabolize glycogen and fat, you are exercising aerobically. As you ride increasingly harder you reach a point where you aren't getting enough oxygen to produce all your energy aerobically. You have reached your threshold, and you add anaerobic energy production. As you get fitter the amount of power that you can produce aerobically will increase. Your LT may also shift upward so you can ride harder and stay aerobic.

To estimate your LT, first identify a time trial course that you can use to test your fitness periodically. Your course should take roughly 30 minutes to complete. The route can be an out and back, loop, or hill climb as long as you don't need to worry about stop signs, traffic, or other interruptions.

Pick a calm day to ride the time trial (TT). Warm up thoroughly for 30 minutes including 5 minutes of hard riding followed by 10 minutes of steady riding. Then ride the course as fast as possible to determine your average heart rate for the 30-minute time trial portion. You want to learn the average heart rate that you can sustain for your TT, so it's important to pace yourself rather than go too hard at the start and then fade. Cool down for at least 15 minutes after your TT. Some heart rate monitors compute average heart rate; if yours doesn't, then eyeball it. You can also do a 30-minute time trial on your trainer, but be sure to have a big fan because overheating will push your heart rate up and give an inaccurate reading.

For a TT of approximately 30 minutes, your average heart rate will be very close to your LT. You could choose a longer course. If your TT takes about 60 minutes, then your average HR will be slightly below your LT; multiply it by 103 percent to estimate your LT. Use your estimated LT to define your training zones:

- Active recovery zone—less than 75 percent of LT
- Weekly long ride zone—76 to 87 percent of LT
- Weekly tempo ride zone—88 to 94 percent of LT
- Intensity work during brisk ride—95 to 100 percent of LT

If your average heart rate for your 30-minute time trial was 160 beats per minute (BPM), then your training zones are the following:

- Active recovery rides—less than 120 BPM
- Weekly long ride—120 to 140 BPM
- Weekly tempo ride—141 to 152 BPM
- Intensity work during brisk ride—153 to 160 BPM

As you get fitter your LT may go up, so you should repeat the TT every four to six weeks. Each time try to do the TT at the same time of day, under similar conditions, and with the same warm-up. If your average heart rate goes up you should adjust your training zones. You can also gauge your progress this way—are you riding the TT faster? If your time is faster, you are fitter even if your LT doesn't change.

Because training zones should be based on fitness, don't use a formula that computes training zones based on maximum heart rate. Maximum heart rate is a function of age and genetics, not fitness, and zones based on maximum heart rate are inaccurate.

You need to interpret your heart rate response during workouts. Environmental conditions (heat, humidity, and altitude) and physiological variations (stress, increased core temperature, medications, and fatigue) may affect your heart rate, and individual responses will be different. Learn how these factors affect you by using your heart rate monitor regularly during your training and by keeping notes on your body's responses during different circumstances.

Power Meters

As explained in chapter 5 (see page 92), power on the bike is a function of both cardio-vascular capacity and muscular power. Heart rate monitors track your cardiovascular workload and improvement and by inference your overall increase in power produc-tion. Power meters measure your actual power production on the bike. Power meters provide the most accurate feedback during workouts and for analysis afterward. If used appropriately, they promote optimum training, but you need to learn how to use them. If you want maximum performance and have the time and discipline to use the data, consider getting a power meter.

If you chose to use a power meter, you will need to determine your functional thresh-old power (FTP), the average power in watts that you could sustain in a one-hour time trial. The standard test for FTP is a 20-minute time trial. Use the same warm-up that you used for the time trial to determine average heart rate at LT. Similarly, pace yourself so that you are producing close to average power for all of the TT and then cool down. Multiply your average power from the 20-minute TT by 95 percent to obtain your FTP.

Use your estimated FTP to determine your training zones:

- Active recovery zone—less than 55 percent of FTP
- Weekly long ride zone—56 to 75 percent of FTP
- Weekly tempo ride zone—76 to 90 percent of FTP
- Intensity work during brisk ride—91 to 100 percent of FTP (Allen & Coggan, 2006)

If your average power for your 20-minute time trial was 180 watts, then your FTP is 171 watts (.95 × 180) and your training zones are the following:

- Active recovery rides—less than 94 watts
- Weekly long ride—95 to 127 watts
- Weekly tempo ride—128 to 154 watts
- Intensity work during brisk ride—155 to 171 watts

As you get fitter your FTP may go up, so you should repeat the time trial every four to six weeks. *See Training and Racing With a Power Meter* (Allen & Coggan, 2006) for detailed information on using a power meter. The recommendations presented here are based on this; we modified them to cap intensity at 100 percent of FTP rather than 105 percent.

You can use your heart rate monitor or power meter to help prevent overtraining. On easy training days, use it to hold yourself back. Your workout may feel too easy, but that's the point.

You can monitor your training efforts with quantitative data from a power meter or heart rate monitor. You can also use your perceived level of exertion as a gauge.

Perceived Exertion

Erika has been running for years and knows how her body feels at different levels of intensity. She gauges her workout intensity using rating of perceived exertion (RPE), a numeric scale designed to quantify effort.

Erika likes the RPE because it is easy to use and requires no equipment. When she is riding or running, she pays attention to her body and how hard she is working. When she started her cycling training, she initially used a heart rate monitor to calibrate her body awareness. She borrowed Kyle's monitor and rode a 30-minute time trial. (Note that LT varies by sport, so Erika's running LT would not be the same as her riding LT.) She then used his monitor on a few rides, comparing the heart rate data with her RPE. Over a few weeks she learned to tune into her body to get an accurate assessment of her exertion. Erika rates her exertion on a scale from 1 to 10, with 1 being the lowest level of exertion. She can maintain an RPE of 1 for many hours and a rating of 5 for an hour; if she were in a flat-out sprint gasping for air, she would be at an RPE of 10.

Here are Erika's ratings during her rides:

- Active recovery—RPE of 1 to 2
- Weekly long ride—RPE of 2 to 3
- Weekly tempo ride—RPE of 3 to 4
- Intensity work during brisk ride—RPE of 5 to 6

Even if you primarily use a heart rate monitor or power meter, RPE is a useful tool. Training by perceived exertion will help you become more aware of your body. Also, heart rate monitors suffer from interference from power lines and other sources of energy, and batteries can fail. When your monitor fails, you can use RPE on your ride, and you see more scenery if you're not constantly looking at numbers!

Coach John has used a heart rate monitor for years and still uses one for intensity work. But he knows his body and much of the time uses a simple RPE scale with four zones:

- Digestion pace—how he rides or walks after a big lunch
- Conversation pace—talking with friends on the long weekend ride
- Headwind pace—riding into a stiff headwind, still talking with friends in short sentences but definitely working
- Sub-barf—his time trial pace, just below the point where he would throw up

Table 6.1 illustrates how to monitor the various training rides in terms of lactate threshold (LT), functional threshold power (FTP), ratings of perceived exertion (RPE), and Coach John's descriptions of perceived exertion.

You can train effectively using either quantitative or subjective feedback. Either method works, so select the one that is most meaningful to you. Try to stay in the appropriate

TABLE 6.1 Comparison of Heart Rate, Power, and Perceived Exertion Training

	Heart rate as % of LT	Power in watts as % of FTP	Rating of perceived exertion	Hughes' perceived exertion
Active recovery ride	<75	<55	1–2	Digestion pace
Weekly long ride	76–87	56–75	2–3	Conversation pace
Weekly tempo ride	88–94	76–90	3–4	Headwind pace
Intensity during brisk ride	95–100	91–100	5–6	Sub-barf pace

zone most of the time for each ride. As your weekly rides get longer you may not be able to stay up in the long ride zone the entire time. Slowing down is OK. If your ride is hilly you may need to climb in the tempo zone. After a climb spin down the back side in the active recovery zone and then resume riding in your long ride zone.

Intensity Workouts

Riders often overlook intensity training for distance events, assuming that just riding longer each week will get them fitter. Although the weekly endurance ride is the key component, you should supplement it with some higher intensity work. These workouts boost your average speed, give you more power to tackle the hills, and make you a stronger rider overall.

Both the 8- and 15-week schedules have a weekly brisk ride, which includes intensity work. The first brisk ride in both programs breaks down like this: 10 to 15 minutes of warm-up; 10 minutes of mixed intensity, which includes both the hard efforts and the recovery periods; and 10 to 15 minutes of cool-down for a total of 30 to 40 minutes.

You can do structured or unstructured hard training. Unless you are training at the elite level, one way of doing intensity work isn't better than another as long as you ride hard, get your heart rate up, and have a little fun, too! Here are some general guidelines:

- *Choose roads with less traffic.* You can concentrate on the intensity workout without worrying about traffic
- *Always warm up and cool down.* This will reduce your risk of injury.
- *Progression is important.* Start with short efforts (two to three minutes) at the lower end of the intensity range (95 percent of LT, 91 percent of FTP, or an RPE of 5) and progress to longer, harder efforts.
- *Do a mix of hard and easy.* During the mixed-intensity portion of the workout, the total recovery time should be at least as great as the total hard riding time.
- *Know when to say when.* Proper intensity is more important than quantity. If you can't get through a workout without sacrificing quality, then cut it short.
- *Partner up*! Training with someone else provides motivation.
- *Stress is cumulative.* If you're recovering from an illness or dealing with other life stressors, skip a hard workout.

A structured intensity workout has defined work and rest periods. For example, a 1:1 workout would consist of one minute of hard riding followed by one minute of easy riding. Both periods are important, so during the work interval ride hard and during the recovery period ride at your active recovery pace. If you ride too hard during the rest break you won't recover fully and won't be able to go hard during your subsequent work efforts.

Structured Intensity Workouts

Here are some structured intensity workouts. For each, the workout for the hard work intervals should be 95 to 100 percent of LT, 91 to 100 percent of FTP, or an RPE of 5 or 6. The recovery intervals should be less than 75 percent of LT, less than 55 percent of FTP, or an RPE of 1 or 2. Always warm up before and cool down after these mixed intensity workouts:

- *One-to-one*. Pick a number between one and five, which will be your work and rest number, for example, three. Ride hard for three minutes and then recover for three minutes. Repeat the three minutes of hard riding and three minutes of recovery several times to complete the planned intensity portion of the workout. As your training progresses you can use larger numbers.

- *Ladder*. Go hard for a minute and recover for a minute. Then hammer for two minutes and recover for two. Then do three hard and three easy. Work your way back down by doing two hard and two recovery and then one hard and one easy.

- *Descending*. Ride four minutes hard and four minutes of recovery, three minutes hard and three minutes easy, two minutes hard and two easy, and finally one hard and one easy. In this workout the duration of the pain lessens as you progress!

- *Hill repeats*. Find a hill that takes three to four minutes to climb. Hammer up the hill, turn around, ride back down, and spin a bit to recover before tackling the hill again. Repeat several times, each time trying to go a little faster to the top. Or you can see how far you can climb in three minutes from the bottom and try to go a little farther up the hill each time.

- *Distance intervals*. Pick a course that takes three to five minutes to complete. Ride the course as fast as you can, note your time, recover, and repeat, trying to go just a little faster.

- *Time trial*. Whether you train with a heart rate monitor, power meter, or RPE, ride a baseline time trial every four to six weeks. Each time you ride the course challenge yourself to go faster. Note the results in your training log and recalculate your heart rate if you're using a heart rate monitor or your power training zones if you're using power meter.

Unstructured Intensity Workouts

You don't have to be a slave to numbers on a heart rate monitor. Here are some ways to incorporate intensity without any special equipment:

- *Hammer the hills*. Ride with friends and challenge each other on climbs.

- *Fly home*. Weather changing? Almost late for your child's sporting event? Time to pedal hard.

- *Ride the wind*. If there are no hills in your area, ride into the wind and then turn around to recover.

- *Ride in fast groups*. Go on a faster club ride. If the group is too challenging, tell the leader that you will hang on for a while—don't feel obliged to complete their ride. To ride with a racing club you'll need to learn how to ride in a pace line (see page 124).

- *Ride in club races*. Enter local citizen races. Push yourself in a time trial against other competitors.

- *Ride and play*. Have fun by sprinting for mailboxes with your friends. Or ride fast for a hundred pedal strokes every time you see a car of a certain color. During a group ride, have someone jump ahead for a couple of minutes. Everyone chases, and then someone else makes a break. The rides should not be formal; just use your imagination and ride hard.

For more information on the benefits of intensity training and types of workouts, see John's publication *Intensity, How to Plan and Gauge the Most Effective Training* in the resources section.

Riding in Pace Lines

Riding in an organized pace line takes skill. Above about 15 miles per hour (24 km/h), aerodynamic drag, even if there is no wind, is the primary impediment to riding speed. If riders share the workload of overcoming aerodynamic drag, those drafting can save as much as 25 percent of their energy. Attending a clinic is the best way to learn pace line riding.

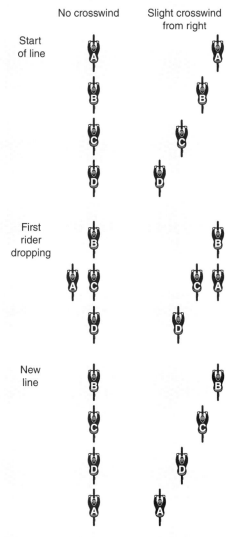

Adapted from Panzera, 2010.

▶ Rider A rides at the front of a line of riders, from two to a dozen or so. Riders at the back of a longer line tend to get whipsawed as speed variations ripple through the line.

▶ In a nonracing pace line, rider A sets a pace so that all riders can stay together rather than some having to struggle to hang on.

▶ Rider A takes a short turn, or pull, at the front for one to two minutes.

▶ Short pulls keep the average speed higher because a rider drops off the front before he or she fatigues significantly.

▶ If there is no crosswind, rider A checks carefully for traffic behind and then moves to the traffic side of the line, signaling to rider B that she or he is dropping to the back. Rider A drops toward the traffic side so that the rest of the pace line doesn't have to look out for traffic from the rear while passing A.

▶ Rider A pedals slightly slower than the line and pulls in behind the last rider. If traffic approaches from behind while A is dropping, then A should get into the pace line immediately.

▶ If there is a crosswind, rider A drops to the windward side of the pace line so that the pace line isn't disrupted as A drifts to the back.

▶ Rider B takes the lead position and is careful not to increase the pace. A new rider who gets to the front may be tempted to increase the pace to show how strong she or he is. This will unnecessarily tire the following riders. The goal is to work as a team and move forward more efficiently.

▶ On level ground rider B is careful to ride at the same speed as rider A did. On rolling terrain rider B rides so that his or her perceived exertion or heart rate is only slightly higher than when rider B was drafting rider A.

▶ Rider B pulls for just a minute or two and drops back. Rider C takes the lead.

▶ If riders don't have the same fitness, they can vary the duration of their pulls.

However you approach it, by incorporating intensity workouts, you will increase your average speed during long rides, be stronger in the hills, and be able to stay with a group when the pace picks up.

Nutrition

Think about the energy systems that provide fuel for your muscles (see chapter 3). When you use the aerobic system during your long and recovery rides, you metabolize both glycogen and fat for energy. When you speed up a bit at tempo pace you're still burning fat but start using more glycogen. During your brisk rides you continue to burn a mix of fuels, but during the hard efforts you rely primarily on glycogen. Your body can store enough glycogen for only 60 to 90 minutes of hard riding or several hours of endurance riding. So, you need to eat during rides.

Refer back to the information on pages 61 and 62 on how to estimate your caloric expenditure while riding. Kyle weighs about 170 pounds (77 kg) at the end of his baseline conditioning. If he rides at 15 miles per hour (24 km/h) he's burning about 750 calories per hour. Erika is lean from running and weighs 100 pounds (45 kg). At 15 miles per hour she's expending about 450 calories per hour. Even light people use a lot of energy!

Remember from chapter 4 that we recommend consuming 25 to 60 grams, or 100 to 240 calories, primarily from a mix of carbohydrate, during each hour of riding for training rides of a few hours. As your rides get longer, you should eat a mix of carbohydrate totaling 60 to 90 grams, or 240 to 360 calories, every hour plus a bit of protein and fat. If you're built like Kyle, eat at the upper end of the range; if you're more like Erika, the lower end is good. You digest the food better if you nibble on several different foods during each hour, rather than eating just one food once an hour. Eat fruit, cookies, bagels with peanut butter, breakfast bars, energy bars, sports drinks, and other foods that taste good to you. You should also drink just enough to satisfy your thirst during rides. Table 6.2 on page 126 includes nutritional information for popular and easy-to-consume foods and drinks.

One product provides no performance advantage over another. Sports drinks, bars, and gels are more convenient than regular food but also cost more and won't make you ride better. Always read the labels on food products to learn about total calories and calories from carbohydrate. Then choose what tastes good and sits well in your stomach.

Recovery

Recall from chapter 3 that your body gets stronger during rest, not while working out, so adequate recovery is critical during the weeks and months leading up to your event. Several practices will help you recharge your body and perform at your best.

Daily Recovery

The quality of tomorrow's workout depends on what you do today to recover. Spending a little time each day on recovery will help you maintain your energy level and enthusiasm. Pay attention to how you feel overall during your training.

TABLE 6.2 **Sample Foods and Drinks to Consume While Cycling**

Food	Amount	Calories	Carbohydrate (g)	Percentage carbohydrate
Apple	1 med.	100	25	100
Bagel, plain	1 med.	250	47	75
Banana	1 med.	105	27	100
Clif Bar (chocolate chip)	1	240	44	73
Cookie (Oreo)	2	160	28	70
Fruit Newtons (Fig Newtons)	2	110	22	80
Granola bar (Nature Valley)	1	90	15	66
Gu	1 packet	100	25	100
Hammer Bar (chocolate chip)	1	220	25	45
Hammer Gel	1 packet	92	23	100
Luna Bar	1	180	27	60
Peppermint Patty	1	140	31	89
Pop Tart	1	210	37	70
PowerBar (chocolate)	1	240	45	75
Raisins	1.5 oz	130	34	100
Three Musketeers	1	260	46	70
Beverage	Amount	Calories	Carbohydrate (g)	Percentage carbohydrate
Accelerade	8 oz (240 ml)	80	15	75
Chocolate low-fat milk	8 oz (240 ml)	155	26	67
Coke	8 oz (240 ml)	108	27	100
Fruit juice (orange)	8 oz (240 ml)	110	26	95
Gatorade	8 oz (240 ml)	60	15	100
Instant breakfast (Carnation)	1 packet	130	27	83
V-8	8 oz (240 ml)	45	10	90

Data from Clark and Hegmann 2005 and selected grocery stores and manufacturers.

- *Stretching.* Your training program becomes more difficult as you progress. Stretching at least three times a week will relieve local soreness and prepare you for the next ride.
- *Nutrition.* You burn more calories per hour riding than you're eating on the bike. Afterward, be sure to refuel and rehydrate so that you are ready for the next day. If you are trying to lose weight, eat a little less throughout the day rather than skip a postride meal.
- *Sleep.* Sufficient sleep is important for both training and overall health. If possible, get to bed a little earlier, and when in bed avoid watching television or reading. Let your brain turn off.

Weekly Recovery

Besides daily recovery, doing the following each week will help your overall revitalization:

- *Active recovery.* Both long and hard rides produce waste products and stiff muscles. Active recovery rides, walks with the dog, playing catch, or swimming help you recover faster.
- *Massage.* Riders in the peloton receive regular massage. If you can't get a massage, you can give yourself one on the weekend.
  - *Homemade massage lotion.* Mix 8 ounces (240 ml) of rubbing alcohol, 8 ounces of witch hazel, a little wintergreen (for warmth), and a little olive oil (for body).
  - *Position.* Sit on a towel on the bed or on an exercise mat on the floor.
  - *Warm-up.* Apply massage lotion and start with brisk, light, up-and-down motions with your hands on one quadriceps and around the knee. Continue for a few minutes until the muscles feel warm.
  - *Stretch.* Then sit with the knee of the warm leg slightly bent and the muscles relaxed. Grab the quadriceps of that leg with both hands and move the right hand slightly to the left and the left hand to the right, stretching the muscle. Then reverse directions. Knead the quad for a few minutes. Use your fingertips to make circular motions where the quad attaches on both sides of the knee.
  - *Flush.* After stretching, apply more massage oil to the quad. Stroke gently from the knee to the hip for a couple of minutes. Then stroke in the opposite direction using more pressure with the heel of your hand. Gradually increase the pressure to work out any knots. After the quadriceps, work on the hamstring and then the calf. Repeat on the other leg.
- *Hot tubs and saunas.* If you do not have existing health problems, sitting in a hot tub or sauna for a short time will help you relax. This session will increase your core temperature and cause you to sweat; don't forget to keep a water bottle handy.

Problem Areas

During long or intense rides microtrauma occurs in your muscles. If the daily and weekly recovery suggestions described in the preceding sections don't relieve your soreness, try icing or roller massage:

- *Icing.* To ice, wrap two or three trays of cubes in a towel so that one side of the ice pack has just one layer of towel. Dampen that side and place it over the affected muscle or joint. Although messy, the damp towel conducts the cold better than ice in a plastic bag does. Ice the area for 15 to 20 minutes. The purpose of icing is to reduce inflammation. If you ice longer, your body will send blood to the affected area to keep it from freezing, which will increase inflammation. If you are nursing an injury, two or three icings a day may work best. If you have point tenderness, try an ice massage. Freeze a paper cup of water and then peel some of the cup away so that it looks like an ice cream cone. Rub the ice on the sore spot.
- *Foam rollers.* Use a hard foam roller (the same kind we recommend for the exercises in chapter 3, see page 52) to relieve pressure. Because you use your body weight on the roller to work the muscle, the massage will be deeper than if you just knead with your hands. Roller massage, done correctly, can be more effective than hand massage, but it may be more painful as you work the knots out.

Training Adjustments

The most successful athletes listen to their bodies rather than slavishly follow a plan. Keeping a training log will help you monitor your performance over time. The three best indicators of potential overtraining are your attitude, your performance, and your resting heart rate. When it's workout time, are you excited to get on the bike? Are you doing your workouts about as fast as you did last week? Has your morning resting pulse before you get out of bed increased by more than 10 percent? If one of these indicators is off for a day, it may be insignificant, but if your motivation lags, if you aren't riding well, or if your morning heart rate is up for several days in a row, you may need a second recovery week. For a recovery week, cut the total volume about in half while maintaining the mix of ride types. For example, if the plan is a long ride of 5:00, a tempo ride of 90 minutes, and a brisk ride of 90 minutes including 30 minutes of mixed intensity, you could do a long ride of 2:00 or 2:30, a 45-minute tempo ride, and a 45-minute brisk ride including 15 minutes of mixed intensity. If you are still lacking snap, take a very easy week with just a few recovery walks or rides. Preventing overtraining is easier than recovering from it. If you add a recovery week do not try to make up the volume the next week. Instead, rewrite your program so that you continue to ramp up progressively.

B ecause a systematic approach to training for your century yields better results, the 8- and 15-week training plans outlined in this chapter make use of these principles:

- ▶ *Progressive overload.* You gradually increase your total weekly volume.
- ▶ *Individuality.* You choose from a range of workout times to accommodate your fitness level and available time.
- ▶ *Specificity.* You are on your bike a majority of the time to build cycling endurance and power.
- ▶ *Variation.* You do various intensities of rides along with supplementary training.
- ▶ *Recovery.* You practice regular recovery and use the recovery week and taper period to maintain the delicate balance of training and rest.

In the next chapter, we look at what to do in the last weeks leading up to the event: gathering specific information about event, refining the training taper, dealing with preride jitters, taking in proper preride nutrition, and checking your equipment. We talk about the event itself, including pacing, eating and drinking, and managing any problems that arise.

CHAPTER 7

Conquering the Century and 200K

It's countdown time—the big day is getting close! Like Kyle and Erika, you have designed and followed a training plan based on one of the programs in chapter 6. The weekly mix of long rides, active recovery, and faster workouts has improved your fitness and you are excited about your century or 200K event. Your preparation during the last couple of weeks before your event will help you have a successful ride.

In this chapter we describe the key elements to focus on during those weeks. We look at the event day—from what to do before the ride to how to manage your energy until the finish line. We also provide several checklists to help you get ready and then to ride your ride. Keep these checklists handy so that you can refer to them in later chapters.

Assessment and Planning

Think back to your self-assessment and goals from chapter 2. Is this your first century? Are you trying for a personal best? Completing a first century or 200K is different from riding your fastest 100 miles or 200 kilometers. Your goals may have changed during your training, so reaffirming your goals for the ride will make it easier to plan for your event. Then take the necessary steps to plan for your ride. Learn about the ride, determine how you will get to the event, and develop a specific event plan.

Learn About the Ride

Learn as much as you can about the ride. Here are some suggestions:

- *Use your resources.* Most events have websites that provide ride information. Some sites may have discussion forums where you can get advice from riders who have done the event. Contact the organizers directly with any concerns that you have.

- *Terrain.* Where are the hills? If your event starts with a 1,000-foot (300 m) climb, you should pace yourself carefully at the start. How steep are the climbs? How long are they? Some event websites include a course profile.

- *Cue sheets.* Most events have a cue sheet (see figure 7.1) that gives turn-by-turn directions from the start to the finish and the locations of rest stops. Organizers typically don't publish the cue sheet until a week or two before the event in case last-minute changes are necessary. When you get it, read it several times to learn how to follow the directions. If anything is unclear, contact the event organizers rather than risk getting lost during your ride. MapQuest, Google Maps, and other mapping software may be useful, but they occasionally have mistakes. Make a couple of copies of the cue sheet and put each in a separate plastic bag to carry during the event in case one gets wet, torn or lost.

- *Weather.* What is the typical weather for the area? Is rain possible? What about wind? Several websites give average temperature, precipitation, prevailing wind, and other conditions for a particular location and time of year.

- *Rules.* Study all the rules in advance and note any that may affect how your ride. For example, some events may not allow the use of aero bars.

- *Road conditions.* Check shortly before the event to learn whether any road construction will affect your riding. For example, when Dan participated in the 2009 Great Alaska Century (Fireweed 100), several miles of pavement were torn up and he had to ride on broken gravel.

- *Rest stops.* How many rest stops will there be? If the event has just one or two, you will have to carry more food and drink on the bike. What kind of food and drinks will they have? Rest stops typically feature fruit, bagels, cookies, water, and some kind of sports drink. Will they have your preferred food? Where are the rest stops? If a rest stop is located just before a major climb, you don't want to eat a lot and then have to climb. Perhaps you should put food in your pocket to carry to the top of the climb and then eat. On the other hand, an aid station before a long descent is a great place to refuel.

- *Sag support.* Many rides have sag wagons—vehicles driven by volunteers who patrol the course to help riders and relay information to the organizers. Some events provide mechanical support, whereas others offer only a ride to the finish in case of mechanical problems.

- *Emergency contacts.* Is a specific number provided for you to use in an emergency? Write this number on your cue sheets and program it into your cell phone. Be aware that cell phone service may be unreliable in some areas.

- *200-kilometer brevets.* Brevet rules require you to carry a brevet card and get signatures at designated locations (controls). Learn in advance where the controls are. Find out beforehand whether the brevet includes rest stops and other support, as an organized century does, or whether the ride is unsupported. If the ride is unsupported you'll need to carry some provisions and buy more along the way. Review Jenny Hegmann's suggestions on Eating Store Food (page 71).

You should learn as much as possible about the details of your event and clear up any confusion that you may have. Even if you have done the ride for the past 20 years, details can change. The day of the event is not the time to discover something you weren't expecting.

CENTURY CHALLENGE – JUNE 1:
HILL VALLEY CYCLING CLUB

Stage	Elapsed	Turn	Notes
0.1	0.1	L	Jones Road (W)
0.3	0.4	L	Smith Street (W)
0.2	0.6	R	Willow Road (N)
6.8	7.4	L	Highway 23 (W) – not signposted
4.9	12.3	-	through Ashley Road – *store is on right*
1.5	13.8	-	Kwik Stop – *Best store until rest stop*
1.8	15.6	R	Highway 21 (N)
1.0	16.6	L	Highway 10 (W)
1.0	17.6	R	Highway 23 (N)
1.6	19.2	L	Highway 12 (W)
7.1	26.3	-	Cross US-35 – Rest stop #1 on corner
1.2	27.5	R	Across bridge to Route 29 – *watch gratings if wet!*
3.4	30.9	L	Highway 27 (N)
3.3	34.2	R	Highway 35 (E)
6.0	40.2	L	Highway 23 (N)
1.7	41.9	L	to stay on Highway 23
4.5	46.4	R	Route 27 – *watch for traffic – obey stop sign*
3.0	49.4	-	Stay on Route 27
0.9	50.3	-	Rest stop #2 on right – *lunch available*
10.1	60.4	-	Supermarket on left
3.9	64.3	-	Porta-pottys on right behind baseball field
2.4	66.7	L	Route 15 (W)
5.3	72.0	-	Rest stop #3
15.5	87.5	-	Route 15 becomes Highway 40
5.0	92.5	R	Route 20
4.0	96.5	L	Route 24
6.0	102.5	L	into Hill Valley Elementary School – finish area!

FIGURE 7.1 **Familiarize yourself with the cue sheet ahead of time and keep it handy during the event.**

Traveling to Your Event

You can just drive to the start of an event close to home. On the other hand, by traveling you can ride a century or 200K with new terrain, different scenery, and the opportunity to meet other riders. Whether your event is across town or across the country, plan how to get there.

Driving to the event　If you are driving here are some points to remember:

- Make sure that you know how to get to your event. Nothing is more frustrating than getting lost and arriving at your event behind schedule.
- If you are carpooling, everyone should be on the same page regarding meeting location and time.
- Are there any special parking arrangements? Some events have a dedicated parking area away from the start.
- Use the checklist on page 138 to pack all your gear the night before and double-check that you load everything in the car. You don't want to arrive at the start without your shoes!
- If possible put your bike inside your car where it is protected from weather and accidents. If you use a roof rack, make sure that your bike is securely fastened. We don't like tailgate racks because the bike becomes a bumper in a rear-end collision.

Flying to the event　If you fly to the event, you (or your shop) will need to pack your bike in a cardboard bike box or hard-shell case. Cardboard boxes are flimsy and should be reinforced. Hard-shell cases are expensive, so some shops rent them. A bike needs to be packed correctly to minimize the risk of damage. See the resources section for a good description from Adventure Cycling of how to pack your bike in a cardboard box.

After your bike is packed you can take it on the plane with you or ship it by a commercial carrier such as UPS or FedEx. Either way, the bike can be insured and tracked, which is important if it is misrouted or damaged. Taking the bike with you on a flight may be more convenient because you don't have to pack and ship it in advance and it will arrive at the destination with you. On the other hand, doing the paperwork and dragging your bike around the airport may be a hassle. Airline fees are becoming increasingly expensive, and shipping by commercial carrier may be cheaper. You send your bike to whatever address is most convenient—that of a relative, friend, or bike shop, for example. But this means packing and shipping it well in advance of your event.

Destination services　If you are traveling to your event, make lodging reservations early, because many establishments fill up early, particularly for popular events. When picking your lodging, contact the hotel directly to make sure that another event that might disrupt your sleep isn't going on.

Locate the nearest bike shops in advance and learn what services they provide. Leading up to the event, nearby bike shops probably will be busy. If you ship your bike, will they assemble it for you for a charge? If so, send it early so that they have enough time to put it together. If you prefer certain brands of sports drink and energy bars, can you buy these at the local shop or will you need to bring them? If you use specialized equipment, such as aero wheels, does the shop have a knowledgeable mechanic and parts in case a wheel is damaged in transit? For the best service, talk with them in advance and establish rapport.

What to Do When It Hurts or Isn't (as Much) Fun

By Paul Carpenter

Winner, Race Across the West 2008, Professor, Sports Psychology, Department of Kinesiology and Physical Education, Northern Illinois University, DeKalb, Illinois

Part of good planning and training includes contingency plans for when things go awry. In longer events you will likely have to overcome some adversity. Here are some mental strategies to keep in mind when the going gets tough.

> ▶ *Don't panic.* Assess the situation. On any long ride it is likely that something is going to hurt or that some problem will arise. Distinguish between pains that you can overcome and pains in which discretion is the better part of valor.
>
> ▶ *Relax.* Take deep breaths, focus on pedaling, and align your breathing with your pedal strokes to refocus (away from the pain) and regroup (allowing you to make a reasoned decision).
>
> ▶ *Stay optimistic.* Don't think negatively and talk yourself into a hole that you cannot get out of. Remain confident in the knowledge that you are well prepared.
>
> ▶ *Engage in positive self-talk.* Make positive affirmations—I can do this, I can overcome, I've trained for this, I am well prepared, I have done this before.
>
> ▶ *Be task oriented.* What do you need to do to continue riding? How can you fix what ails you? Focus on what you can control rather than the things that are out of your control.
>
> ▶ *Focus on small goals.* Small successes will lead to bigger successes. Ride 30 more minutes. Get to the next rest stop. If you keep pedaling you will reach your destination. Try to avoid getting off the bike at the first sign of difficulty because once you get off, it's hard to get back on.
>
> ▶ *Look at adversity as an opportunity.* Focus on why you entered the event. Don't be afraid to adjust your goals if the situation warrants it.
>
> ▶ *Take five.* Give yourself some time mentally. Don't quit at the first difficulty.

Remember, a challenge met and adversity overcome are much more satisfying than an objective easily achieved.

Creating Event Scenarios

Now that you have gathered specific information about your event, plan how you intend to tackle the ride in terms of your goals, pacing, and time in rest stops. Look back at your weekly long rides. You probably had some great rides, some average rides, and some not-so-good rides.

The same happens with events. Although we'd like to do our best on every ride, circumstances may require us to reevaluate our expectations. Think about your big ride in terms of three possible scenarios:

1. You are riding a great ride. You are pacing yourself properly, spending the right amount of time in rest stops, and getting adequate food and fluid. Keep doing what you're doing but don't get too excited. A century is a long day, and although you feel great early, if you go too hard you might wear yourself out by mile 80 (km 130).

2. You are having a normal day. Keep up on your food and fluid and watch your pacing. Take advantage of the rest stops but don't linger.

3. You are not having a good day. Don't worry—it happens to all of us. Slow down a bit, pay attention to your nutrition, and concentrate on riding *your* ride. Energy levels and emotions often fluctuate significantly during an event. Take a couple of extra minutes in the rest stops to stretch and regroup.

Kyle is analytical, so he pulls out his training log and copies of the cue sheet. Referring to his long rides he writes his best scenario on a cue sheet, noting the ride start time, his expected arrival time at each rest stop and his time off the bike, and his projected finish time. He does the same for an average ride and then for a tough day to gain a sense of how his scenarios might unfold.

Erika is more intuitive. She enjoys yoga and progressive relaxation. She decides to try visualizing her three scenarios on three successive evenings before the event using the technique described on page 136. She spends about an hour each time visualizing each ride in detail. She does the tough ride the first night, the average ride the next night, and finishes with the great ride so that she feels positive heading into the event.

Training

During the last few weeks before your event, the training emphasis shifts from improving physical conditioning to rehearsing for the ride and maintaining fitness while storing energy for the event.

When preparing for races, pro teams ride the course to train and develop race-specific tactics. If you live near your event you can do the same. Break your century into sections and ride those parts on different days so that your body becomes accustomed to the demands of the course and you learn to follow the cue sheet. Do one or several rides that include the parts of the course that you find particularly hard, such as some of the hills, so that when you encounter them during the event you know that you can meet the challenge. If you can't ride the course, train on similar terrain.

In your training you taper the last two weeks before the event. The purpose of the taper is to maintain fitness while storing energy for your event. This close to the event, you can't get any fitter, but you can become run down. This is not the opportunity to make up for lost time. Both the 8- and 15-week programs in chapter 6 have the same taper.

Week 8 and Week 15, Taper

- Long ride of 2:30 to 3:30 the weekend before your century. This ride is about half the duration of your longest ride and will maintain your endurance.
- A midweek moderate tempo ride of 60 to 90 minutes and a midweek brisk ride of 60 to 90 minutes including 15 to 20 minutes of mixed intensity. These two rides will maintain your power.
- An active recovery ride of 40 to 60 minutes and an optional second recovery ride of 20 to 30 minutes. These rides will keep you loose.
- Two core strength sessions of 10 to 20 minutes and three stretching sessions of 10 to 20 minutes. In combination with the recovery rides, these sessions will help you recuperate from all the hard training.
- No resistance training.

Week 9 and Week 16, Century

- Midweek tempo ride of 30 to 40 minutes
- Two active recovery rides of 20 to 30 minutes
- Two core strength sessions of 10 to 20 minutes and three stretching sessions of 10 to 20 minutes

While tapering, use the recovery techniques described in the last chapter. Stretching, massage, foam roller massage, and sufficient sleep will help you feel fresh for your ride.

Mental Preparation

During the taper you should prepare your mind as well. The psychological component has a significant effect in endurance sports. Doing simple relaxation and visualization exercises can lower heart rate and blood pressure, increase blood flow to muscles, decrease muscular tension, increase concentration, and boost confidence.

Many techniques are popular and effective, including listening to soothing music, yoga, tai chi, and meditation. The more you practice a technique, the more benefit you'll receive. Progressive muscle relaxation and visualization can be especially helpful when preparing for an event.

Progressive Muscle Relaxation

To perform progressive muscle relaxation, sit or lie down in a quiet place. Put on some calming music if you like. Starting with your left foot, tense all the muscles in your foot by scrunching up your toes for 5 seconds while holding your breath. Then exhale smoothly for 30 seconds as you relax your muscles. Move up your body, tensing and relaxing each area in turn:

- Left calf
- Left thigh
- Repeat with right foot, calf, and thigh
- Left hand and forearm
- Whole left arm
- Repeat with right hand, forearm, and whole arm
- Abdomen
- Chest muscles
- Neck and shoulders
- Jaw and face

This technique progressively relaxes all your major muscles and teaches you to differentiate between a relaxed and tensed muscle. Many of us spend a lot of time with tensed muscles and do not realize it. Over time this can lead to tension headaches, fatigue, and stress. After you get the feel for progressive relaxation, you can use it to monitor muscle tension during the day and learn to relax consciously.

You can build on progressive relaxation with guided imagery. Imagine yourself in a calming place such as a beach and engage all your senses to see, hear, smell, and feel all aspects of the situation—the waves, the gulls, the salty ocean, the sun, and the breeze. You'll relax more if you use the same locale each time. You can practice progressive relaxation throughout the year, which benefits you generally.

You can use these techniques more specifically to help with your riding. To prevent or treat the buildup of nervous energy as you train and especially at the start of an event, find a quiet place to sit, focus on relaxing your muscles, and imagine yourself in your calming spot.

Visualization

Through visualization, or mental rehearsal, you use all of your senses to imagine riding the event and performing at your best. John used this technique before he set the course record in the Boston–Montreal–Boston 1,200-kilometer ride.

Several days or more before your event, start with progressive relaxation and go to the calming place in your mind. Imagine yourself at the start of the event. Don't think about it but put yourself into the scene. Use all your senses. What do you see? The bright colors of riders with bikes everywhere. What sounds do you hear? People socializing and support staff checking in riders. What do you smell? The scent of fresh coffee and baked goods. Most important, focus on how you feel. Imagine yourself rolling up to the start line relaxed, focused, and ready for a great ride. Hear yourself clicking into your pedals. Feel yourself starting smoothly and riding like you did on one of your best long rides. Feel how effortless the pedaling feels. See the road disappearing beneath your tires. Continue to visualize yourself riding the entire event. The more time you spend doing this and the more vivid and convincing you can make the images, the less nervous you'll be on the day of the century.

As with other skills, relaxation and visualization techniques require practice to achieve proficiency. Be patient and diligent and you will improve. Training the mind results in increased confidence, better performance, and a more enjoyable experience. For more information see John's article on mental training techniques listed in the resources section.

Equipment Preparation

After your hard training and careful planning, the last thing you need is trouble with your bike. Take your bike to the shop for an inspection and tune-up about two weeks before the event. This cushion will give them time to order any necessary parts and allow you to go for several test rides after the tune-up. If you are proficient at working on your own bike, you can do this yourself.

As noted earlier, establishing a friendly rapport with your shop helps. Bike store staff are often overloaded, especially at the start of the season or before important events. Bringing bagels or coffee for the staff when picking up your bike shows shop employees that you appreciate their service. They are likely to remember your thoughtfulness should you find yourself in a jam.

You should have already tested your clothing thoroughly. Don't wear a new piece of clothing during the event, even one from a familiar manufacturer. If you have sensitive skin, wash your riding clothes in the same laundry detergent that you use for your regular clothes.

Table 7.1 is a preride equipment checklist that you should keep handy for your rides, including the longer rides described in later chapters.

Don't wait until the last minute. Check your gear several weeks in advance. If you need to replace items on your list, get them right away.

TABLE 7.1 **Ride Equipment Checklist**

Whether you use a bike shop or take care of your bike yourself, consider replacing these items:
Tires and tubes
Chain (if there are more than 1,500 miles [2,400 km] on it)
Cassette or freewheel (if worn or with every third new chain)
Computer batteries (if more than a year old) and clean contacts with fine sand paper
Cables (shift and brake)
Brake shoes
Handlebar tape
Also check these items:
Seat pack for wear
Tubes, patches and fresh glue, and pump or CO_2 cartridges
Bladder, bottles, and flasks for leaks. To check a bladder close it, blow air into it and squeeze it near your ear listening for leaks. Similarly, close a bottle or flask and squeeze it, listening for leaks.
Bottles, bladder, and flasks for cleanliness. A moldy or dirty bladder, bottle or flask can make you sick, so clean or replace it.
Cleats for tightness and wear
Clothing clean and in good repair

From J. Hughes and D. Kehlenbach, 2011, *Distance Cycling* (Champaign, IL: Human Kinetics).

Nutrition

Food is your fuel, so pay extra attention to your nutrition during the last couple of weeks. In chapter 4 you calculated your daily caloric requirement. If you are trying to lose weight, you might have cut back your calories by as much as 20 percent. Starting two weeks before the event, eat your full quota of calories so that your fuel tank is full.

To top off your glycogen stores, during the last few days before the event, increase your intake of carbohydrate and reduce the amount of fat and protein. Your daily intake should include

- 70 to 75 percent of total calories from carbohydrate,
- 15 to 20 percent of total calories from fat, and
- 10 percent of total calories from protein.

Be careful that when you increase the carbohydrate you don't increase the fat with butter or rich sauces. Your body stores the additional glycogen with water, so don't worry if you gain a bit of weight when loading up with carbohydrate.

You have experimented to find the foods and drinks that work best for you; practiced eating sufficient calories and drinking to satisfy your thirst; and learned to handle, unwrap, and consume food and drink while riding. Based on what you've learned, assemble a variety of items to take to the event, including nutrition for before, during, and just after your ride. Although most events provide some food and drink, they may not be your preferred choices. If you like a particular sports drink and don't know whether the event provides it, bring powdered sports drink so that you can add water and make your own. Resist the temptation to try something new.

You will be taking a lot of gear to the event, and the comprehensive packing list in table 7.2 will minimize the possibility of forgetting something.

TABLE 7.2 **Event Packing List**

Bike items:
Bike
Seat pack
Spare tubes and patch kit
Tool kit (see chapter 5)
Frame pump or CO2 inflators
Computer, heart rate monitor, and power meter (if you use one)
Floor pump
Bottles or hydration pack
Clothing items:
Helmet and mirror
Jersey
Shorts
Gloves
Socks
Shoes
Headband or head cover
Arm and knee or leg warmers
Wind vest, jacket, or raincoat
Glasses
Clean clothes for after the ride

Nutritional items:
Water
Sports drink to carry and powdered favorite sports drink if not available at rest stops
Favorite foods to carry such as fruit, cookies, bars, and gels
Postride recovery food and drink
Personal items:
Directions to start
Cue sheets and ride emergency phone number
Driver's license or ID
Personal emergency contact information
Cell phone programmed with an ICE (in case of emergency) number
Medical insurance card
Prescription medications
Sunscreen and lip balm
Hygiene kit
Money
Camera
Small notebook or business cards to exchange contact information with people you meet

From J. Hughes and D. Kehlenbach, 2011, *Distance Cycling* (Champaign, IL: Human Kinetics).

Final Preparation

The 24 hours before an event will be busy, and you may find all the details a bit overwhelming. Here's a checklist to keep you organized and help you relax (table 7.3):

TABLE 7.3 **Preride Checklist**

The night before the ride:
Eat a good dinner to top off your tank. Eat familiar food, nothing new, before the event.
Pack as much as possible so you don't waste energy scrambling around on the morning of the event.
Use your checklists to check your equipment and pack all but the last-minute items.
Double-check each item or have someone check for you. A different set of eyes might spot things that you have overlooked.
Relax! Do whatever helps you wind down and get a good night's sleep.

(continued)

Table 7.3   (continued)

The morning of the ride:
Finish getting everything ready early.
Review your ride plan. You can do it!
Use the relaxation and guided imagery exercises.
Have a good breakfast of familiar foods. Eat primarily low-glycemic-index carbohydrate with some protein and fat to avoid swings in blood sugar levels.
Drink fluids but be careful. With the added excitement of the event, liquid might go right through you.
Leave early to give yourself plenty of time to get to the venue.
Just before the ride:
Unpack your bike, clothes, and gear and check in before socializing.
Perform a basic bike and equipment check:
• Tires hard?
• Tires clean?
• Brakes working?
• Shifting smoothly?
• Bottles or bladder full?
• Seat pack, spare tubes, tool kit on bike?
• Pump or CO_2 inflators on bike?
• Computer, heart rate monitor, and power meter (if you use one) ready?
• Helmet, gloves, and riding shoes ready?
• Cue sheet and a few snacks readily accessible?
• Driver's license, health card, emergency contact information, cell phone, and other personal items from table 7.2 in jersey pocket or seat pack?
Restrooms tend to get busy. Go early so that you don't miss your start.
Be sure to grab your car keys when you lock the car.

From J. Hughes and D. Kehlenbach, 2011, *Distance Cycling* (Champaign, IL: Human Kinetics).

On the Road

It's show time! All your hard work in training and preparation is done. Now relax, take it all in, and have fun. For a successful ride pay attention to these key things:

Pace yourself   When the gun goes off, some riders go out fast. Unless you're going for a personal best, avoid getting caught up with them. Choose your groups wisely and pace yourself. In the excitement of the start, you may go faster than you should, so take it easy for the first 30 minutes. Remember that the group riding your pace is often behind you! If you are using a heart rate monitor, keep in mind that your heart rate may be elevated compared with what you experience on training rides, so you may be better off using perceived exertion as a guide. With a power meter current wattage fluctuates a lot. Try to keep it in the same range as you do during your long training rides.

Check your cue sheet Put one copy of the cue sheet in a map holder on your handlebar, carry it in your jersey pocket, or tuck it up one leg of your shorts for quick reference. Stow the other copy in another location. Some organizers paint arrows on the pavement to show the turns, but if other rides have been routed through the same area, determining which arrows to follow can be difficult. Don't assume that other riders are following the course correctly; double-check each turn yourself.

Safety: Dealing With Obstacles in the Road or Shoulder

Roads are dirty. You will run into glass, gravel, and rough pavement, and you may encounter potholes, tires, and other large obstacles. How you handle these may be the difference between a good and not-so-good ride. The hazard management process that follows will usually keep you out of trouble:

1. *Anticipation*. Always look ahead to anticipate problems, even if you are riding in a group.

2. *Awareness*. Be aware of your surroundings. Are you with other riders? Is traffic approaching from the rear? These circumstances will limit your options for reacting to the obstacle.

3. *Assess*. Determine the risk and consequences presented by the obstacle, including the following:

   - Rough pavement, which may be uncomfortable
   - Glass, which might cause a flat
   - Gravel, which could cause you to lose control
   - A pothole or piece of tire, which could cause a crash

4. *Warn others*. If you are riding in a group call and point out the problem.

5. *Decide*. Based on your surroundings, the type of obstacle, the risk, and the potential consequences, decide what to do. In some cases the best course of action is to ride over the obstacle.

6. *Recover*. If you've chosen to ride over glass, stop immediately and check your tires for any shards. Start by spinning each wheel against your gloved hand. Then inspect each tire visually. If you've ridden over something more substantial, check your tire pressure and spin each wheel to be sure it's still in true. This will take a few minutes—less time than you'd spend fixing a flat somewhere down the road!

Water-filled potholes are a special problem. You don't know how deep one is, what the bottom surface is, or how sharp the edges are. If possible, avoid riding through these.

On your active recovery rides you can practice handling several kinds of problems:

▶ After riding over glass, brush your tires with a gloved hand while riding on the tire. Have a good grip on the handlebars and keep looking down the road. Then put one hand on the tire in front of the brake so that the rotating wheel doesn't drag it into the brake.

▶ Ride through gravel by slightly loosening your grip on the handlebars so that the front wheel can find its own line. Keep applying power smoothly to the rear wheel so that it doesn't skid.

Practice the hazard management process until it becomes second nature.

Ride with a group Riding with a group increases the fun; however, pay attention to your ride even during a fun conversation. Even if you aren't the first rider, look down the road for potential problems and point them out to your group. Ride smoothly in a straight line and signal or call out before you move or change speed. Don't overlap front and rear wheels.

Ride in a pace line If it's windy or the pace is above 15 miles per hour (24 km/h), you can save a lot of energy by riding in an organized pace line. Remember the protocol from chapter 6: Ride at a pace everyone can sustain, take short pulls, look carefully for traffic before you drop to the back, drop to the traffic side of the line if a crosswind isn't blowing, and drop to the windward side if it is. Be cautious when riding in a pace line with unfamiliar riders who may not know the protocol.

Eat and drink The first hour goes by quickly. Start eating in the first hour. Depending on your body size we recommend consuming a mix of carbohydrate totaling 60 to 90 grams, or 240 to 360 calories, plus a little protein and fat, during each hour of riding and drinking to satisfy your thirst. Nibbling on a variety of carbohydrate during each hour will work better than eating one thing on the hour. Use your experience from the weekly long rides to guide you; what worked on them will work on the century. If you might forget to eat or drink, set your watch to remind you.

Take advantage of rest stops Rolling into an aid station during your ride feels great. Take advantage of what they offer but use them wisely. View them not as places to rest but as resupply stations. If you have tight muscles, stretches using your bike will loosen you up (see figures 7.2 through 7.4).

When you arrive at a rest stop, park your bike carefully to avoid thorns and other potentially hazardous debris. Before leaving do a quick bike check: Are your tires hard? Are they clean? Are your brakes working?

Enjoy the company of others but avoid lingering so long that you get stiff. Use the restroom, fill your bottles and pockets, and get back on the road. Before you leave, thank

FIGURE 7.2 **Hamstring stretch.**

FIGURE 7.3   **Quadriceps stretch.**   FIGURE 7.4   **Back rotation stretch.**

the volunteers because without them rides like this could not exist. When reentering the road watch for cars and other bikes and ease back into your pace as you did at the start.

Mentally manage the ride   During your century, problems may occur. Don't panic—almost anything can be solved. Take a deep breath, relax, and diagnose the problem. Is the problem with the bike? Riding with a soft tire or a rubbing brake can be a drag—literally. Are you getting repeated flats? Make sure that nothing is embedded in the tire or protruding from the rim strip. If you are down mentally, have you forgotten to eat or drink? If your legs are tired, did you go out too hard? Mentally review your three basic scenarios. If you have forgotten to eat, don't try to make up the calories immediately because doing so may give you digestive problems. Instead, just get back on schedule. If you have gone out too fast and your legs are trashed, slow down for a while, regroup, and adjust your expectations. Your energy level and emotions will fluctuate during the ride. You may find that after slowing down for a while your energy will return. Above all, whatever happens, remember that this is *your* ride. You still can have fun and finish.

Enjoy the experience   Whether this is your first or hundredth century, enjoy it. Get your head away from your electronics and look around you. Discover the beautiful scenery right in front of you. Chat with other riders who come and go. You may find new riding partners who become lifelong friends. Carry a small camera in your seat pack or jersey pocket, take lots of photos, and offer to share them with others. By relaxing and putting the fun factor ahead of your performance, you'll have fond memories for years to come.

After the Ride

Finishing a century or 200-kilometer ride, especially your first one, may produce mixed emotions. You are glad that the long day is over. You feel proud of your accomplishment and are ready to celebrate. You may have a twinge of sadness when you see the finish line that marks the end of a long journey. As you cross that line, give yourself a hearty pat on the back. One hundred miles or 200 kilometers on a bike in one day is no easy feat.

Recovering from your century or 200K starts the moment that you get off the bike. Right away reach for some fluids, preferably an electrolyte replacement drink, and start drinking enough to satisfy your thirst. Eat 500 to 1,000 calories of moderate- to high-glycemic-index carbohydrate with a little bit of protein within a few hours after finishing, preferably something salty. If you do not feel like eating after such a demanding day, drink a smoothie-type beverage, chocolate milk, or a commercial recovery drink.

As soon as possible, change out of your sweaty cycling clothes into something dry and comfortable. Shower if you can or use a restroom and baby wipes to clean up and prevent skin irritations. During the ride you may have been drinking and eating a lot of food that contains sugar. Brushing your teeth can make you feel better and help protect your teeth.

Postride stretching will help with the inevitable stiffness and make the drive home less painful. You have a good feel for the muscles that are prone to tightness after long rides, so while you are enjoying the postride festivities, stretch. You may find many others doing the same. You can do the same stretches that we illustrated earlier for rest stops.

Enjoy the company of other cyclists and make new friends. Before you leave, give a heartfelt thanks to the volunteers for their hard work. They are the unsung heroes of cycling events.

Take time to savor your accomplishment, preferably in the company of others, as you begin your recovery.

Courtesy of Alaska Digital Visions.

After you are home, relax, enjoy yourself, and have a celebratory dinner. It's OK to reward yourself but try to eat a wholesome meal with quality carbohydrate and protein. Go easy on the alcoholic beverages and remember that your body is still recovering from the hard day. Make sure to drink extra water if you have a beer with dinner. Taking an easy walk after dinner may help your digestion and reduce muscle soreness.

Before you head to bed, grab your training journal or a piece of paper and put down your experiences with and reflections about the ride. Note what you enjoyed, what was hard, what worked, what didn't, what you would have done differently, what you learned, and any other thoughts that come to mind. The more information you record, the easier it will be to plan for your next event. Remember that preparing involves many factors, and you want to figure out what works best. Keeping track of your events will help you develop as a cyclist and remind you of your accomplishments.

Finally, do more stretching and perhaps self-massage or use the foam roller to help loosen your muscles before going to bed.

Conquering the century or 200K takes more than simply riding your bike. Completing an event requires assessment and planning, readying yourself physically and mentally, preparing your equipment, staying well fueled and hydrated, using good technique, and mentally managing the ride.

Whether you are a first time rider or a century or 200K veteran, paying attention to these factors will help you perform at your best, be safe, and enjoy your day on the bike.

The century bug bites hard! After you have one or two under your belt, you might be looking for new challenges. In the next chapter we describe how to train for several centuries in a season as well as 300-kilometer and 200-mile (320 km) events. In later chapters we explore how to prepare for and ride multiday events.

CHAPTER 8

Ultimate Training for Ultra Events

After riding a century or two, you may want new challenges. You can accomplish almost anything on a bicycle with the right approach. Riders like you have crossed continents and even circled the globe under their own power. In this and following chapters we help you decide what events are right for you, how to prepare, and how to keep the fun factor high throughout your preparation and events.

This chapter serves as an introduction to what's out there beyond the century or 200K. We describe getting ready for and riding several centuries and 200Ks in a single season as well as 300K (186-mile) events and double centuries. We provide an 8-week program for improving your century performance, a 4-week maintenance program for riding multiple centuries within a single season, and a 12-week program for riding a double century. Again, we use *century* to include 200Ks and *double century* to include 300Ks. In chapter 9 we discuss two- to three-day touring, both supported events and credit-card style outings, and in chapter 10 we apply the principles of riding short tours to the longer brevets and supported and unsupported tours of a week or more.

You learned many skills in getting ready for and completing a century. In these chapters we apply the same expertise to longer distances and teach you some new techniques. We continue to focus on the areas that are essential to success: assessment and planning, mental preparation, physical training, equipment preparation, nutrition, and riding technique.

Assessment and Planning

Start your planning and preparation for a new event by reflecting on why you ride. Cycling is a great way to keep in shape, share time with others, and explore the world. Sometimes we get caught up with the details and lose sight of the big picture. Riding is much more than being a slave to a training plan. Regardless of your goals, never lose sight of why you ride. Enjoy the simple pleasures that come with spending time on your bike.

People all over the world ride bikes for different reasons. What are your reasons? What do you like? To help you select your next events, grab a pen and answer the questions in figure 8.1 on page 148 as thoroughly as possible.

FIGURE 8.1 CYCLING QUESTIONNAIRE

Question #1: As you develop as a cyclist, what do you like about riding?

Are you looking for a new challenge, or are you happy with your riding? _____

Do you like riding by yourself or with a group? _____

Do you get pleasure from helping other riders? _____

What else do you enjoy about riding? _____

Question #2: What seems exciting to you?

Riding more challenging centuries? _____

Completing several centuries a year? _____

Touring overnight on your bike? _____

Going farther on one ride? _____

Exploring new routes, terrain, and scenery? _____

What else seems exciting? _____

Question #3: What are your strengths and weaknesses?

You should be familiar with how your body responds to training and events and be able to identify your strengths and weaknesses.

Do you have the endurance to finish a long event? _____

Do you have your nutrition figured out, or do you run out of energy late in a long ride? _____

_____

Are you a strong climber? _____

Does the wind give you trouble? _____

Are you comfortable in a group, or do you get nervous? _____

How well do you manage anxiety before your events? _____

What are your other strengths and weaknesses? _____

Question #4: Were you able to maintain focus and energy while training for your century?

If not, why did you run out of enthusiasm? Was your training volume excessive? Did other work, social, or personal factors interfere?

_____

(continued)

If you lost enthusiasm during training, preparing for longer events may be difficult. You can still have fun by riding more than one century in a season, helping other riders get through their first one, or riding weekend tours.

Question #5: How much time do you have to train throughout the week?

_____

Training for longer events requires more training time. Be realistic about the amount of time that you can devote to your training. Time should also be available for family, work, social, and other needs.

Question #6: What are your goals and aspirations for family, work, school, and so on?

_____

_____

Question #7: Given your answers to the first six questions, what are your cycling goals?

_____

_____

Cycling goals should be **SMART**—specific, measurable, attainable, realistic, and testable. Goals don't have to be complicated. Completing a three-day charity tour is a **SMART** goal.

By answering these questions, you have a profile of your interests and goals that will help you decide which new events will be right for you. As we progress through the next chapters, we refer back to these questions and their relationship to your training and goal setting.

What events pique your interest? Do a bit of research, grab a calendar, and write down the ones in which you would like to participate as well as any other commitments (work, family, social,) that will affect your schedule.

In chapter 6 we outlined two training programs that used basic training principles to prepare riders for a single century. As you start planning for other distance cycling events, two new training concepts apply: athletic maturity and periodization.

Athletic Maturity

Athletes develop over several years of participating in a sport and gain athletic maturity. With experience you know more about how much and what kinds of training bring improvement and when to back off. As you log more distance, you become better equipped to handle the inevitable psychological, physical, and mechanical issues that arise during rides.

Over years of aerobic training, the body adapts, and this adaptation is cumulative. You are more mature as an endurance athlete if you have been active in another endurance sport. To a certain extent this adaptation can be transferred to cycling.

As you mature you ride more economically with more efficient power transfer to the pedals and less wasted upper-body motion. Further, you master the skills that foster economy of effort: riding at your best pace, riding in a group, cornering safely without unnecessary slowing, climbing efficiently, and so on.

After a few years of riding you have your bike dialed in: bike fit and preferred saddle, shorts, pedals, and shoes. You know which foods and drinks work for you in what quantities and when to eat and drink.

As you consider additional events assess your athletic maturity. Are you fairly new to endurance sports? Or do you have an endurance background but are new to long-distance cycling? Or do you have a number of long-distance events under your wheels?

If you are new to long-distance cycling focus on building your experience by riding more centuries, 200Ks, or weekend tours. If you have mastered these events you may be interested in longer events. Or you may chose to continue to ride the types of events that you know but do them faster, more frequently, or more comfortably.

Periodization

Whether you want to ride several events in one season or a significantly longer event, you should plan for an entire season instead of one event. To do so, you should organize training volume and intensity into different phases to achieve specific goals—a process called periodization. Recall the house analogy from chapter 3. You start building a house by laying a foundation that will support the entire structure and allow for future additions. In training you lay your base. During this phase you develop endurance, improve the aerobic energy system, train your body to metabolize fat and spare glycogen, and learn to be comfortable on the bike during longer rides.

After you've laid the foundation for a house, you construct the house itself—the framework, walls, and floors. After you have built your base in training, you move into the intensity phase to increase your power. Your average speed increases, and you climb better. If you don't lay a solid foundation when you build a house, the foundation may not support the structure. If you don't build a sufficient training base, your body may not be able to handle the demands of intensity training.

The next step in building a house is adding the finishing touches that make it a personal home: the landscape, the interior decorations, and the furniture. During the peaking phase of your training you focus on specific preparation for your event, such as training on parts of the actual course, riding back-to-back days to prepare for a weekend tour, or practicing riding your bike with the gear that you need for the tour. You also continue your mental preparation.

After you've built your training pyramid, you taper with a week or two of easier riding to store up energy for the event. Figure 8.2 illustrates the way each phase of training builds on the previous one.

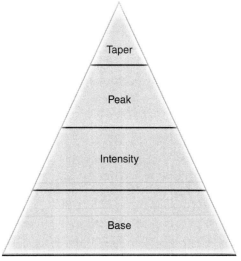

FIGURE 8.2   **The training pyramid.**

The Bucket List: New Things to Do on Your Bike!

By Pete Penseyres

Penseyres started serious cycling on camping trips on his tandem with his wife and set the transcontinental record for two tandems, drafting (1979). He won the solo Race Across America in 1984 and 1986, setting the long-standing speed record of 15.4 miles per hour (24.8 km/h) for 3,107 miles (5,000 km), and set the men's transcontinental tandem record with Lon Haldeman (1987). He raced in a fully faired recumbent on the four-man team that set the RAAM record (1989) and set the four-man team age 50 plus RAAM record in 1996. Penseyres trained for all these races by commuting. Most recently he's helped new riders enjoy RAAM by coaching and racing on eight-person teams (2006, 2007, and 2008). He has master's nationals jerseys for the individual road race and, with the help of six great tandem partners, another 11 for tandem road races and time trials.

▶ *Explore.* Find new ways to get from one place to another using roads or paths that either can't be accessed by a motor vehicle or would require too much patience to find unless you were on your bike. Most of us did this kind of exploring as kids with our first bikes and recall the sense of freedom and possibility; exploring can be equally exciting and rewarding for adults.

▶ *Socialize.* Ride with a group of beginning cyclists and share their joy of covering impossibly long distances of 10 miles (16 km) or more under their own power. Answer their questions and ask your own about their lives. Everyone has a story to tell. A midride stop for coffee, snacks, or lunch is a great location for story time and getting to know your new friends.

▶ *Mentor.* Help others become better cyclists so that they will want to ride more. You will have more friends to ride with, and more cyclists on the roads will increase motorists' awareness and everyone's safety.

▶ *Commute.* There is no better way to get to and from work than by bike. The benefits range from the obvious cost savings, reduced carbon footprint, and improved health and fitness to the less obvious advantages of using the time to reduce stress, do serious training, solve problems, and store memories of events that no motorist can experience. You will have entertaining stories that no one but another bike commuter will believe.

▶ *Go carless.* Think of how you could ride your bike each time you need to go somewhere. Set up a utility bike with panniers or baskets to carry groceries or a change of clothes to attend noncycling meetings or events, visit friends or relatives, or ride any other time you start to head for your car.

▶ *Tour.* Take vacations by bike either on your own or with friends or an organized group. You will see the countryside better, have more and better contacts with people, build memories, maintain fitness, and add to your expanding repertoire of stories.

▶ *Instruct.* Become a certified USA Cycling coach or a League of American Bicyclists instructor and enjoy helping others become safer and more skillful. The process of obtaining certification will improve your own cycling knowledge and skills.

▶ *Diversify.* Ride as many different types of cycles as you can. Road, mountain, cruiser, tandem, recumbent, ordinary, unicycle, and tricycle are all types to add to your bucket list of things to do before you rust out.

Overzealous riders often organize the year as an inverted pyramid. These riders spend the least amount of time developing a base, more time with intensity, and the greatest amount of time trying to peak. This mistake usually results in overtraining and increases the possibility of getting injured and burned out. To ride an endurance event, you need endurance, which you build during the base phase.

Training

Whether you decide to train for a century or a 1,200-kilometer brevet, the concepts of training stay the same. To develop as a cyclist, you use the principles of progressive overload, recovery, individuality, specificity, and variation. Pay close attention to individuality—how you are handling the workload and recovery—because more training requires sufficient recovery to get you stronger and keep you smiling on the bike.

We provide three training programs:

8-week century or 200K performance program. If you've ridden a century this season and want to ride a faster one, this program is for you! The first week you ride 4:20 to 6:45 and build to 7:55 to11:00, plus supplementary conditioning.

4-week century maintenance program. If you love riding centuries or 200Ks and want the challenge of riding one a month, here's how! The weekly volume every four weeks ranges from 2:10 to 3:40 through 5:40 to 8:30, plus supplementary training.

12-week double century or 300K program. If you want to test your limits, use this program! You ride 8:20 to 10:30 the first week and peak at 13:05 to 16:00, plus the supplementary workouts.

The types of workouts are the same as those laid out in chapter 6.

- *Long.* Throughout the programs consistently ride either the shorter or longer weekend ride. These rides increase your endurance, train your digestive system, and allow you to test new gear and various foods. As these workouts get longer you may not be able to stay in the long ride zone for the entire ride; slow down and pace yourself so that you can finish the rides. Also, if your long rides are hilly, you may need to climb in the tempo zone and then resume riding in your long ride zone.

- *Tempo.* These slightly faster rides increase your cruising speed. If you are doing the longer weekend rides, then you should also do the longer tempo ride; if you are doing the shorter weekend, rides you may choose the longer tempo rides.

- *Brisk.* These more intense rides include a segment of mixed intensity that helps boost your power and increase your average speed. If you do the longer weekend ride, then you should also ride the longer brisk workouts. If you choose the shorter weekend rides, you may do the longer brisk rides. If you choose the shorter brisk rides, then also do the shorter segments of mixed intensity.

- *Recovery.* These rides help you to recover and have more energy for other rides. You might fit these in by running errands on your bike!

- *Supplementary.* Continue your core strength, flexibility, and resistance-maintenance training.

To get the most from your training, keep the intensity of the workouts within the ranges specified in table 8.1. (See chapter 6 for more information on training by heart rate, power, and RPE.)

TABLE 8.1 **Recommended Workout Intensities**

Ride	Heart rate as percentage of LT	Power as percentage of FTP	Rating of perceived exertion
Long	75 to 87	56 to 75	2 to 3
Tempo	88 to 94	76 to 90	3 to 4
Brisk, mixed intensity, hard effort	95 to 100	91 to 100	5 to 6
Brisk, mixed intensity, recovery effort	less than 75	less than 55	1 to 2
Active recovery	less than 75	less than 55	1 to 2

Two Centuries in a Season

Riding more endurance events doesn't necessarily involve a huge time commitment. If you have been happy training for and riding a century or have limited training time, a great challenge would be to ride more of them! In many parts of the world you can ride an organized century or 200K nearly every weekend. Although that may be a bit much, you could ride two centuries in one season, say one in July and another in September. The rides would be about 10 weeks apart, which would give you time to recover and then prepare for the next one.

How much recovery you need should take into account both your body and your attitude. See how you feel after the first century. If you can't wait to get back on the bike and your legs feel fresh, then a one-week break should be adequate before resuming training. But if your legs are sore and it's a struggle even to look at your bike, allow an extra week of recovery before working out. Listen to your body—it will let you know if it needs a break.

Erika had a great time riding her first century and decides to ride another one with her brother Kyle in September. Her first century went well. Her legs were a little sore, but she is excited about getting back in the saddle. After a week of easy riding, stretching, and self-massage, she feels ready to start training again.

Erika has built her endurance base, and after the recovery break she is ready for the next phases of training: intensity, peaking, and taper. She has a couple of options depending on her goals:

1. If her goal is to complete another century, she could start with week 8 of the 15-week program from chapter 6.

2. If her goal is to improve her performance, she could focus on building her speed and power.

Erika's goal is to improve her performance. Because she'll be riding with Kyle, she won't go faster, but she wants to be strong enough to pace him. Erika has built her endurance for 100 miles (160 km), so the following program focuses on increasing power while maintaining endurance. Every other week she does a long endurance maintenance ride, and during the alternate weeks she does two intensity rides.

If your goal is to complete a second century, refer back to chapter 6. If your goal is to ride a faster or harder century, use the following performance improvement program.

8-WEEK CENTURY OR 200K PERFORMANCE IMPROVEMENT PROGRAM

Weeks 1-3 Intensity Phase
Increase intensity to improve power and maintain endurance.

WEEK 1

Riding

Long ride of 2:00–3:00
Midweek tempo ride of 60–75 minutes
Midweek brisk ride of 40–60 minutes including 10–15 minutes of mixed intensity
Active recovery ride of 40–60 minutes
Second active recovery ride of 20–30 minutes (optional)
Total riding time: 4:20–6:45

Supplementary training

Two core strength-training sessions of 10–20 minutes
Three stretching sessions of 10–20 minutes
One resistance-maintenance training session of 20–30 minutes (optional)

WEEK 2

Riding

Weekend brisk ride of 60–90 minutes including 20–30 minutes of mixed intensity
Midweek tempo ride of 60–75 minutes
Midweek brisk ride of 45–60 minutes including 15–20 minutes of mixed intensity
Active recovery ride of 30–40 minutes
Second active recovery ride of 20–30 minutes (optional)
Total riding time: 3:15–4:55

Supplementary training

Two core strength-training sessions of 10–20 minutes
Three stretching sessions of 10–20 minutes
One resistance-maintenance training session of 20–30 minutes (optional)

WEEK 3

Riding

Long ride of 3:00–4:00
Midweek tempo ride of 60–90 minutes
Mid week brisk ride of 40–60 minutes including 10–15 minutes of mixed intensity
Active recovery ride of 40–60 minutes
Second active recovery ride of 20–30 minutes (optional)
Total riding time: 5:20–8:00

Supplementary training

Two core strength-training sessions of 10–20 minutes
Three stretching sessions of 10–20 minutes
One resistance-maintenance training session of 20–30 minutes (optional)

WEEK 4—RECOVERY

Riding

Weekend brisk ride of 30–45 minutes including 10–15 minutes of mixed intensity
Midweek tempo ride of 30–45 minutes
Second midweek tempo ride of 30–45 minutes
Active recovery ride of 20–30 minutes
Second active recovery ride of 20–30 minutes (optional)
Total riding time: 1:50–3:15

Supplementary training

Two core strength-training sessions of 10–20 minutes
Three stretching sessions of 10–20 minutes
No resistance training

Weeks 5-7 Peaking Phase
Prepare for specific event. If possible train on the course or simulate parts of the course.

WEEK 5

Riding

Long ride of 4:00–5:00
Midweek tempo ride of 60–90 minutes
Midweek brisk ride of 60–90 minutes including 15–20 minutes of mixed intensity
Active recovery ride of 40–60 minutes
Second active recovery ride of 20–30 minutes (optional)
Total riding time: 6:40–9:30

Supplementary training

Two core strength-training sessions of 10–20 minutes
Three stretching sessions of 10–20 minutes
One resistance-maintenance training session of 20–30 minutes (optional)

WEEK 6

Riding

Weekend brisk ride of 60–90 minutes including 20–30 minutes of mixed intensity
Midweek tempo ride of 60–90 minutes
Midweek brisk ride of 60–90 minutes including 15–20 minutes of mixed intensity
Active recovery ride of 40–60 minutes
Second active recovery ride of 20–30 minutes (optional)
Total riding time: 3:40–6:00

Supplementary training

Two core strength-training sessions of 10–20 minutes
Three stretching sessions of 10–20 minutes
One resistance-maintenance training session of 20–30 minutes (optional)

(continued)

WEEK 7—PEAK

Riding

Long ride of 5:15–6:30
Midweek tempo ride of 60–90 minutes
Midweek brisk ride of 60–90 minutes including 20–30 minutes of mixed intensity
Active recovery ride of 40–60 minutes
Second active recovery ride of 20–30 minutes (optional)
Total riding time: 7:55–11:00

Supplementary training

Two core strength-training sessions of 10–20 minutes
Three stretching sessions of 10–20 minutes
One resistance-maintenance training session of 20–30 minutes (optional)

WEEK 8—TAPER

Riding

Long ride of 2:30–3:30
Midweek tempo ride of 60–90 minutes
Midweek brisk ride of 60–90 minutes including 10–15 minutes of mixed intensity
Active recovery ride of 40–60 minutes
Active recovery ride of 20–30 minutes (optional)
Total riding time: 5:10–8:00

Supplementary training

Two core strength-training sessions of 10–20 minutes
Three stretching sessions of 10–20 minutes
No resistance training

CENTURY WEEK

Riding

Long ride—century or 200K
Midweek brisk ride of 30–40 minutes including 10–15 minutes of mixed intensity
Active recovery ride of 20–30 minutes
Active recovery ride of 20–30 minutes

Supplementary training

Two core strength-training sessions of 10–20 minutes
Three stretching sessions of 10–20 minutes
No resistance training

If you are training for a faster 200K you could either add a week with longer rides between weeks 7 and 8, or you could ramp up all the weekly rides smoothly and proportionally to a revised week 7. Plan a final long ride that is two-thirds to three-quarters of the duration of your anticipated 200K.

Multiple Ride Challenges

Several organizations offer programs to challenge you to do one long ride each month. Ultra Midwest started the first program in 2000 to challenge riders to complete a century every month of the calendar year. Ultra Midwest offers online tracking of centuries as well as total mileage. The UltraMarathon Cycling Association offers the Larry Schwartz Year-Rounder award for cyclists who complete a century in every month of the calendar year. Randonneurs USA offers a similar program, the R-12 award, for riders who complete a 200-kilometer brevet for 12 consecutive months. See the resources section for details.

Share the fun of riding a century with your family.

Courtesy of Alaska Digital Visions.

A Season of Centuries

If the century bug has bitten you, you may enjoy the challenge of riding a century or 200K every month of the year. These rides, especially with friends, are just plain fun! You have fewer weeks between events, so you need a program to maintain your fitness between rides. Finding the right balance between training and recovery is highly individual.

Start with a recovery week of easy riding to loosen up after your century. The next two weekends do moderately long rides to maintain your endurance, and during each week do a tempo ride and a brisk ride to keep your legs sharp. Then perform a minitaper during the week of your next century. On page 158 is an example of a maintenance schedule that will help you ride one century per month.

CENTURY AND 200K MAINTENANCE PROGRAM

Riding

Long ride of 1:00–2:00
Midweek tempo ride of 30–40 minutes
Active recovery ride of 20–30 minutes
Active recovery ride of 20–30 minutes
Total riding time: 2:10–3:40

Supplementary training

Two core strength-training sessions of 10–20 minutes
Three stretching sessions of 10–20 minutes
One resistance-maintenance training session of 20–30 minutes (optional)

WEEK 2

Riding

Long ride of 3:00–4:00 (or 4:00–5:00 for 200Ks)
Midweek tempo ride of 60–90 minutes
Midweek brisk ride of 60–90 minutes including 20–30 minutes of mixed intensity
Active recovery ride of 40–60 minutes
Second active recovery ride of 20–30 minutes (optional)
Total riding time: 5:40–8:30

Supplementary training

Two core strength-training sessions of 10–20 minutes
Three stretching sessions of 10–20 minutes
One resistance-maintenance training session of 20–30 minutes (optional)

WEEK 3

Riding

Long ride of 2:30–3:30 (or 3:30–4:30 for 200Ks)
Midweek tempo ride of 60–75 minutes
Midweek brisk ride of 60–75 minutes including 15–20 minutes of mixed intensity
Active recovery ride of 40–60 minutes
Second active recovery ride of 20–30 minutes (optional)
Total riding time: 5:10–7:30

Supplementary training

Two core strength-training sessions of 10–20 minutes
Three stretching sessions of 10–20 minutes
One resistance-maintenance training session of 20–30 minutes (optional)

EVENT WEEK

Long ride—century or 200K
Midweek tempo ride of 30–40 minutes (or if you are fully recovered and want to improve performance, a brisk ride of 40–60 minutes including 10–15 minutes of mixed intensity)
Active recovery ride of 20–30 minutes
Active recovery ride of 20–30 minutes

Supplementary training

Two core strength-training sessions of 10–20 minutes
Three stretching sessions of 10–20 minutes
No resistance training

This program maintains your fitness for four weeks so that you can ride another century or 200K. Start conservatively riding the shorter rides each week so that your legs are fresh for the event. If that works well then you could do the longer rides to prepare for the next one. Then if you would like to improve your performance in the subsequent ride, in weeks 2 and 3 you could change the tempo ride to another brisk ride that includes mixed intensity.

As you become more experienced riding centuries, why not help others? Here are some ideas:

- *Help a first-time century rider*. Remember what your first ride was like? Riding with another rider on the journey, particularly an experienced one, can be helpful for beginners. Share tips and give them encouragement. When the going gets tough, they'll be glad that you are there.

- *Lead*. Some rides recruit pacers to help others reach their time goals. You can pace new riders to finish or pace a fast group, which is a great way to push yourself.

- *Ride with friends or family*. Some events feature shorter distances. For example, you could ride the 25-miler (40 km) with your family, finish the remaining 75 miles (120 km) on your own, and then enjoy the postride festivities together.

- *Support a cause*. You could raise a certain amount of money per mile or kilometer that you ride. Or you could set a time goal; if you take more than that time, you have to match the donations—a little incentive to keep you moving!

- *Volunteer*. Events can always use an extra hand with registration, sag, mechanical support, and at rest stops. Volunteers make organized rides possible. Many events encourage volunteers to preride the course. You get your century and scout the course for any last-minute problems.

By John Lee Ellis, Randonneurs USA, www.rusa.org

▶ *Brevet* means "certified," and *randonnée* means "tour" or "excursion." As in ski randonneuring, the object is to range widely over challenging countryside to complete a course.

▶ Randonnées are deeply rooted in cycling history. The most famous event is Paris–Brest–Paris (PBP), held every four years, which traverses 1,200 kilometers from Paris to Brest and back in France. First held in 1891 as a competitive event, it is now a noncompetitive ride and the oldest endurance cycling event. In the 2007 PBP year, riders completed over 15 million kilometers in randonnées and brevets. Four or five randonnées are held annually in North America, and events of 1,200 kilometers or longer are offered in Asia, Australia, and Europe.

REPRINTED, BY PERMISSION, FROM RANDONNEURS USA.

▶ Brevets offer a personal challenge in a spirit of camaraderie, not competition, and they value persistence over finishing time. Another value is self-sufficiency, which doesn't mean that riders can't help each other but that having private support or even an overly coddling event staff is not in the classic spirit of randonneuring.

▶ The standard distances are 200, 300, 400, 600, 1,000 and 1,200 kilometers. Traditionally, completing a 200-, 300-, 400-, and 600-kilometer series is recognized as Super-Randonneur status and is a season goal for many randonneurs.

▶ Completing a series of 200-, 300-, 400-, and 600-kilometer brevets can qualify riders for Grand Randonnées of 1,200 kilometers or longer, such as PBP.

▶ Riders follow a specified route and carry a card (see figure 8.3), which must be verified at control points along the way where the time of passage is entered. (A 300-kilometer brevet might have two to four intermediate control points, for example.)

▶ The distance must be completed within a time limit, corresponding to an average speed of 15 kilometers per hour (9 mph) including stops. These limits encourage persistence and finishing, even in the face of adversity (mechanical, meteorological, terrain, or physical or mental indisposition), and allow time for helping others. For example, riders have 13:30 for 200 kilometers and 20:00 for 300 kilometers.

▶ A randonneur's primary goal is to finish. In addition, a rider may be trying for a personal best finishing time, seeking maximum scenic enjoyment, riding with friends, helping a novice, testing equipment or strategy for longer events, or any combination. The 600-kilometer event has a cutoff of 40:00. A randonneur who finishes one in 39:50 on a weekend when she or he did not feel sharp, experienced inclement weather, or may have helped out a struggling companion gets the same credit as the rider who breezes through in 25:00. The rider who quits at 400 kilometers because the ride ceased being fun or because a personal best wasn't in sight is not reflecting randonneuring ethos.

- ▶ Riding in groups or alone, fast or slow, with sleep breaks or not, is up to the rider.
- ▶ Brevets are held all over the world, and riders can qualify for randonnées worldwide.

Randonneurs USA sanctions brevets in the United States. The resources section has a list of randonneuring organizations around the world.

Rider's Last Name: _____	**Brevet de Randonneurs Mondiaux**
Rider's First Name: _____	
Address: _____	

Rider's Last Name: _____

Rider's First Name: _____

Address: _____

RUSA Member #: _____ ☐ Applied for

Club / ACP Code: Rocky Mountain Cycling Club / 906002

_____
RIDER's signature at the FINISH

The ride was done in: _____ hours _____ minutes

_____
Signature of the ORGANIZER

IMPORTANT! <u>DNF</u>: 303-604-1163 or 303-579-5866

MAIL TO: 2155 Dogwood Circle, Louisville CO 80027

Brevet de Randonneurs Mondiaux

Randonnée of
200 KM
STOVE PRAIRIE
May 1, 2010
Mead, Colorado (USA)

SPONSORED BY
Rocky Mountain Cycling Club

VERIFIED & VALIDATED EXCLUSIVELY BY
Audax Club Parisien

Mead Hwy. 66 at I-25 08:00 0 km	Time:			
LaPorte Vern's Store – Rd 54G 10:16 to 13:08 77.0 km (47.9 miles)	Time:			
Stove Prairie Stove Prairie School – Rist Canyon Rd. 11:26 to 15:48 117.1 km (72.8 miles) *??? Westbound Road:* _____	Time:			
Loveland Sandy's Conoco – US-34 at Glade Rd. 12:34 to 18:20 155.4 km (96.6 miles)	Time:	Secret Checkpoint:		Time:
Mead Hwy. 66 at I-25 13:53 to 21:30 204.3 km (127.1 miles)	Time:	Bike Inspection:		

FIGURE 8.3   **Control card.**

Whether you are riding two centuries for the season or one a month, remember the basics:

- Tailor the training rides to your particular events. The more specific to your event that you can make the preparation, the more successful your ride will be.
- Pay attention to nutrition both on and off the bike. Wholesome meals throughout the day, good on-bike nutrition, and adequate fluids will keep you riding well.
- Train hard but also rest hard. More training requires careful recovery to avoid over-training and burnout. Keep up with the stretching, self-massage, and foam roller work, and try to get enough sleep each night.
- Listen to your body and modify the training plan to your individual needs.

300-Kilometer and 200-Mile Events

If you have ridden several centuries or 200Ks without struggling, you're ready to prepare for a 300K or double century. You can find events of approximately these lengths in many countries.

Double centuries are two centuries ridden continuously as a 200-mile (320 km) single-day event. The metric equivalent is the 300K (186 miles), some of which are organized as brevets. In this section we use the term *double century* to cover both doubles and 300Ks because the training is the same. Just like centuries, doubles come in many forms. Check the website of the event or other resources to learn the details.

You use the same training principles for a double century as you used for a century, although the training volume is greater. To prepare for a double, follow these guidelines:

- When estimating your time for a double, recognize that your pace will be slower than it is for a century. If you ride centuries in 7:00 a double may take 16:00 or more. If you ride 200Ks in 9:00 a 300K may take 15:00 or so.
- Build your long rides to about two-thirds to three-quarters of the duration of the event. For a 16:00 double century you would do a final long training ride of 10:45 to 12:00. For a 15:00 300K you would do a ride of 10:00 to 11:15.
- Ramp up your long rides gradually.
- Because you already have a good endurance base, do the long rides every other week to avoid burnout or overtraining. Do a much shorter endurance ride in the alternate weeks.
- Take a recovery week every four weeks by reducing the long ride to a few hours, cutting back the tempo and brisk rides, and adding active recovery rides.
- Early in the program, do the brisk rides that include mixed intensity in the shorter weeks with shorter endurance rides. Later in the program include a brisk ride each week, but make them shorter in the weeks with the long endurance rides. As you train, if you are riding well, you could substitute a second brisk ride for the tempo ride in the shorter weeks.
- Continue the core strength and flexibility work that you did for the century.

How do you use these guidelines to design a training program? If you have recently completed a century or 200K without any significant problems then you can use the following 12-week program to prepare for your first double or 300K.

12-WEEK DOUBLE CENTURY OR 300K PROGRAM

WEEK 1

Riding

Long ride of 6:30–7:15
Midweek tempo ride of 40–60 minutes
Second midweek tempo ride of 30–45 minutes
Active recovery ride of 40–60 minutes
Second active recovery ride of 20–30 minutes (optional)
Total riding time: 8:20–10:30

Supplementary training

Two core strength-training sessions of 10–20 minutes
Three stretching sessions of 10–20 minutes
One resistance-maintenance training session of 20–30 minutes (optional)

WEEK 2

Riding

Long ride of 3:30–4:30
Midweek tempo ride of 60–90 minutes
Midweek brisk ride of 40–60 minutes including 10–15 minutes of mixed intensity
Active recovery ride of 40–60 minutes
Second active recovery ride of 20–30 minutes (optional)
Total riding time: 5:50–8:30

Supplementary training

Two core strength-training sessions of 10–20 minutes
Three stretching sessions of 10–20 minutes
One resistance-maintenance training session of 20–30 minutes (optional)

WEEK 3

Riding

Long ride of 7:15–8:00
Midweek tempo ride of 60–90 minutes
Second midweek tempo ride of 45–60 minutes
Active recovery ride of 40–60 minutes
Second active recovery ride of 20–30 minutes (optional)
Total riding time: 9:40–12:00

Supplementary training

Two core strength-training sessions of 10–20 minutes
Three stretching sessions of 10–20 minutes
One resistance-maintenance training session of 20–30 minutes (optional)

(continued)

WEEK 4—RECOVERY

Riding

Long ride of 2:00–3:00
Midweek tempo ride of 30–40 minutes
Midweek brisk ride of 40–60 minutes including 10–15 minutes of mixed intensity
Active recovery ride of 40–60 minutes
Second active recovery ride of 20–30 minutes (optional)
Total riding time: 3:50–6:10

Supplementary training

Two core strength-training sessions of 10–20 minutes
Three stretching sessions of 10–20 minutes
No resistance training

WEEK 5

Riding

Long ride of 8:00–9:00
Midweek tempo ride of 60–90 minutes
Midweek brisk ride of 40–60 minutes including 10–15 minutes of mixed intensity
Active recovery ride of 40–60 minutes
Second active recovery ride of 20–30 minutes (optional)
Total riding time: 10:20–13:00

Supplementary training

Two core strength-training sessions of 10–20 minutes
Three stretching sessions of 10–20 minutes
One resistance-maintenance training session of 20–30 minutes (optional)

WEEK 6

Riding

Long ride of 3:30–4:30
Midweek tempo ride of 1:30–1:45
Midweek brisk ride of 60–75 minutes including 15–20 minutes of mixed intensity
Active recovery ride of 40–60 minutes
Second active recovery ride of 20–30 minutes (optional)
Total riding time: 6:40–9:00

Supplementary training

Two core strength-training sessions of 10–20 minutes
Three stretching sessions of 10–20 minutes
One resistance-maintenance training session of 20–30 minutes (optional)

WEEK 7

Riding

Long ride of 8:45–10:00
Midweek tempo ride of 1:15–1:45
Midweek brisk ride of 40–60 minutes including 10–15 minutes of mixed intensity
Active recovery ride of 40–60 minutes

Second active recovery ride of 20–30 minutes (optional)
Total riding time: 11:20–14:15

Supplementary training

Two core strength-training sessions of 10–20 minutes
Three stretching sessions of 10–20 minutes
One resistance-maintenance training session of 20–30 minutes (optional)

WEEK 8—RECOVERY

Riding

Long ride of 2:00–3:00
Midweek tempo ride of 40–60 minutes
Midweek brisk ride of 40–60 minutes including 10–15 minutes of mixed intensity
Active recovery ride of 40–60 minutes
Second active recovery ride of 20–30 minutes (optional)
Total riding time: 4:00–6:30

Supplementary training

Two core strength-training sessions of 10–20 minutes
Three stretching sessions of 10–20 minutes
No resistance training

WEEK 9

Riding

Long ride of 9:45–11:00
Midweek tempo ride of 1:15–1:45
Midweek brisk ride of 40–60 minutes including 10–15 minutes of mixed intensity
Active recovery ride of 40–60 minutes
Second active recovery ride of 20–30 minutes (optional)
Total riding time: 12:20–15:15

Supplementary training

Two core strength-training sessions of 10–20 minutes
Three stretching sessions of 10–20 minutes
One resistance-maintenance training session of 20–30 minutes (optional)

WEEK 10

Riding

Long ride of 3:30–4:30
Midweek tempo ride of 60–90 minutes
Midweek brisk ride of 60–75 minutes including 15–20 minutes of mixed intensity
Active recovery ride of 40–60 minutes
Second active recovery ride of 20–30 minutes (optional)
Total riding time: 6:10–8:45

Supplementary training

Two core strength-training sessions of 10–20 minutes
Three stretching sessions of 10–20 minutes
One resistance-maintenance training session of 20–30 minutes (optional)

(continued)

12-Week Double Century or 300K Program (continued)

WEEK 11—PEAK

Riding

Long ride of 10:45–12:00
Midweek tempo ride of 60–90 minutes
Midweek brisk ride of 40–60 minutes including 10–15 minutes of mixed intensity
Active recovery ride of 40–60 minutes
Second active recovery ride of 20–30 minutes (optional)
Total riding time: 13:05–16:00

Supplementary training

Two core strength-training sessions of 10–20 minutes
Three stretching sessions of 10–20 minutes
One resistance-maintenance training session of 20–30 minutes (optional)

WEEK 12—TAPER

Riding

Long ride of 4:00–6:30
Midweek tempo ride of 60–75 minutes
Midweek brisk ride of 60–75 minutes including 10–15 minutes of mixed intensity
Active recovery ride of 40–60 minutes
Second active recovery ride of 20–30 minutes (optional)
Total riding time: 6:40–10:30

Supplementary training

Two core strength-training sessions of 10–20 minutes
Three stretching sessions of 10–20 minutes
No resistance training

EVENT WEEK

Riding

Long ride—event
Midweek tempo ride of 40–60 minutes
Active recovery ride of 40–60 minutes
Second active recovery ride of 20–30 minutes (optional)

Supplementary training

Two core strength-training sessions of 10–20 minutes
Three stretching sessions of 10–20 minutes
No resistance training

Notice that throughout the program you

- gradually build up your long rides,
- schedule long rides every other week to prevent overtraining and burnout,
- incorporate recovery weeks every fourth week, and
- alternate weeks that include very long rides with weeks that have more intensity.

Remember that everyone responds differently to the demands of life and training, so adjust the schedule to meet your needs. At this point in your development, you should have a good idea of what works and what doesn't. Just make sure that you are still having fun and looking forward to the next ride.

Mental Preparation

While preparing for and riding your first century, you learned that all does not go as planned! The more rides you do and the longer the rides are, the more important the mental factors become. You have developed a repertoire of mental skills; keep applying those skills as you prepare for new rides:

- *Relaxation and visualization techniques.* Practice the relaxation techniques from chapter 7 (pages 135–136). As you develop your techniques, you mentally go at will to your image of a calm place. When a problem develops while preparing for your event, go briefly to your calm place. You'll be in a better frame of mind to assess what's really gone wrong and what you can do about it. Also, practice the visualization techniques to rehearse for a successful event.
- *Ride plans.* Develop several ride plans for your event: your expected ride, a not-so-good day, and an awesome event. For double centuries and 300Ks consider what a slow ride might mean in terms of clothing and lights. Then during the ride mentally adjust to the circumstances.
- *Solve problems.* As your training rides get longer you are more likely to encounter a problem. With a bit of ingenuity you can overcome almost any difficulty. Practicing your problem-solving skills during your training rides will help prepare you for your event. Dead legs? Slow down for an hour and eat and drink. Several flats? Stop and check the tire thoroughly for the culprit. Sore butt? Stand up for a minute every 5 to 10 minutes to relieve the pressure.

Equipment Considerations

Whether you are riding two or more centuries in a season or a double century, you are putting more distance on the bike and on your body, so the effects of any bike or clothing problems are exacerbated. More distance means more wear on all your equipment—your bike, clothing, and accessories. In chapter 5 we talked about performance versus reliability in equipment choices. As the distances become longer, reliability starts to outweigh performance, especially if you don't have mechanical support during the event.

Bike

As you ride more analyze your current setup:

- *How do you feel during and after long rides*? Being a little stiff is normal, but if you experience pain you should look at your equipment choices. For example, do you need a different saddle? Is your hydration pack too heavy?

- *Should your bike fit be reevaluated*? If your fit hasn't been checked in a year then get it reevaluated. A change in strength or flexibility or an injury can affect fit. Describe how you currently feel on the bike and whether you will be riding longer distances. The shop may suggest ways to make your bike more comfortable, such as a different stem or handlebar.

- *Is your bike functioning properly*? As the distance adds up, wear occurs. To prevent shifting problems, periodically check the chain and cassette for wear and the cables for wear and proper tension. For safety's sake, inspect your brakes, wheels, and tires regularly.

- *Consider using lower gears*. Your legs may not have the same zip if you're riding a century a month. Likewise, you won't feel as fresh in the second half of a double century as you did in the first half. Switching to compact chain rings, a triple crank set, or a lower gear cassette will ease the strain on your knees and help you deal with the fatigue that builds over longer rides. Even on longer supported rides you may want to carry a bit more gear (e.g., clothing), and lower gearing will help.

Clothing

You tested the clothing for your first century, which will probably suffice for more centuries in summer. For centuries in other locales or not in summer, you may want more clothes. For longer events you can also use your century clothing. But because you will start earlier and ride later, you might be riding in temperatures that vary by 30° F (17 °C) or more, depending on your locale. For some centuries and longer rides you may need to wear arm and knee or leg warmers and a windbreaker. The knees have poor circulation; to prevent injury keep them covered until it's 60 °F (16 °C). When the day warms up stow your extra clothing in your jersey pocket, seat pack, or hydration pack. We use a larger seat bag so that we can keep our hydration packs relatively light and our pockets available for food and cue sheets.

Also, the more you ride, the greater the chances are that you will experience inclement weather. Every cyclist will have to ride in inclement weather eventually, and the right clothing can even make it enjoyable. You need a clothing system to deal with the weather common in your area. How often do you encounter rain? Riding in the Pacific Northwest often involves many hours of rain, so riders need good raingear. If you ride in a warm climate that has sporadic showers but not sustained rain, you may get away with a light, quick-drying rain shell. Also, consider your goals. If you are trying for a PR, you may want to travel light, carry less gear, and put up with some discomfort if necessary.

When choosing clothing think about dressing in layers for better insulation and greater flexibility. For your torso start with a wicking layer, a thin layer of synthetic or wool material that will draw moisture away from your skin. Stay away from cotton, which retains moisture. A few sheets of newspaper on your chest also can help keep you warm, and you can dispose of them at a rest stop. If you sweat a lot, however, the ink may rub off on you a bit. For your legs you can wear either knee or leg warmers, or you may choose lightweight tights, perhaps with a windproof and rainproof material on the front of the legs. Don't forget a layer for your head, hands, and feet; take a thin balaclava to go under your helmet and cover your face if necessary, light glove liners to wear under your cycling gloves, toe warmers to fit over the toes and cleats of your shoes, and a shower cap from a motel as an emergency rain bonnet. As the day warms up, you can shed your base layer to stay cool.

On top of your base layer wear the insulating layer, usually your favorite cycling jersey. If you expect colder conditions you might also wear a thermal vest or long-sleeve wool or synthetic jersey over your regular jersey. We prefer wool because it stays warm even when wet. The best thermal vests have a windproof front and rear pockets for carrying gear.

Safety: Two-Lane Roads

Many of your rides will be on scenic, quiet country roads with light traffic and good shoulders. Some of your outings, however, will be on busier roads that present challenging conditions. Here are some tips to keep you safe:

▶ As noted earlier, wear bright clothing, use a rear view mirror, and ride predictably.

▶ Anticipate potential problems. If a car is coming toward you check your mirror. Is traffic also approaching from the rear? Or are multiple cars approaching from ahead? Might one pull into your lane to pass the others? In both situations, is the road wide enough for two vehicles and you? Or should you get off the road?

▶ Ride near the right edge of the usable portion of the road, that is, the section where you can ride without increased risk of a flat or a fall from junk on the road. The physical edge of the road may have gravel, broken pavement, broken bottles, and so forth. Don't ride where you would increase the risk of either hitting something or having to swerve suddenly to avoid an obstacle.

▶ If you are approaching a blind driveway on your right, check for traffic behind you and then move farther into the roadway or slow down so that a driver exiting the driveway will see you in time to yield.

▶ Be alert to situations where you won't be visible to a driver approaching from the rear; in those situations stay right. Examples include riding around a blind curve to the right and riding over the top of a hill because you won't be visible immediately to a driver coming up the hill behind you.

▶ On a highway with a useable shoulder ride 3 to 4 feet (1 m) to the right of the traffic. Even on a highway with a very wide shoulder ride here to ensure that you are visible and to give yourself an escape zone in case of a problem. You may need to move more to the left when approaching an intersection, especially if the driver from the rear will be turning right.

▶ Your ears can also provide useful cues. Is a vehicle coming down a blind driveway? But don't rely exclusively on your ears, because background noise or wind can obscure sounds.

▶ Drivers tend to be more considerate of a group of riders, but they need more room to pass a group. Be careful not to obstruct traffic.

Finally, you want an outer layer. A wind vest might be sufficient for riding in the morning chill. If the forecast is for possible showers or sustained wind, you may want a lightweight windbreaker. Some windbreakers have removable sleeves to give you more flexibility. If you anticipate hours in the rain, you need a specialized cycling raincoat with a breathable fabric. Any cycling outer layer should be bright for safety and close fitting so that it doesn't billow in the wind. The best coats have two-way front zippers and zippers in the armpits to provide ventilation when needed, as well as a rear flap that extends over your buttocks when on the bike.

Clothing choices are personal. Some people want to feel warm all the time, whereas others prefer to feel cool. As with your other riding equipment, test all your clothing items to determine what does and does not work.

In Chapter 10 we discuss clothing choices in more detail in relation to touring (pages 215–216). In chapter 11 we discuss hypothermia, which can occur even in relatively mild conditions (pages 236–237). You can develop hypothermia riding at 50 °F (10 °C) in rainy, windy conditions! Choosing the proper combination of base, insulating, and outer layers will help keep you warm, dry, and safe.

Lights

Even in the off-season you can usually ride a century in daylight, and during summer you can complete most double centuries and 300Ks in daylight. For a few events, however, you may need to ride in the dark for an hour or so at the start. As you develop your ride plans consider whether you might finish in the dark if you're riding your slow scenario. If you might need lights, then take the basics: a simple battery-powered headlight on your handlebars and a battery-powered taillight on your seat stays. If you might be riding at night, visibility is critical, so use reflective material. Good cycling vests and coats have reflective strips. Reflective tape on your wheels and frame works well. If you prefer not to put tape on your bike, then reflective ankle bands are effective and easy to stow when not in use. Investing in a lighting system also gives you more training flexibility because you can start or finish rides in the dark, such as when commuting. We discuss lighting and night riding in more detail in conjunction with the longer events in chapter 10 (pages 217–219).

Nutrition

By now you know the principles of nutrition and should have a good idea of what works during training and in events. The key is applying what you know:

● *Daily nutrition*. Are you eating regular meals with a balanced, varied diet, sufficient to provide the energy that you need to train? Periodically logging your intake may help you stay on track and ride well.

● *Training rides*. Continue to apply what works on your centuries and perhaps experiment with different foods during training. On longer training rides, pay attention to your food choices—what you like on centuries may not work for 200-mile or 300-kilometer rides. Have you noticed any warning signs that you are not eating enough? Some people get cranky; others become lightheaded. Varying your food choices while riding may help you eat on regular intervals or reduce digestive problems. Are you drinking just enough to satisfy your thirst? Or are your wrists getting puffy around your gloves or your ankles getting puffy around your socks? This condition indicates that you are retaining fluid and should stop drinking until you urinate the excess fluid and the swelling goes down.

- *Recovery*. Proper recovery after your long rides lays the foundation for effective training in the following week. In the first few hours after getting off the bike, eat 500 to 1,000 calories of moderate- to high-glycemic-index carbohydrate to help replenish your glycogen stores. Take in a little protein as well and continue drinking fluids as you recover.

- *Preride*. Increase the carbohydrate and decrease the fat and protein in your diet three or four days before an event.

Final Preparation

As with your first century, you may feel a bit overwhelmed as you approach your next event, whether it's another century, a 300K, or a double century. Practice progressive relaxation for several nights before and the morning of your event. Use the equipment, event packing, and preride checklists in chapter 7 (pages 137–140) to help you get organized and reduce ride stress. You might also make a short rest stop checklist on a file card to carry on 300-kilometer and 200-mile rides.

On the Road

As with other events, the start will be exciting and possibly stressful. Before you start, visualize getting into your pace and letting the faster riders go ahead. Ride your own ride. Use the pace from your long training rides as a guideline. If after the first half hour you are riding faster, force yourself to slow down. Holding yourself back in the beginning is much better than running out of energy later in the day. Your heart rate may differ during an event because of excitement, so you may want to use RPE or your power meter to guide your pace.

A fairly constant level of effort rather than consistent average speed is the most economical over the course of the event. If you push up the climbs and then have to recover on the downhills or hammer with a group and then get dropped, you use more energy than you will if you ride at a fairly consistent heart rate, power output, or RPE. By measuring out your energy in a controlled fashion, you'll have more zip in your legs in the last stretch.

As you start riding farther, nutrition during the ride becomes more important. The first hour goes by quickly—start eating and drinking during this time. Depending on your body size, remember to eat a mix of carbohydrate totaling 60 to 90 grams, or 240 to 360 calories, plus a little protein and fat during each hour of riding and to drink to satisfy your thirst. Eating a mix of carbohydrate during each hour is easier to digest than eating one food at the end of every hour. Use your experience from the weekly long rides to guide you; if it worked for those rides, it will work for the double century. If you think you might forget to eat, set your watch to remind you.

If you ride with others, you may meet new cyclists with whom you can talk to help pass the time. Also, you can help one another through mental tough times and with bike problems. Remember, though, to be safe while in a group. Recall the basics of group riding. Pay attention to your ride. Watch for and call out hazards. Ride a straight line and signal or call out before you move or change speed. Protect your front wheel. In a pace line remember the protocol of short pulls at a consistent effort, dropping to the traffic side if no wind is blowing, or dropping to the windward side if there is a crosswind.

Draw on your mental training—your relaxation techniques and your image of a calm place. When a problem develops, go briefly to your calm place and then identify what has gone wrong and what you can do about it.

Break down the ride. A 200-mile or 300-kilometer ride can seem impossibly long. John finds that rides usually fall into three parts:

1. At the beginning he feels fresh and enjoys riding.
2. During the middle it seems endless.
3. Finally, he smells the barn!

During your rides recognize and accept when you are in the long, hard middle. Stop thinking about how hard it is. Talk to your companions, focus on the scenery, or plan your celebratory dinner.

Similarly, whether the ride is great, normal, or subpar, follow your plans and enjoy the ride. Stay focused on the immediate short-term goal. How do you race the Race Across America? One time station at a time. How do you ride a double century? One rest stop at a time.

Use aid stations in a way that fits your ride plan and goal. If you are trying to ride a personal best, finish before dark, or meet an event cutoff time, as you approach a rest stop develop a mental checklist of what you need to do there. As you arrive agree with any riding companions how long you'll stop. View the aid station as a refueling stop. Get food and drink to go and consume some while you are taking care of other tasks such as removing clothing, putting on sunscreen, or stretching if you feel tight. Check your bike and be ready to depart with your friends. If time is less of an issue talk with others but don't stay too long lest you get stiff. As you get on your bike thank the volunteers. When reentering the road watch for cars and other bikes and gradually reestablish your rhythm.

To prepare for and ride several centuries or longer events you can draw on the same principles you used for your first century. As you look for new opportunities, consider what draws you to riding. Is it getting fitter? The physical challenge? The camaraderie? Keep referring back to your personal assessment and don't lose sight of what matters to you. As you ride more frequently or ride longer distances, take care that you still enjoy them overall, despite some low moments. As Pete Penseyres recommends, look for ways to integrate cycling into your life, help others, and have fun.

Training doesn't have to be complex. Keep the basic principles (volume progression, intensity, overload and recovery, specificity, and individuality) in mind, and you can prepare for anything—multiple centuries in a season, a double century, a 300K, or, as we describe in the next chapter, two- to three-day rides, both supported rides and credit-card touring rides.

CHAPTER 9

Mastering the Multiday

Now that we have the principles for preparing for longer one-day events, let's apply them to multiday events. Back-to-back days on the bike can be a lot of fun! You can use two- to three-day rides to build up your skills and confidence for longer tours and brevets. Many experienced randonneurs began with weekend touring and continue to tour as a fun change of pace.

In this chapter we focus on preparing for a two- to three-day supported or credit-card tour. If you plan a weekend camping tour, you can use the same process; refer to the section on camping gear (pages 213–216) in the next chapter, which covers longer events. You prepare for weekend rides about the same way you do for a century, although there are a few new considerations. We apply the same key success factors—assessment and planning, training, mental preparation, equipment, nutrition, and technique—to prepare for and ride weekend events. We also provide detailed information on a nightly routine to optimize recovery.

You can do many types of weekend events. You can set out with a couple of friends for a quiet weekend ride through the countryside, or you can join thousands of other riders in an organized ride to raise money for a charity. Throughout the chapter, we refer to two general types of weekend rides: supported and unsupported. Supported rides are logistically easier. You simply sign up and pay the registration fee or fulfill the fund-raising requirement. The organizers take care of the route, rest stops, mechanical support, food, transport of your gear, and overnight accommodations. All you have to do is ride. Many charity organizations, commercial operators, and bike clubs throughout the world offer two- and three-day rides. Unsupported tours take more planning, because you are responsible for all the details. These types of rides range from credit-card touring (covered in this chapter), in which you carry the bare essentials, stay in motels, and eat in restaurants, to weekend camping trips. You pick where you want to go, with whom you want to ride, and when you get on your bike!

Assessment and Planning

Before you sign up for a supported tour or plan your own adventure, ask yourself what you want out of the tour. Do you want an easy weekend of riding with friends or family or a demanding tour through mountainous terrain? Do you like time to yourself or lots of social interaction? Look at the many options to see what best fits your goals and consider the information in table 9.1.

In a supported tour, most (if not all) of the planning will be done. Even so, you should find out as much as you can about the event. Check the website, talk to veteran riders or the organizers, find out about support, look at the terrain, study the cue sheets if available, and get answers to any questions that you have. You will invest a lot of time and possibly money in an organized tour, so make sure that all your concerns are addressed.

For an unsupported tour, you do the planning yourself. Honestly assess your experience and be realistic in developing your plan and choosing your route. A three-day tour in the mountains might look great on paper, but if you haven't spent much time in the hills, your plan may be too ambitious. Getting ready for an unsupported tour takes more time because you are responsible for all the logistics. Remember that your other obligations (work, family, school, and so on) will reduce the time that you have to prepare.

You can draw on many resources to plan your tour. You can start with maps to get a general overview of your intended route. Be careful with road maps for drivers, which may show only major routes and other roads that may be unsuitable for riding. Some organizations offer maps specifically for cyclists that give information on road conditions, climbing gradients, points of interest, places to shop, and lodging options. (Remember to check on the hours of services.) Make sure that you get a current edition before you head out. These maps are usually weather resistant and are designed to fit in a cue sheet holder or the map compartment of a handlebar bag. Many cities, states, and nations

TABLE 9.1 Comparison of Supported and Unsupported Rides

Supported rides	Unsupported rides
• *Everything is planned.* You simply show up and ride. But organized rides may not be offered where you want to ride.	• *Planning is up to you.* You have to choose a safe route, resupply points, meal stops, and overnight accommodations. You may enjoy the planning.
• *Number of riders.* Most supported rides have large groups of riders—some charity events host hundreds or even thousands of riders.	• *Choose your own group or go solo.* You can go with a bunch of friends or head out on your own.
• *No Flexibility.* Generally speaking, you can't deviate from the route or ride schedule.	• *Spontaneity.* Stop and chat with locals, take a more scenic route, or go home early.
• *Support.* Organizers provide aid stations, mechanical support on the road, and hot dinners and breakfasts.	• *Self-sufficient.* You need to find supplies, perform your own basic repairs, and, in case of serious problems, arrange your own support.
• *Logistics are taken care of.* Organizers usually transport your gear during the day.	• *Requires a bit more gear.* Some bikes, especially racing bikes, may not handle well with larger loads.
• *Cost.* Organized rides can be expensive, particularly if they include luxurious accommodations and gourmet cuisine.	• *Cost.* Your own weekend ride will cost far less than most supported events, other than club tours.
• *Raise money for a cause.* Weekend rides often benefit charitable organizations.	• *Family friendly.* Even if they do not cycle, they can meet you at the end of the day.
• *Preparation.* Many rides feature training support to help you prepare for the event and forums to update you on ride details.	

Planning Resources

Adventure Cycling Association

The mission of the Adventure Cycling Association (ACA) is to inspire people of all ages to travel by bicycle for fun, fitness, and self-discovery. The ACA produces maps specifically designed for bicycle travel. More than 35,000 miles (56,000 km) have been charted throughout the United States and southern Canada. The ACA also offers tours ranging from introductory trips during which you learn the basics of traveling by bike to the TransAm tour, a self-contained 4,253-mile (6,845 km) trek from Yorktown, Virginia, to Florence, Oregon. The ACA can be reached at www.adventurecycling.org or 800-755-2453.

League of American Bicyclists

The mission of the League of American Bicyclists (LAB) is to promote bicycling for fun, fitness, and transportation and to work through advocacy and education for a bicycle-friendly America. The LAB offers courses in bicycle safety, commuting, motorist education, and kids' cycling. You can become an LAB cycling instructor and help cyclists in your community. In May of each year, the League of American Bicyclists promotes bike month, encouraging people to get out and ride to work or school. The LAB can be reached at www.bikeleague.org or 202-822-1333.

offer free downloadable cycling maps on the Web, and many online communities can give you firsthand accounts of touring in a certain area. Also on the Web you can find mapping software such as Map My Ride (www.mapmyride.com) and Google Maps (maps.google.com/biking) that can be used in conjunction with maps to plan route segments, measure distances, and help with your general planning. In planning your route, consider the following:

- *Length of day*. Even if you can comfortably ride a century in one day, the cumulative fatigue from three 100-mile (160 km) days, especially if you are carrying a bit of gear, may make the trip less enjoyable. Particularly for your first weekender, consider 50- to 75-mile (80 to 120 km) days.
- *Terrain*. You should be comfortable riding a hilly century before planning a hilly weekend tour.
- *Availability of supplies*. A route that has stores during the day and overnight locations reduces what you need to carry on the bike.
- *Where do you want to stay?* Will you stay in a B&B, hotel, or motel, or would you rather camp? (Camping is covered in the next chapter.)

In addition, consider whether services will be available if you have mechanical, physical, or weather-related problems and set up a communication schedule to let others know your progress.

Training

How do you train for back-to-back days on the bike? For weekend rides we follow the periodization model from chapter 8, progressing from the bottom up:

- The base period when you build the endurance to carry at least some of the load that you expect to carry for your weekend trip

- The intensity phase when you develop power while maintaining endurance
- The peak period when you do back-to-back rides carrying all the gear for your tour but for shorter distances
- The taper when you maintain fitness while storing energy for the event

The principles of training also apply here—specificity, progression of overload, adequate recovery, and individual considerations.

Let's say that you have signed up for a 150-mile (240 km), two-day weekend tour (about six hours of riding each day). Before beginning our 12-week plan to train for the tour, build up to at least a four-hour ride using one of the century training programs. Then start this plan, which uses workouts similar to those from chapter 6. To get the most from your training, keep the intensity of the workouts within the ranges specified in table 9.2. (See chapter 6 for more information on training by heart rate, power, and RPE.)

- *Long.* Throughout the programs consistently ride either the shorter or longer weekend ride. Start the first week by carrying some of the gear for the tour and add more gear each week until you're training with all your equipment by week 9. These rides maintain your endurance, accustom you to riding with a loaded bike, and allow you to test new gear or different foods. Following the principle of specificity these workouts build to back-to-back rides totaling 7:00 to 10:00 in the peak week. Do these rides primarily in the long ride zone; however, you may need to climb hills in the tempo zone and as the rides get longer pace yourself in the recovery zone to finish the ride.
- *Tempo.* These slightly faster rides increase your cruising speed. As with the other training programs, if you are doing the longer weekend rides, then you should also do the longer tempo and brisk rides; if you are doing the shorter weekend rides, you may choose the longer tempo and brisk rides.
- *Brisk.* These more intense rides include a segment of mixed intensity that helps boost your power and increase your average speed. If you do the shorter brisk rides, then also do the shorter segments of mixed intensity.
- *Recovery.* These rides help you to recover and have more energy for other rides. You may substitute another activity for the second recovery ride, such as hiking with your family, shooting hoops in the driveway, or swimming, but you should try to ride your bike at least four days a week.
- *Supplementary.* Continue your core strength, flexibility, and resistance-maintenance training.

TABLE 9.2 **Recommended Workout Intensities**

Ride	Heart rate as percentage of LT	Power as percentage of FTP	Rating of perceived exertion
Long	75 to 87	56 to 75	2 to 3
Tempo	88 to 94	76 to 90	3 to 4
Brisk, mixed intensity, hard effort	95 to 100	91 to 100	5 to 6
Brisk, mixed intensity, recovery effort	less than 75	less than 55	1 to 2
Active recovery	less than 75	less than 55	1 to 2

12-WEEK PROGRAM FOR 150-MILE (240 KM) TWO-DAY WEEKEND TOUR

Weeks 1–3 Base Training Phase

Continue building the endurance base and get used to riding with some of the equipment for your planned tour. Test any new gear.

WEEK 1

Riding:

Long ride of 3:30–4:30
Midweek tempo ride of 50–75 minutes
Second midweek tempo ride of 50–75 minutes
Active recovery ride of 30–40 minutes
Second active recovery ride of 20–30 minutes (optional)
Total riding time: 5:40–8:10

Supplementary training:

Two core strength-training sessions of 10–20 minutes
Three stretching sessions of 10–20 minutes
One or two resistance-maintenance training sessions of 20–30 minutes (optional)

WEEK 2

Riding:

Long ride of 4:00–5:00
Midweek tempo ride of 60–90 minutes
Second midweek tempo ride of 50–75 minutes
Active recovery ride of 30–40 minutes
Second active recovery ride of 20–30 minutes (optional)
Total riding time: 6:20–8:55

Supplementary training:

Two core strength-training sessions of 10–20 minutes
Three stretching sessions of 10–20 minutes
One or two resistance-maintenance training sessions of 20–30 minutes (optional)

WEEK 3

Riding:

Long ride of 4:30–5:30
Midweek tempo ride of 60–90 minutes
Second midweek tempo ride of 60–90 minutes
Active recovery ride of 30–40 minutes
Second active recovery ride of 20–30 minutes (optional)
Total riding time: 7:00–9:40

Supplementary training:

Two core strength-training sessions of 10–20 minutes
Three stretching sessions of 10–20 minutes
One or two resistance-maintenance training sessions of 20–30 minutes (optional)

(continued)

WEEK 4—RECOVERY

Riding:

Long ride of 1:00–2:00
Active recovery ride of 30–40 minutes
Active recovery ride of 30–40 minutes
Total riding time: 2:00–3:20

Supplementary training:

Two core strength-training sessions of 10–20 minutes
Three stretching sessions of 10–20 minutes
No resistance training

Weeks 5–7 Intensity Phase
Add intensity while continuing to build endurance and test equipment.

WEEK 5

Riding:

Long ride of 5:00–6:00
Midweek tempo ride of 45–75 minutes
Midweek brisk ride of 45–60 minutes including 10–15 minutes of mixed intensity
Active recovery ride of 30–40 minutes
Second active recovery ride of 20–30 minutes (optional)
Total riding time: 7:00–9:25

Supplementary training:

Two core strength-training sessions of 10–20 minutes
Three stretching sessions of 10–20 minutes
One resistance-maintenance training session of 20–30 minutes (optional)

WEEK 6

Riding:

Long ride of 5:00–6:00
Midweek tempo ride of 60–90 minutes
Midweek brisk ride of 60–75 minutes including 15–20 minutes of mixed intensity
Active recovery ride of 30–40 minutes
Second active recovery ride of 20–30 minutes (optional)
Total riding time: 7:30–9:55

Supplementary training:

Two core strength-training sessions of 10–20 minutes
Three stretching sessions of 10–20 minutes
One resistance-maintenance training session of 20–30 minutes (optional)

WEEK 7

Riding:

Long ride of 5:00–6:00
Midweek tempo ride of 1:15–1:45
Midweek brisk ride of 75–90 minutes including 20–25 minutes of mixed intensity
Active recovery ride of 30–40 minutes

Second active recovery ride of 30–40 minutes (optional)
Total riding time: 8:00–10:35

Two core strength-training sessions of 10–20 minutes
Three stretching sessions of 10–20 minutes
One resistance-maintenance training session of 20–30 minutes (optional)

WEEK 8—RECOVERY

Riding
Long ride of 1:00–2:00
Active recovery ride of 30–40 minutes
Active recovery ride of 30–40 minutes
Total riding time: 2:00–3:20

Supplementary training:
Two core strength-training sessions of 10–20 minutes
Three stretching sessions of 10–20 minutes
No resistance training

Weeks 9–12 Peaking phase
Do specific training with back-to-back rides carrying all the equipment for the event. Depending on your schedule, you have two alternatives:

    a. Back-to-back rides of approximately equal length on Saturday and Sunday or
    b. A longer ride on Saturday and a shorter tempo ride on Sunday

Whichever plan you choose, stick to that schedule throughout the program.

WEEK 9

Riding:
    a. Back-to-back long rides of 3:00 to 4:00 or
    b. a long ride of 5:00–6:00 on Saturday and a tempo ride of 1:00–1:30 on Sunday
Midweek brisk ride of 60–90 minutes including 15–20 minutes of mixed intensity
Active recovery ride of 20–30 minutes
Second active recovery ride of 20–30 minutes (optional)
Total riding time: a. 7:20–10:30; b. 7:20–10:00

Supplementary training:
Two core strength-training sessions of 10–20 minutes
Three stretching sessions of 10–20 minutes
One resistance-maintenance training session of 20–30 minutes (optional)

WEEK 10

Riding:
    a. Back-to-back long rides of 3:30 to 4:30 or
    b. a long ride of 5:00–6:00 on Saturday and a tempo ride of 1:30–2:00 on Sunday
Midweek brisk ride of 60–90 minutes including 15–20 minutes of mixed intensity
Active recovery ride of 20–30 minutes
Second active recovery ride of 20–30 minutes (optional)
Total riding time: a. 8:20–11:30; b. 7:50–10:30

(continued)

Supplementary training:

Two core strength-training sessions of 10–20 minutes
Three stretching sessions of 10–20 minutes
One resistance-maintenance training session of 20–30 minutes (optional)

WEEK 11—PEAK

Riding:

    a. Back-to-back long rides of 4:00 to 5:00 or
    b. a long ride of 5:00–6:00 on Saturday and a tempo ride of 2:00–2:30 on Sunday

Midweek brisk ride of 60–90 minutes including 15–20 minutes of mixed intensity
Active recovery ride of 30–40 minutes
Second active recovery ride of 30–40 minutes (optional)
Total riding time: a. 9:30–12:50; b. 8:30–11:20

Supplementary training:

Two core strength-training sessions of 10–20 minutes
Three stretching sessions of 10–20 minutes
One resistance-maintenance training session of 20–30 minutes (optional)

WEEK 12—TAPER

The taper is the same for both programs.

Riding:

Long ride of 1:00–2:00 on Saturday
Tempo ride of 60–90 minutes on Sunday
Midweek brisk ride 40–60 minutes including 10–15 minutes of mixed intensity
Active recovery ride of 30–40 minutes
Second active recovery of 30–40 minutes (optional)
Total riding time: 3:10–5:50

Supplementary training:

Two core strength-training sessions of 10–20 minutes
Three stretching sessions of 10–20 minutes
No resistance training

EVENT WEEK

Riding:

Long rides—weekend tour
Midweek tempo ride of 40–60 minutes
Active recovery ride of 30–40 minutes
Second active recovery of 30–40 minutes

Supplementary training:

Two core strength-training sessions of 10–20 minutes
Three stretching sessions of 10–20 minutes
No resistance training

In this program, you build your endurance for three weeks while carrying more and more of your gear. After a recovery week, for three weeks you develop your power while maintaining your endurance and increasing the amount of gear that you carry. Another recovery week leads to three weeks of peaking that involves back-to-back rides with all your equipment. Finally, you taper to maintain fitness while storing energy for the tour.

Because riding for multiple days requires dealing with more gear (detailed in the next section), we suggest practicing each element during training rides so that nothing new occurs during the event. Use your long training rides to master these two key skills:

1. Practice handling your loaded bike. Your loaded bike will balance differently, rock more dramatically when you stand, and corner differently. It will also decelerate more slowly when you brake, accelerate more slowly, and climb more slowly.

2. Practice riding at a touring pace. With a loaded bike you travel more slowly, for the same level of effort, than you do during your centuries. Pay attention to your heart rate, power meter, or RPE. Learn to accept your speed and enjoy the ride, rather than try to force the pace.

Equipment

The bike that you use for one-day events may work for two- to three-day outings, especially supported events that won't require you to carry much. If you plan a credit-card tour, look at your intended route and the availability of supplies during the day and at night. For a supported tour study the event's website to learn about the route and what you'll need to carry. With this information you can assess whether your century bike and accessories are adequate.

Bike

Is the route similar in difficulty to the centuries that you've ridden? Are your bike, wheels, and gearing adequate for the climbing and any rough roads? Fatigue builds over several days, especially if significant climbing is required, so lower gearing may make the ride more enjoyable. Using pedals and shoes with recessed cleats, such as Shimano SPDs, or touring shoes and pedals with traditional clips and straps makes it easier to walk around. Review the questions about bike setup from chapter 8 (page 167). If you need to make changes, give yourself plenty of time to get used to them.

Just as you do for one-day events, check your bike thoroughly about two weeks before your event so that you have plenty time to test everything and make last-minute adjustments. If you have a shop do this, explain what kind of tour you plan to do. Refer back to chapter 7 (page 137) for specifics on what to check on the bike or go online to http://tinyurl.com/49ha5wb.

Some tour operators provide a bike and all its accessories, so you may have an opportunity to ride a top-of-the-line bike during the event. If this is the case, find out as much as possible about what kind of bike it is, whether they will have your size, and whether you need to bring your own shoes, pedals, saddle, or other equipment.

Clothing

If you are going on a supported tour the clothing that you use for centuries may be adequate during the day. But because you will be riding for several days during which conditions may vary, you may want to carry a bit more clothing. Review the recommendations in chapter 8 (pages 167–169). For a credit-card tour, you want to carry as little extra clothing as possible. You can use the same pair of shorts for two to three days as well as the same base layer and jersey; change out of them immediately after riding and air them out over night. Take underwear, running shorts, and a second base layer to wear around town (also as backup in case the first one gets wet in the rain). These items and your windbreaker probably will suffice. If conditions may be cooler, carry a second heavier jersey or thermal vest and tights or light rain pants to wear on and off the bike as necessary. If you are riding with road shoes and cleats, take a light pair of sandals to wear off the bike. If you have access to a hot tub, include your swimming suit! As with shorter events, inspect and test every item that you plan to wear.

Accessories

On a weekend tour you need to carry a bit more gear. Even if the event is fully supported, room for extra food and clothing will make your ride more comfortable. For both supported and credit card tours, organization is key, and we recommend using several of the following to keep your gear organized:

- *Jersey pockets.* Your pockets worked well for snacks, cue sheets, and other small items on your centuries, and they are equally handy on weekend tours.
- *Handlebar bags.* Handlebar bags are very convenient to hold things you want handy while riding (maps/cue sheets, food, camera, sunscreen, lip balm, etc.). Before purchasing one, check that it fits on your bike, particularly if your bike has dual control shifting and brake levers—make sure that you will still be able to operate the levers with the bag in place. Be careful not to put too much weight in the handlebar bag, lest you change the handling of the bike.
- *Frame packs.* Various small bags fit on the top tube behind the stem and in the front of the frame behind the headset, which are also useful for snacks, lip balm, etc.
- *Hydration pack.* Hydration packs often include pockets and straps for carrying gear; however, 50-100 oz of water plus gear will feel very heavy by the end of the day.
- *Seat pack.* Some seat packs expand to provide more capacity and in addition to holding your repair kit can accommodate rain gear and warmers.
- *Rack trunk bags.* A rack trunk is a larger bag that attaches to a rack over the rear wheel. Touring bikes usually have attachment points for racks; racing bikes do not. On racing bikes a rack with a quick-release clamp can be attached to the seat post and may be further anchored with small bungee cords to the rear wheel dropouts. Rack trunks carry more than expandable seat packs. With both rack trunks and seat packs the center of gravity is high, causing the bike to sway more, so avoid overloading them.

Balancing Life

By Dan McGehee

McGehee holds the UltraMarathon Cycling Association road record for 100 miles (160 km)—3:56:03, or 25.42 miles per hour (40.91 km/h). He has won the Cochise County Cycling Classic 10 times and holds the record for the 252-mile (406 km) course—10:26. He is the father of three and an optometrist.

Balance in life is a matter of perspective. If riding your bike is the number one priority in your life, then you have to fit in your other activities and responsibilities around it. This circumstance is applicable to only a select number of cyclists, who are probably getting paid to ride. But for us working stiffs, the issue is not allowing the bike (in my case known as the mistress) to displace or eliminate the more important responsibilities in our lives. That sounds good on paper, but the lines blur in real life, especially when preparing for a big event. The question for me is this: How many things can I add to my life before cycling creates an imbalance? I want to be competitive in the events that I do, but I do not want my family life or professional aspirations to suffer as a result.

Assuming that you are an avid cyclist, your family and your work associates know that you love to ride. They may even show significant interest in your bike, your apparel, the event that you just did, or the distance that you are logging. Do not assume that they care about your cycling as much as you do—chances are they don't. Don't forget that they have their own interests and hobbies. This is also true with training partners and other cyclists whom you know. They have their own goals. But do you ride to impress others or to satisfy an inner drive that makes you want to test yourself? By developing a balanced perspective about why you train and ride, and by hearing about the experiences of others, you may learn how better to fit your cycling into your daily life.

A relatively structured training program is critical to achieving balance. Look at your year as a whole, your goals both on and off the bike, and the major events in which you want to perform at your best. The more activities and responsibilities that you have away from the bike, the less time you have for major events. All the secondary cycling events are a bonus, and you can use them to train (or skip one or two) to stay on track for your peak performances. I have found that record attempts are easy to do, while races with set dates and times are inflexible. A race director is not going to reschedule because my son has a tennis tournament, I'm on call for the office, or my daughter has to be carted back to college.

Training through secondary events on my calendar increases my mental resolve, because I have to work harder to achieve a solid finish. These events test my ability when I'm already fatigued from the heavy training in the previous weeks. After filling in the calendar with the critical days and events for your family life and office responsibilities, you can figure when other events can fit in and count backward from there to plot your training schedule. Over the years, I have experimented and modified my program to help determine how best to reach peak performance, but I am still a work in progress. Working with a cycling coach can add an instant level of experience to your program. Although even the best coach will need months to gain a solid understanding of your abilities, weaknesses, motivations, and so on, working with a professional eliminates much of the long-term trial and error.

But don't forget that at the end of your big event, season, year, career, and perhaps your life, you are going to ask yourself whether all the training and sacrifice was worth it. I hope that you will be able to answer a profound yes, but not at the expense of the more important things in your life.

Using a combination of these accessories will balance the load better on the bike. For example, you could have a handlebar bag or frame pack with just the essentials, jersey pockets or a hydration pack with a bit of food and a windbreaker strapped on, and an expandable seat pack or rack trunk (see figure 9.1).

Develop a packing system and use it during your training rides. Figure out the best place to store each item and always keep it there. On the tour you should know where

FIGURE 9.1 **A balanced, lightly loaded touring bike.**

each piece of gear is. Use plastic bags to organize and protect your gear. Even if a bag claims to be waterproof, take extra precautions. Label bags if they are not see-through. See the packing list for tours at http://tinyurl.com/49ha5wb.

Mental Preparation

The techniques that you learned to prepare mentally for single-day events will serve you well as you prepare for a multiday tour.

- *Checklists.* Use the sample lists provided here and in previous chapters to develop personal checklists so you can assemble everything you need and not have to worry about forgetting something. Prepare your checklists at the start of the peaking phase in training and refine them on your weekend rides.

- *Event scenarios.* Just as you did for other rides, come up with three plans for each day of the tour—a great day, a slow day, and your anticipated day—so that you can adjust your expectations as necessary. If you are planning a self-supported tour include the hours of services (when cafes are open, when you can check into lodging and so forth) to anticipate any problems with different scenarios. Set up a communication schedule to keep others informed about your progress.

- *Progressive relaxation.* Use your relaxation skills to calm down during training and the night before the event starts so you can sleep soundly.

- *Visualization.* Starting the week before the tour, visualize each day of the tour one day at a time. If you can visualize the full tour several times, the actual experience will feel familiar rather than intimidating. (Progressive relaxation and visualization are explained in chapter 7 on pages 135–136).

Nutrition

As you began training for your first century, you developed an eating approach to meet your nutritional needs. Since then things may have changed:

- *Weight loss.* By riding more and eating less you may have lost weight. Recalculate your caloric requirements for both exercise and activities of daily living based on your current weight.
- *Increased volume.* You train more for a weekend tour than you do for a century, so your weekly caloric requirement increases.
- *Heavier bike.* If you lost 10 pounds (4.5 kg) off your waist but added 15 pounds (7 kg) of bike gear, your energy needs will change.
- *Changing habits.* Developing new habits takes persistence. The dietary changes that you planned may not have become daily habit.

We recommend reviewing chapter 4 (pages 61–62), reestimating your caloric needs, and keeping a food journal for a week to see how you are doing.

If you are riding in a supported event, find out what food will be offered during rest stops and meals. If you have any dietary restrictions, contact the organizers to see whether they can accommodate your needs.

A few days before the tour, be sure to do the following:

- *Top off your glycogen stores.* Increase the proportion of carbohydrate in your diet.
- *Hydrate fully.* Drink extra water, which you need to store the additional glycogen, and lay off alcohol.
- *Dinner and breakfast.* Eat familiar foods the night before and the day of the event.

Refer to chapter 7 (pages 137–138) for detailed suggestions on preevent nutrition.

On the Road

Let's ride! Here's how to apply the success factors during your event.

Managing the Mental Issues

As events become longer, either in number of days or total distance, mental factors become more important. Sport psychologists have learned that an optimal level of excitement will allow you to perform at your best, as illustrated in figure 9.2.

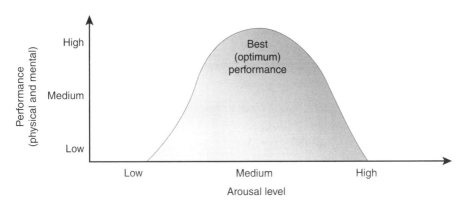

FIGURE 9.2 **Athletes perform best when their level of arousal is neither too high, nor too low.**

If you're not excited about the tour, you'll be flat on the road, and if you are too nervous, you'll waste energy that you could put into the ride. You've learned several mental skills to manage your energy productively. Use your checklists to keep your equipment organized and reduce stress. Use your relaxation skills to calm down each evening of the ride and perhaps the morning of each stage. From your preride visualizations, you know whether they help you feel calm about a ride or tend to get you excited. If visualizing is calming, then doing so each evening of the tour will help you relax. But if visualizing gets you excited, it could interfere with sleep. During each day use your event scenarios to adjust to the kind of ride that you are having.

To these we add three new skills:

- *Time management.* For a century you can hang out at the rest stops, finish, get in the car, and go home. On a tour, at the end of the ride, the day is not over. Manage your stops during the day so that you have enough time in the evening to take care of necessary business and relax.

- *Organization.* As described in the earlier section on equipment, organizing your gear and keeping it in order will help you manage time.

- *Routine.* As part of your event planning, develop a routine from the time you get off the bike in the afternoon until you get on the bike the next morning. List all the things that you need to do and plan the best order in which to do them. See the tips in the section on recovery later in this chapter.

When you arrive at the start of a supported tour, sign in and check your gear before socializing. Larger events typically have rider meetings to go over the route, safety issues, rules, and so forth. Pay close attention to the organizers. They have a tough job keeping everyone safe and happy throughout the tour.

If you are touring on your own, check and double-check your bike and supplies. Review your ride scenarios, schedule for keeping in touch with family and friends, and your plan for mechanical, physical, or other problems. After that, hop on the bike and have a great time!

Pacing

You've learned all the skills that you need to ride 100 miles or 200 kilometers. Now just apply the same skills to riding back-to-back days. Ride at a comfortable pace. Tours (both supported and unsupported) have no competitive element, no timing, and no awards, so relax and enjoy your ride. If you race or ride fast one-day events, you need to adjust your speed. Use the following methods to ride at a sustainable pace.

- *Heart rate, watts, or RPE.* Use your heart rate monitor, power meter, or RPE to keep the pace down. Remember that you'll be riding on consecutive days, so conserve your energy.

- *Back-to-back training pace.* Ride the pace that you rode on your back-to-back rides during the final weeks of training.

- *Second-day pace.* Start the first day at the speed that you expect to ride the second day when your legs are tired.

- *Ride with a group.* Unless you are on a solo tour, ride with a group. If you can maintain a normal conversation, your pace is right. If you are struggling to talk, the group is too fast, so drop back and find another group.

Problem Solving

By preparing thoroughly for your event you can help prevent or mitigate most problems. Start by doing your homework. Make sure that the tour is right for you before you sign up for an event or plan your own. Then use the information that you've gathered to test and train with all your equipment in various weather conditions. Before a tour, check that your bike and other gear are ready. The week before the tour reread the relevant material in this book and practice relaxation and visualization techniques.

Unfortunately, problems may still arise. With the right approach, you can address nearly anything and continue. Use these pointers:

▶ *Stay calm*! Take a minute to eat and drink before trying to solve a problem. Use your relaxation skills to calm down. Put things in context. How bad is it really? There's a big difference between delay or discomfort and real catastrophe, so try to keep things in perspective.

▶ *Diagnose*. What is going on? Determine what kind of problem you are dealing with and take steps to fix it. For example, if you feel unusually fatigued, consider the possible causes and solutions. Did you go out too fast at the start? (Adjust your pace.) Are you eating on schedule? (Get back on track.) Is one of the brakes rubbing? Is one of your tires low? (Make a simple adjustment.)

▶ *Accept and adapt*. If you can solve a problem, that's best, but if you can't, you probably can adapt and still ride. Sometimes your attitude makes all the difference. Suppose that your rear shift cable breaks. How do you choose to interpret the incident? If you think that you can't finish the ride and become angry, your performance will suffer. Instead of getting flustered, pause and assess the situation. You could interpret this occurrence as an opportunity to finish the ride on a four-speed. Position the derailleur on the most useful cog and jam a stick into it to hold it in place. Start riding and choose among your four gears: big chain ring, small chain ring, and sitting or standing in each! If you come to a very steep hill, get off the bike, reposition the stick so the derailleur is on a larger cog, and up you go. You'll have one heck of a story to tell at the end of the day!

▶ *Don't worry about elements not in your control*. Fretting over rain, headwinds, or other things that nature may throw at you just wastes energy. Embrace the good days with the not-so-good days. Riding during inclement weather will make the pleasant days seem all that much better!

▶ *Group dynamics*. Riding in a group we usually enjoy each other's company. Occasionally, you may run into people with whom you do not get along. During a large event such as a century, 300K, or weekend tour, just ride with another group. On a smaller organized tour, however, you may find yourself riding and spending time off the bike with people whom you don't enjoy. Before booking a tour, talk with the tour organizer and find out what kinds of people usually participate. The organizer should try to match your riding style, goals, and interests to one of their tours. If you meet someone on a tour who rubs you the wrong way, treat it like a headwind. Don't waste energy fretting.

● *Put fun above performance*. Try not to worry about your overall time. Weekend tours usually feature great scenery and good company. If you look around and socialize, you will remember the ride for years to come.

● *Use a reminder*. If you tend to ride too fast during events, set an alarm on your heart rate monitor, tape a note to your handlebars, or come up with a saying that you can use to help you slow down.

If you practice these techniques during your training rides, you'll be less tempted to hammer early in the tour and more likely to have a great time for the entire weekend.

Nutrition

To have the energy to ride for several days, you need to pay particular attention to your nutritional intake. Unlike with one-day events, you'll be back on the bike the next day covering more distance. Think in terms of calories in versus calories out over the course of each 24-hour period. You should take into account calories expended both during the ride and used the rest of the 24 hours, when you are both active and sleeping.

If you weigh 150 pounds (68 kg) and ride at 15 mile per hour (24 km/h) on a lightly loaded bike, you burn about 675 calories per hour. During six hours of riding you'll use about 4,000 calories. Over the remaining 18 hours, you're relaxing or sleeping, but not very active, so you'll use another 2,000 calories, yielding a total of 6,000 calories over 24 hours. That's a lot of calories!

We recommend consuming a mix of carbohydrate totaling 60 to 90 grams, or 240 to 360 calories, every hour on longer rides. If you consume 75 grams, or 300 calories per hour, you would eat 1,800 during the ride, leaving another 4,200 to be consumed off the bike for recovery immediately after the ride, at dinner, as a snack before bed, and during breakfast the next morning.

Try not to guess at these figures. Developing a written plan may seem tedious but will ensure that you are adequately fueled. Your performance during the event depends heavily on proper nutrition on and off the bike.

Recovery

Yogi Berra was right: "It ain't over till it's over." Unlike one day rides, the end of your day on the bike starts the recovery process to get you ready for the next day of the event.

After-Ride Routine

What you do the first few hours after the ride affects your energy level and how your body feels, both in bed and on the bike the next day.

- *Nutrition and hydration.* Just as you did after your longer rides, within a few hours after riding consume 500 to 1,000 calories of moderate- to high-glycemic-index carbohydrate along with a little protein to help replenish your glycogen stores. Continue drinking fluids as you recover.

- *Hygiene.* Get out of your riding clothes and into something dry as soon as possible. Shower if you can or use baby wipes to clean up. Brush your teeth. You'll feel much better.

- *Stretch.* Walk around and stretch if you are stiff.

- *Elevate.* Lie down with your legs propped up so your feet are about a foot (30 cm) above your heart to improve the circulation in your legs.

- *Ice.* Ice if you are sore. Ice is usually available on supported tours and at convenience stores.

- *Self-massage.* Rub your legs using the techniques described in chapter 6 (pages 127–128).
- *Nap.* A short nap after your postride snack, especially with your legs elevated, does wonders for your recovery.

Nightly Routine

Participants usually have a lot of fun in the evening on weekend tours. Supported events typically feature a group meal and possibly entertainment. On unsupported rides you can enjoy time with your friends or family. On either kind of tour, evenings are an opportunity to relax and reflect on the day.

Although you enjoy relaxing and socializing, you also need to get ready for the next day. Here are suggestions for an evening routine:

- *Unpack and set up.* Get your gear and unpack. If you are camping, set up your tent. Be careful about bike and personal security.
- *Prepare for the next day.* Get your clothes, cue sheet, maps, snacks, and so on ready for the next day so you aren't scrambling around the next morning.
- *Check your bike.* Use the lists in the equipment maintenance section on page 192 to check your bike.
- *Have a good dinner.* Emphasize carbohydrate, stay fully hydrated, and avoid alcohol.
- *Continue to pay attention to your recovery.* Stretch if you didn't earlier. Treat any sore spots with ice or massage.
- *Relax.* Stop socializing a bit before bedtime and spend some quiet time doing progressive relaxation and perhaps visualizing the next day.

Morning Routine

Day 2 arrives, and you've had a good night's sleep! Following a routine will get you ready for another day of fun with the bike.

- *Stretch.* You may be a little stiff. Take a short walk and do some simple stretches to get ready for the day's ride. The dynamic stretches in chapter 3 are particularly good before a ride (pages 50–52).
- *Breakfast.* Top off your tank with a good breakfast, fill your bottles, and get your snacks.
- *Pack your gear.* Use your personal checklists and packing system, which helps you avoid leaving items behind. Nevertheless, double-check your gear before you start.
- *Review the route.* Look at the day's rest stops, store locations, climbs, and so forth. If you're on an organized tour, attend any rider meetings. If you are on your own, review the day's plan with your companions. If you have any questions or concerns, address them now.
- *Pace yourself.* When you start riding take a little time to ease back into your rhythm.
- *Have a great day!*

John lives in Boulder, Colorado, in the foothills of the Rocky Mountains. He loves to climb for hours and then come flying down, sharing the road with cars and other cyclists. Here are his tips for descending safely:

▶ *Look back frequently.* As you go faster the wind noise makes it much harder to hear traffic, so look frequently in your rearview mirror.

▶ *In the hooks.* You are more stable if your hands are in the bends of the handlebars, right behind the brake levers, rather than on top of the brake hoods. You also have better control of the brake levers.

▶ *Inside pedal up.* When you go around a corner, put the pedal nearest the inside of the corner at the top (12 o'clock) and the outside pedal at the bottom (6 o'clock). When descending S-curves, shift the pedal position for each corner.

▶ *Butt back.* As you descend, the slope angle puts more of your weight on the front wheel. As you brake your effective center of gravity moves forward. To balance both of these, slide your butt back a couple of inches (about 5 cm) in the saddle. The easiest way to do this is to place the pedals in the 3 and 9 o'clock positions, lift your butt off the saddle, and with your hands push the bike forward slightly under you.

▶ *Use primarily the front brake.* For the reasons just noted you have much more weight on the front wheel, so the rear wheel is more likely to skid. Your front brake provides most of the braking power. Use both brakes. Brake hard enough with the front to slow down and just enough with the rear brake to keep control.

▶ *Lean the bike.* The bike will be more stable if you lean into the corner.

▶ *Countersteer.* Pro racers use this technique for cornering instead of turning the handlebars. Put your weight on the outside pedal (6 o'clock). Then with a straight arm push down on the handlebar nearer the inside of the corner. Countersteering is the fastest way to lean your bike over and you'll corner more quickly if you countersteer.

▶ *Brake early.* When you apply the brakes, the forces make the bike stand up more rather than lean into the corner. When the bike stands up it goes straight rather than makes an arc around the corner. Slow down before a corner so that you don't have to brake in the corner and destroy your line.

▶ *Ride the tangents.* If traffic is clear, and only then, you can go through a curve faster if you straighten out the curve. For a left-hand curve start at the right edge of the road, check for traffic, cut the tangent near the center-line, and exit to the right edge of the

The countersteering technique.

road. For a right-hand curve, double-check for traffic behind you, move to the centerline of the road, ride the tangent near the right-hand edge of the lane, exit the curve near the centerline, and then return to your normal position on the road.

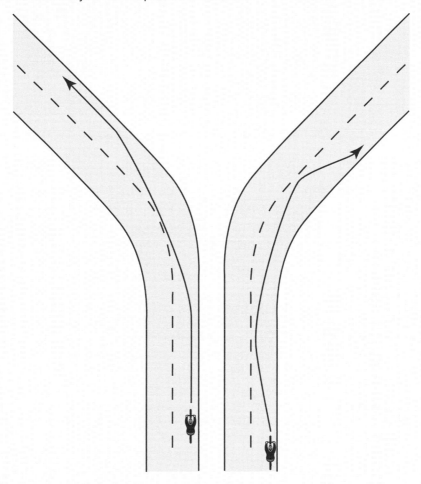

Riding the tangents.

▷ *Take the lane.* If you are descending at the speed of traffic, ride in the main traffic lane, just as a motorcycle does.

▷ *Practice.* As with everything we teach in this book, practice the pieces so they become habit and you won't have to think about them during your event. On a recovery ride go to an empty parking lot, stand up a few water bottles to define a course, and practice cornering around them. Learn to shift your butt back when you don't have to worry about traffic. Try countersteering. A racing club in your area may offer a clinic that includes cornering skills.

After mastering these techniques you'll have better control over your bike, be safer, and can roll away from your friends.

Equipment Maintenance

Preventive maintenance is much better than emergency repairs! On a tour you should do three types of preventive maintenance regularly:

Rest Stop Maintenance

Just as you did on one-day rides, perform these quick checks on your bike at every stop:

- Spin your wheels slowly against your gloved hand to clean the tires and inspect them for any cuts. Check that the wheels are still true and that the brakes are centered and not rubbing.
- Check the tire pressure. Snap your fingernail briskly against the tire. The sound should be a "ping" rather than a "thunk."
- Squeeze the brakes to make sure that the cables aren't wearing and stretching.

Nightly Maintenance

At night, check your tires:

- Air pressure—the correct air pressure minimizes the possibility of flats caused when the tube is pinched against the rim. You can use a floor pump with an accurate gauge, carry a small pressure gauge, or use the "ping" test.
- Condition—make sure that they are clean and have no cuts.

Check your wheels:

- Trueness—spin the wheels. They should not wobble.
- Quick releases—they should be secure but not too tight.
- Check that the brake shoes are centered and close to the rims.
- Check the shifting for clean operation and proper indexing.
- Inspect your helmet and adjust if necessary.

If you had a flat, patch and test the tube so it's ready for the next day. Or throw it away and put a new one in your seat pack.

Periodic Maintenance

If your bike was overhauled before the tour it should perform fine. But with heavy use components occasionally loosen up. Every few nights check that these items are tight:

- Crank arms
- Pedals
- Chain ring bolts
- Seat post bolt and seat mounting bolts
- Brake pads, brake mounting, and brake cable connection bolts
- Front and rear derailleur mounting and cable connection bolts
- Bolts or screws of water bottle cages and other accessories
- Stem bolts

- Headset for easy movement without too much play
- Hubs for spinning without too much play
- Bottom bracket for smooth rotation without too much play
- Shoes and cleats for loose screws or bolts
- Gear bags for firm attachment and excessive wear

One day on a bike is good, and multiple days can be even better. Depending on your budget and preferences, you can do weekend events that are supported or unsupported, including as many or as few luxuries as you wish. As with one-day events, success depends on proper planning, training, pacing, mental preparation, equipment, and nutrition.

You've expanded the concepts and skills you learned for one-day rides to include 300-kilometer brevets and double centuries. You've learned how to plan and train for multiple days of riding, select and carry more equipment, organize your gear and routine, manage your nutrition over a 24-hour period, pace yourself for longer distances, and recover overnight so that you are ready to ride again the next day.

Supported and unsupported touring open up new avenues in your cycling experience. You will meet different people because touring tends to attract riders less interested in competition and more interested in having fun, people who add to the enjoyment of the tour. With supported charity events, you make a positive contribution in helping others.

In chapter 10 we take the concepts and skills covered previously and apply them to preparing for and enjoying longer tours and brevets.

Ultradistance Riding

Perhaps you are curious about how far you can go on your bike. After one-day events and weekend rides consider ultradistance rides such as the following:

- Cross-state events in the United States, such as Cycle Oregon, the Register's Annual Great Bicycle Ride Across Iowa (RAGBRAI), and Bicycle Ride Across Tennessee (BRAT)
- Supported tours ranging from one-week trips, both commercial and club trips, to cross-country expeditions such as those offered by PAC Tour and the Adventure Cycling Association
- Self-contained touring, either with a credit card or camping out
- 400-, 600-, 1,000-, and 1,200-kilometer brevets

Lists of cross-state events, commercial tour operators, and brevet organizers around the world are included in the resources section.

Any of these events will give you a great challenge and allow you to experience a new world of cycling possibilities. With the proper approach you can complete these demanding and rewarding events. In this chapter we discuss both multiday tours (supported and unsupported) and brevets because they require similar preparation and skills. Many randonneurs ride a 600-kilometer brevet as a two-day tour with a short sleep break and a 1,000- or 1,200-kilometer brevet as a three- or four-day tour with short sleep breaks. Brevets and touring both involve assessing your athletic maturity before selecting and planning appropriate events; training for multiple days in the saddle; selecting and carrying more equipment; managing nutrition over several 24-hour periods; employing mental skills to prepare for the event, coping with the challenges, and solving the inevitable problems; using proper techniques including pacing yourself; and recovering for the next day.

In this chapter we extend the competencies that you've already developed in the areas essential for success: assessment and planning, physical training, mental techniques, proper equipment, good nutrition, and riding skills. Specifically, we provide an 8-week program to train for multiday tours and 12-week plan for 200, 300, 400, and 600 kilometer brevets.

Curiosity

By Ken Bonner

Bonner has been an ultracyclist for 22 years. He holds several UltraMarathon Cycling Association (UMCA) sanctioned point-to-point cycling records in Canada. He set the overall course record of 50:34 for the Rocky Mountain 1200 in British Columbia in 2008 at age 66 and the overall record of 63:39 for the Granite Anvil 1200 in Ontario in 2009. Bonner is a member of Randonneurs USA, UMCA, and BC Randonneurs Cycling Club and has ridden at least 37 1,200-kilometer events.

"Curiosity killed a cat!" ("Diff'rent," Eugene O'Neill, 1921).

Although many long-distance cyclists are satisfied with completing a 100-mile or 200-kilometer event, others seek to accomplish longer distances. Why? The same macho motivating factors that exist for shorter racing distances drive some cyclists, but for most long-distance cyclists curiosity is the driving force. How long can I ride? How fast can I ride that long? What training is best for me? How will I cope with extreme weather, such as high winds, torrential rain, snow, heat, and cold (often all within the same event)? How much and what type of food, drink, clothing, and ride support do I need? What tools and backup equipment do I need to overcome mechanical problems? What will cause physical pain, where, and when? What is a good pain management plan? How long can I function without sleep? What is a good sleep management plan? Riders' stories related to their quests to answer these questions are learning tools for others.

I've encountered a variety of challenges on long rides, such as riding in the wilderness and breaking my chain and chain tool; standing on the edge of the road holding onto my bike as the wind blew it horizontally and lightning crashed all around; running out of tubes, patches, and tires in the middle of nowhere with 200 kilometers to ride; sleeping in bear country in the rain on the side of the road; and running out of fluid with 50 miles (80 km) to go in 100 °F (38 °C) heat.

I've also met some wonderful people, both riders and ordinary folks. During a Colorado Last Chance 1200K, I was fixing a flat tire at night on an isolated country road about 50 miles from Boulder when a pickup truck stopped behind me. The headlights lit my bike for me, but no one got out. Pickup trucks are not good news in my part of the world! I finished my repair job and then the driver climbed down from the cab. A friendly woman! After hearing my story, she was so impressed with my accomplishment that she wanted to shake my hand—a black, greasy hand! "No, you don't," I said. Not to be dissuaded, she grabbed and pumped my hand before driving off into the night!

My hero is the long-distance cyclist who perseveres and overcomes adversity. Wally, a long-distance cyclist I know, was a sedentary white-collar professional with many time constraints who decided to take up cycling. Wally's goal was to lose a little weight, explore the neighborhood, and maybe get fit physically. One thing led to another, and a 1,200-kilometer brevet became his next challenge. The outcome was a did not finish (DNF). Undaunted, Wally tried to finish two more 1,200-kilometer brevets. Outcomes were two more DNFs! Most folks would have found a new goal after the first DNF, but not Wally. The following season, Wally completed *four* 1,200-kilometer brevets! Curiosity may have killed a cat, but as the more recent proverb asserts, "Satisfaction brought it back!"

Assessment and Planning

What do you want out of your next event? What excites you? Do you have a dream trip that you have always wanted to do? Would you like an easy tour for your entire family, or do you have your eyes set on one of Lon Haldeman's PAC Tours that crosses the United States averaging more than 100 miles (160 km) every day (www.pactour. com)? Many types of ultradistance events may suit your goals and budget:

- *Supported multiday tours.* You can take a trip with a commercial tour operator, participate in an organized cross-state ride, join your club's annual tour, or have a noncycling friend or family member drive a support vehicle and spend time with you along the way and at night. These trips often allow for ample time off the bike to enjoy the company of others and may include breaks during the day to explore local attractions.

- *Self-contained touring.* Grab your credit card and a change of clothes or pack your bike with all the necessities—food, camping gear, and clothing—and head out on your own two-wheeled adventure for as long as you like. Riders have crossed continents and even circled the globe on their bikes. You can go with friends or enjoy a solitary journey. The choice is yours.

- *Brevets.* Join the sport of randonneuring and use your skills to complete a specified course through checkpoint controls within designated time limits. Series of 200-, 300-, 400-, and 600-kilometer brevets are organized in many parts of the world. These events allow you to tackle rides of progressively greater distances and share the experience with like-minded riders. You can also use these rides to prepare for 1,000-, 1,200-kilometer and longer brevets.

After determining the general type of event that appeals to you, realistically assess your athletic maturity. Before you embark on a tour of a week or more or a brevet series, within the last month or two, you should have completed a two- or three-day tour, or a 150-mile one-day ride (or even better a 300-kilometer or 200-mile ride), or ridden one century or 200K per month for three or four months.

If a tour interests you, use your riding experience to project how far you might be able to ride on a tour. For example, if you ride centuries at an average of 14 miles per hour (22.5 km/h) including off-the-bike time (about 7 hours total), you might average 13 mph (21 km/h) riding a bike equipped for a credit-card tour and cover 90 miles (145 km) in 7 hours. You might average only 10 miles per hour (16 km/h) on a bike loaded for camping and cover 70 miles (115 km) in a day. Remember that fatigue builds each day, so by midweek you could be 1 to 2 miles per hour (1.5 to 3 km/h) slower. We recommend getting experience with pacing and cumulative fatigue on a one-week tour before attempting a longer one.

If a brevet series excites you, you need the same athletic maturity as someone who is contemplating a multiday tour. You should have recently completed a ride of 150 miles (240 km) or more, a two- to three-day tour, or a century or 200K each month for several months. You should be able to finish a 200K in 9:00 to 10:30 (a century in 7:30 to 8:30). Review your postride notes about these events to see whether you had any significant problems with fatigue, discomfort on the bike, nutrition, pacing, or mood during the rides. Preparing for and riding brevets will hone your skills, but you should have mastered the basics in earlier rides.

Long-distance ventures require a considerable investment of time and, for some events, money. As with other events, use resources such as websites, clubs, and other riders to gather information about the options. Refer back to table 9.1 on page 174 for a comparison of supported and unsupported rides and think about the information that follows. Work patiently through the considerations in the planning stage to select an appropriate next challenge because the preparation and event will take time away from your family and other priorities.

Organized Tours

Before you decide to take a particular tour, do some research. Tour organizers usually handle all the planning and logistics, allowing you to relax and enjoy the ride. The organizer usually takes care of the route, provides some support during the day, and arranges lodging and possibly meals, which make an organized tour an attractive option if you don't have the time or desire to set up your own trip.

Tours vary considerably in difficulty, ranging from rides featuring multiple days in the mountains, including climbs used by professional racers, to those that cater to families and have relaxed days on the bike to take in local attractions. Based on your experience, in similar terrain if possible, estimate how long each day would take you and whether the individual days are comparable with your riding experience. Given your physical condition now, after training for eight more weeks would you be able to ride back-to-back days of similar duration to the tour days and complete a ride comparable to the hardest day of the tour, without difficulty? If not, either plan an easier tour or build up your experience base before selecting and training for a weeklong tour.

After degree of difficulty, consider your budget. The more support provided during the day, the better the quality and variety of meals offered, and the more extravagant the lodging is, the higher the price you will pay. Tours run from US$500 per person for a weeklong camping tour with minimal support during the day to thousands of dollars for fully catered tours with high-end lodging and fine meals.

Inquire what kind of support will be offered during the day. Some tours provide sumptuous rest stops and rolling bike shops in case of mechanical problems, whereas some club tours provide only a cue sheet that outlines the route for each day. Will guides ride with you, or are you responsible for following the cue sheet? Some organizers provide space in a sag vehicle in case you or another member of your party gets tired of riding. If you want to tour with riders who may be less than enthusiastic about long days in the saddle, they can ride for part of the route, hop in the van, and meet you at the end of the day. Other tours don't plan to carry tired riders in a vehicle but will make space if you get hurt or have a serious mechanical problem. Check with the tour operator about the policy for providing sag space.

What kind of lodging do you want? Accommodations range from campgrounds to bed and breakfasts and everything in between. The type of accommodation may affect your sleep, which could in turn affect your riding and enjoyment the next day. Also, find out what kinds of meals are included. Meals range from group cooking by the participants to group meals in fine restaurants to dining on your own. Meals should be an enjoyable part of your tour. If you plan to tour with family or friends consider their preferences. You may have a sense of adventure and enjoy camping, whereas others might look forward to more comfort at the end of a long day and a restaurant meal.

Will you bring your own bike, or would you like one supplied to you? If you use the organizer's bike, you don't have to pack, ship, and unpack your own. All you have to do is ride! If they provide the bike, find out about it. Some companies offer top-of-the-line bikes and components. Do you normally ride a bike with bar-end shifters? Can you adapt to a bike with dual control levers? Bring your own pedals, shoes, saddle, and helmet to make your riding more comfortable and check that the tour operator can accommodate any special needs.

A bike tour can be more than just pedaling through the countryside. You can choose among wine-tasting tours, rides through historical areas, and tours with other themes. Tour leaders or guides can make or break a trip, so find out about them. How long have they been leading trips? Are they native to the area or knowledgeable about the region? If the tour is in a foreign country, do they speak the local language? A reputable outfitter should provide you with references on all aspects of the tour. Contact these people to find out what they liked and didn't like. A fully supported tour can be a substantial investment. Read the fine print, especially regarding cancellation (you may want to consider travel insurance). To avoid surprises, make sure that the organizer addresses any concerns.

Self-Contained Tours

You can have fun planning your own tour as you pore over maps and talk with family or friends. But before unrolling the maps think realistically about your athletic maturity, an especially important consideration when planning longer unsupported rides. Then ask yourself these questions: How long could you ride each day? How long do you want to ride each day? Would you like to have fun with another hobby, such as fishing or photography, in addition to pedaling? How would you prefer to spend the nights? How much time do you have to prepare, given your family, work, and other commitments?

You have a great degree of flexibility in planning your own tours. You choose your length of days based on your ability and interests. You decide whether to ride all day or to spend the morning riding and the afternoon exploring the town, hiking, fishing, or taking pictures. You choose where you want to go—close to home or in another part of the country? You decide whether you'd rather stay in B&Bs in quaint towns, decent motels, or campgrounds.

After you have a general idea of your type of tour, unfold a map and look at route options for each day. A topographical map is particularly helpful because back-to-back days in the hills will be much different from days ridden on flat terrain. Given the type of accommodations that you prefer, identify a number of potential overnights. These might be a full day's ride apart or considerably closer together by the direct route but also connected by scenic alternative routes. Then consider towns and supply points en route and at night so you know what you need to carry. The individual days should be comparable in duration to your past rides, while carrying all the gear for the tour, either credit-card style gear (discussed in chapter 9 on pages 181–184) or camping gear (discussed in this chapter). During the planning process, reach out for help. Consult online forums or cycling groups and contact local bike shops or clubs. Other riders may have traveled the route. Most cyclists love to describe their experiences, which may save you problems down the road. Finally, if you will be traveling in the peak season, make reservations.

Before you finally pick a route, figure out a plan in case you have physical, mechanical, or other problems. Can you rely on public transit as backup? Or friendly locals? Or will you need to call for help? Will cell phones work? If not, are public telephones available? Make a plan for keeping in touch with others and communicating in case of an emergency.

Brevets

Riding brevets, because of the distances covered and camaraderie, can be among the most satisfying cycling activities. Are you curious to see how far you can ride? On the longer brevets, you spend considerably more time riding every 24 hours (and see more country!) and significantly less time off the bike than on even the hardest multiday tours.

For most brevets you cover 300 kilometers (186 miles) or more in 24 hours. Because of the time constraints, riders complete brevets of 600 kilometers (373 miles) and longer with minimal sleep. How much sleep do you want or need? Are you willing to ride at night with lights? Riding at night can be wonderful, and watching the sun come up on your bike is magical. But people who suffer significantly from sleep deprivation or have poor night vision may have difficulty riding at night. Think about all these factors and whether you would enjoy the test of covering long distances within the time limits shown in table 10.1. If so, you're ready for the challenge of brevets!

TABLE 10.1 **Brevet Time Limits**

The brevet distance must be completed within a time limit including stops.	
200 km	13:30
300 km	20:00
400 km	27:00
600 km	40:00
1,000 km	75:00
1,200 km	90:00

Mental Preparation

The longer the event is, the more strongly your mental skills will affect your performance and enjoyment of the ride. You already have learned the relaxation and visualization techniques (pages 135–136 in chapter 7) to help prepare for an event. You can also use power words and images during the ride to perform better. Start by free associating: Write down the words that describe you as an endurance rider. Perhaps you think of your riding as strong, steady, and smooth and your attitude as focused, persistent, and relaxed. Visualize specific images that each power word evokes for you. "Steady" and "smooth" might evoke the image of a migrating flock of birds. "Relaxed" might remind you of a cat snoozing. You can use each word and image to help in specific situations. Just had another flat? Say "relaxed" several times and visualize the cat stretching before you tear the tire off the rim. Tired, discouraged, and a long way from the finish? Repeat "steady" and "smooth" and imagine you and your companions riding like that flock of migrating birds.

Because preparing your mind is as important as training your body, our training plan for the brevets (presented in the next section) includes scheduled time each week for practicing progressive relaxation, developing power words, and visualizing each brevet. We also recommend practicing these techniques during your preparation for a tour to help calm those inevitable butterflies during the weeks and days leading up to the start and to give you tools to use during the tour.

Starting with your centuries, you developed an expected plan for your event and alternate scenarios for both great rides and tough ones so that you were prepared for all possibilities. You also developed three scenarios for 300Ks or double centuries and weekend tours and used the scenarios to help you decide what clothing and equipment you might need. The longer the ride is, the more detailed the scenarios should be in the following areas:

- *Time management.* As described in chapter 9, you need to manage your time on weekend tours so you have sufficient time at the end of the day. On longer tours time management becomes more important because your riding speed will decay. Although your riding speed might be 15 miles per hour (24 km/h), not including rest stops, on day 1, you may be pedaling at only 12 miles per hour (19 km/h) on day 7. What effect should your slower pace have on the time that you spend off the bike during each day's ride later in the tour? A weeklong tour probably also includes more day-to-day variation, in both distance and terrain, so you need to create a time management strategy for each day.

- *Nutrition.* In chapter 9 we also introduced the concept of managing your nutrition over a 24-hour cycle on weekend tours. If you don't eat quite enough on a weekend tour, your performance won't suffer much, but as the daily riding time or number of days gets longer, managing your nutrition becomes critical. If you weigh 150 pounds (68 kg) you can store about 1,800 calories of glycogen. If you are riding a multiday tour or longer brevet and not eating enough every 24 hours, you will progressively deplete your glycogen stores. Your event plan should include a specific nutritional plan to eat enough daily carbohydrate.

- *Brevets.* On every brevet you must reach each control by a specified time and finish within the time allowed. For each brevet your three scenarios should project riding speed and budget the time off the bike so that even with the slowest scenario you reach each control and finish within the time limits with a bit of a safety margin. When projecting your riding speed, remember that your pace will decay by at least 1.5 kilometers per hour (1 mph) every 24 hours. Brevets of 600, 1,000, and 1,200 kilometers all have time cutoffs that don't allow for full nights of sleep. For these longer brevets, estimate your riding speed and then your total on-the-bike time for the event. Subtract this from the hours allowed for the event to determine your available off-the-bike time. Then allocate your off-the-bike time among time at controls, sleep breaks, and a safety margin. Create three scenarios based on different riding speeds and different amounts of time off the bike. If you are disciplined at controls and are having an average ride, you probably can get three or four hours off the bike at night—not luxurious but enough to keep you going.

- *Drop bags.* Some organizations take one or more small gear bags to planned overnight controls on brevets. Pack a change of cycling clothes, comfort items like your toothbrush, extra batteries and bulbs, extra tubes, and perhaps a tire. If you prefer sports nutrition products to regular food, send ahead your favorite food and drink, and perhaps a meal replacement drink such as Ensure for a quick pre-bed meal and breakfast.

For brevets of 400 kilometers and longer, many riders create a detailed spreadsheet to project the different variables (riding speed, off-the-bike time, nutrition, sleep breaks) from control to control for the duration of the brevet.

Training

You know how to prepare for a century, a 300K or double century, and a weekend tour. Getting ready for a longer tour or brevet requires a similar systematic approach based on the same concepts.

As you prepare, pay attention to all your success factors: improving physical conditioning and recovery, sharpening techniques such as pacing and time management, following a 24-hour nutrition plan, and practicing your mental skills. The longer the event is, the more these aspects of athletic maturity come into play. Some people develop quickly, whereas others improve over many years of riding. In your journal note how you respond when the training volume or intensity increases, how you feel mentally and physically at different times of the program, when your motivation is high and when it is low, how training, family, and work affect one another, and any other factors that seem to affect your riding. In particular, review the problems that develop and the ways in which you solve them. Throughout your preparation, keep in mind what cycling means to you and what you get out of it.

Multiday Tour Training

This training program for multiday touring assumes that you plan a weeklong tour riding five to six hours a day, either on a supported tour or when carrying camping gear. We again use the concept of periodization for this 8-week schedule. Before training for a multiday tour you should have recently completed a weekend tour, a century each month for three or four months, or a 300K or double century. If you finished one of these in the last few weeks, you have already completed the base phase of training. You have built your endurance with long rides and are comfortable with your bike and equipment. If a month or more has passed since you rode one of these, do several weeks of endurance training from one of the earlier programs until you can complete a five- or six-hour ride without difficulty. Weeks 1 through 3 of this program build your endurance for back-to-back rides and introduce more intensity training to build your power. Week 4 is a recovery week. Weeks 5 through 7 focus on peaking to get you ready for your event. You train with the gear and loads that you will use on your tour. Finally, in week 8 you taper to recover and store energy for the trip.

This program prepares you for a week of back-to-back days using a rhythm of alternating hard weeks with much easier weeks.

Week 1: High volume with back-to-back endurance rides on the weekend. We also include one midweek intensity ride as well as a recovery jaunt.

Week 2: Low volume with back-to-back tempo workouts on the weekend and two midweek intensity rides along with a recovery outing.

Week 3: Longer back-to-back rides on the weekend with similar midweek training.

Week 4: Low-volume recovery week.

Weeks 5 through 8 follow the same rhythm.

Training for multiday touring uses the same types of workouts as the other programs. To get the most from your training, keep the intensity of the workouts within the ranges specified in table 10.2. (See chapter 6 for more information on training by heart rate, power, and RPE.)

TABLE 10.2 **Recommended Workout Intensities**

Ride	Heart rate as percentage of LT	Power as percentage of FTP	Rating of perceived exertion
Long	75 to 87	56 to 75	2 to 3
Tempo	88 to 94	76 to 90	3 to 4
Brisk, mixed intensity, hard effort	95 to 100	91 to 100	5 to 6
Brisk, mixed intensity, recovery effort	less than 75	less than 55	1 to 2
Active recovery	less than 75	less than 55	1 to 2

- *Long.* Throughout the programs, consistently ride either the shorter or longer weekend rides. Start the first week by carrying some of the gear for the tour and add more gear each week until you're training with all your equipment by week 5. These rides maintain your endurance, accustom you to riding with a loaded bike, and allow you to test new gear or different foods. Remember that you may go a bit harder to climb hills but stay at the long ride intensity for most of the ride. As the rides get longer you may not be able to stay at the long ride intensity. That's OK—listen to your body.
- *Tempo.* These slightly faster rides increase your cruising speed. As with the other training programs, if you are doing the longer weekend rides then you should also do the longer tempo and brisk rides; if you are doing the shorter weekend rides you may choose the longer tempo and brisk rides.
- *Brisk.* These more intense rides include a segment of mixed intensity that helps boost your power and increase your average speed. If you do the shorter brisk rides then also do the shorter segments of mixed intensity.
- *Recovery.* These rides or other activities help you to recover and have more energy for other rides.
- *Supplementary.* Continue your core strength, flexibility, and resistance-maintenance training.

The following program represents the optimal plan. You could reach your goal with less preparation, but the tour won't be as enjoyable.

This program prepares you for a week of five- to six-hour days. If you have the athletic maturity to consider a tour with longer days, you could modify this program by keeping about the same proportions among the types of rides. For example, if you plan to do a tour of seven- or eight-hour days, then increase the training volume for each ride in this program by about 25 percent. Before starting a modified program remember to build your base sufficiently so that you easily can handle the volume of the first week.

8-WEEK MULTIDAY TOUR PROGRAM

Weeks 1–3 Intensity Phase
Build endurance for back-to-back rides, increase power for carrying loads, test any new equipment, and progressively increase the amount of equipment that you carry so that by week 5 you are training with all your equipment.

WEEK 1

Riding:

Back-to-back long rides of 3:00–4:00 each (total 6:00–8:00)
Midweek brisk ride of 60–90 minutes including 10–15 minutes of mixed intensity
Midweek tempo ride of 60–90 minutes (optional)
Active recovery ride of 30–40 minutes
Second active recovery ride of 20–30 minutes (optional)
Total riding time: 7:30–12:10

Supplementary training:

Two core strength-training sessions of 10–20 minutes
Three stretching sessions of 10–20 minutes
One resistance-maintenance training session of 20–30 minutes (optional)

WEEK 2

Riding:

Back-to-back weekend tempo rides of 60–90 minutes (total 2:00–3:00)
Midweek brisk ride of 60–90 minutes including 15–20 minutes of mixed intensity
Second midweek brisk ride of 60–90 minutes including 10–15 minutes of mixed intensity
Active recovery ride of 30–40 minutes
Second active recovery ride of 20–30 minutes (optional)
Total riding time: 4:30–7:10

Supplementary training:

Two core strength-training sessions of 10–20 minutes
Three stretching sessions of 10–20 minutes
One resistance-maintenance training session of 20–30 minutes (optional)

WEEK 3

Riding:

Back-to-back long rides of 3:30–4:30 (total 7:00–9:00)
Midweek brisk ride of 60–90 minutes including 15–20 minutes of mixed intensity
Midweek tempo ride of 60–90 minutes (optional)
Active recovery ride of 30–40 minutes
Second active recovery ride of 30–40 minutes (optional)
Total riding time: 8:30–13:20

Supplementary training:

Two core strength-training sessions of 10–20 minutes
Three stretching sessions of 10–20 minutes
One resistance-maintenance training session of 20–30 minutes (optional)

WEEK 4—RECOVERY

Riding:

Long ride of 1:00–2:00
Active recovery ride of 30–40 minutes
Active recovery ride of 30–40 minutes
Midweek tempo ride of 60–90 minutes (optional)
Total riding time: 2:00–4:50

Supplementary training:

Two core strength-training sessions of 10–20 minutes
Three stretching sessions of 10–20 minutes
No resistance training

Weeks 5–8 Peaking Phase
Continue back-to-back rides on alternate weekends carrying the equipment and loads that you will carry for your tour. You could do overnight trips.

WEEK 5

Riding:

Back-to-back long rides of 4:00–5:00 (total 8:00–10:00)
Midweek brisk ride of 60–90 minutes including 15–20 minutes of mixed intensity
Midweek tempo ride of 60–90 minutes (optional)
Active recovery ride of 20–30 minutes
Second active recovery ride of 20–30 minutes (optional)
Total riding time: 9:20–14:00

Supplementary training:

Two core strength-training sessions of 10–20 minutes
Three stretching sessions of 10–20 minutes
One resistance-maintenance training session of 20–30 minutes (optional)

WEEK 6

Riding:

Back-to-back weekend tempo rides of 1:30–2:00 (total 3:00–4:00)
Midweek brisk ride of 60–90 minutes including 20–25 minutes of mixed intensity
Second midweek brisk ride of 60–90 minutes including 15–20 minutes of mixed intensity
Active recovery ride of 20–30 minutes
Second active recovery ride of 20–30 minutes (optional)
Total riding time: 5:20–8:00

Supplementary training:

Two core strength-training sessions of 10–20 minutes
Three stretching sessions of 10–20 minutes
One resistance-maintenance training session of 20–30 minutes (optional)

(continued)

WEEK 7—PEAK

Riding:

Back-to-back long rides of 5:00–6:00 (total 10:00–12:00)
Midweek brisk ride of 60–90 minutes including 15–20 minutes of mixed intensity
Midweek tempo ride of 60–90 minutes (optional)
Active recovery ride of 30–40 minutes
Second active recovery ride of 30–40 minutes (optional)
Total riding time: 11:30–16:20

Supplementary training:

Two core strength-training sessions of 10–20 minutes
Three stretching sessions of 10–20 minutes
One resistance-maintenance training session of 20–30 minutes (optional)

WEEK 8—TAPER

Riding:

Long ride of 1:30–2:00 one weekend day
Tempo ride of 60–90 minutes the other weekend day
Midweek brisk ride of 40–60 minutes including 10–15 minutes of mixed intensity
Active recovery ride of 30–40 minutes
Second active recovery of 30–40 minutes (optional)
Total riding time: 3:40–5:50

Supplementary training:

Two core strength-training sessions of 10–20 minutes
Three stretching sessions of 10–20 minutes
No resistance training

EVENT WEEK

Riding:

Long ride—event starts on weekend
Midweek tempo ride of 40–60 minutes
Active recovery ride of 30–40 minutes
Active recovery of 30–40 minutes

Supplementary training:

Two core strength-training sessions of 10–20 minutes
Three stretching sessions of 10–20 minutes
No resistance training

Safety: Night Riding

Longer brevets include riding in the dark. Some randonneurs spend lots of time and money on lighting systems, but riding technique is more important than lumens.

▶ Ride in the road when possible, not on the shoulder. Car tires tend to keep the roadway clean. The shoulder has more glass and other debris, which isn't visible at night.

▶ You can easily become focused just on your cone of light or the taillights of another rider. Learn to scan the road constantly looking for cues illuminated by the moon, stars, or other light bouncing from the pavement.

▶ When riding with others, ride side by side rather than drafting. A conversation when riding side by side will help keep you alert, and at night riding safely behind someone is difficult because of poorer visibility and increased reaction time.

▶ Speed and effort are more difficult to judge at night. Without illuminated electronics, you won't have any data. Learn to listen to your body and use RPE without any external cues.

▶ You're more likely to hit an invisible bump. Ride with the slightly loose grip of a mountain biker so that you can roll over rough patches without getting thrown.

Brevet Series Training

Randonneuring clubs throughout the world host many brevets each year. The standard series of 200-, 300-, 400-, and 600-kilometer brevets often are held a month apart. If riding brevets interests you, this program will help you prepare for a series by riding each brevet as endurance training for the next brevet and using the endurance workouts between the brevets to maintain your endurance and practice event skills. For the program we assume that you have used either of the century (200 km) programs to complete a 200-kilometer brevet in 9:00 to 10:30, averaging 19 to 22 kilometers per hour (12 to 14 mph) including off the bike time, without difficulty within the last month. We also assume that the brevets are scheduled four weeks apart, giving you three weeks to recover and prepare for the next one, similar to a schedule of riding one century each month. We assume as well that you are riding to complete the series of brevets, not to achieve maximum speed.

The training plan assumes the ranges of finish times including brief stops at checkpoint controls shown in table 10.3. The ranges take into account differences in terrain and conditions.

TABLE 10.3 **Assumed Brevet Finishing Times for Training Series**

Distance	Time	Approximate speed km/h	Approximate speed mph	Allowed time
200 km	9:00 to 10:30	22 to 19	14 to 12	13:30
300 km	14:30 to 16:30	20.5 to 18	13 to 11.25	20:00
400 km	21:00 to 23:30	19 to 17	12 to 10.5	27:00
600 km	34:00 to 37:30	17.5 to 16	11 to 10	40:00

Recognizing the principle of individuality, your brevet times may vary. Your speed may decline more from the 300K to the 400K because the 400K includes some night riding. The time for the 600K does not include a sleep break. If you can train to finish the 600K in about 34:00 including stops at controls, then you would have time for a 3:00-4:00 sleep break.

Training for brevets uses the same types of workouts and intensities as the other programs (see table 10.2 on page 203). The program assumes that the brevets are four weeks apart. The weekend training rides follow this general structure, and the detailed program follows:

- *Recovery ride on the first weekend after the brevet.* A 60- to 90-minute ride to recharge your batteries. Have fun but keep the intensity down in the active recovery zone. If you are more experienced, you could do an endurance ride of 2:00 to 3:00.

- *Endurance ride on the second weekend after the brevet.* These rides of 5:00 to 10:00 maintain your endurance and should be in the long ride zone. You may need to go a little harder climbing steeper hills or slower as the ride gets longer. During the program try to increase the pace every four weeks so that by week 11 (midway between the 400K and 600K) you are averaging 22 to 24 km/h (13.75 to 15 mph) including time off the bike. This will build your cruising speed so that your overall speed doesn't decay as much from fatigue during the longer brevets.

- *Rehearsal ride on the third weekend after the brevet.* Practice your pace for the next brevet carrying the same gear on these shorter endurance workouts. Because fatigue builds significantly during brevets of 300 kilometers and longer, you won't be able to ride the entire brevet as hard as you do your normal endurance rides. To help manage your brevet pace, see the tips for multiday events in chapter 9 (pages 186–188). Use this rehearsal ride to practice eating and drinking, managing your time off the bike, and double-checking all your gear.

The endurance ride on the second weekend provides flexibility in the schedule. If you have only two weekends between brevets, omit week 2. If you have more than three weekends you may add additional endurance weeks like week 2, but don't do too much!

Each week includes a midweek tempo ride, one or two active recovery sessions, and supplementary core and flexibility training. Some weeks include a midweek brisk ride with mixed intensity.

The longer your event is, the more mentally demanding it is. Don't neglect your preparation. Each week includes two midweek 20- to 30-minute mental training sessions as follows:

- *First week—analyze.* The week after the brevet go over the ride. What went well? What problems did you encounter? What do you need to test and resolve before the next brevet? Based on what you learned, develop your three scenarios for the next brevet.

- *Second and third weeks—preride.* During these weeks visualize riding the next brevet (refer back to chapter 7) and practice your power words and images.

- *Fourth week—relax.* During the week before the brevet practice your relaxation skills (refer back to chapter 7).

12-WEEK BREVET SERIES PROGRAM

WEEK 1—200-KILOMETER BREVET

Riding:

Long ride of 200 kilometers in 9:00-10:30
Midweek tempo ride of 30–40 minutes
Active recovery ride of 20–30 minutes
Active recovery ride of 20–30 minutes (optional)
Total riding time: 9:50–12:10

Supplementary training:

Two midweek mental rehearsal sessions of 20–30 minutes relaxing and visualizing the brevet
Two core strength-training sessions of 10–20 minutes
Three stretching sessions of 10–20 minutes

WEEK 2—RECOVERY

Riding:

Long ride—recovery ride of 1:00–1:30 or endurance ride of 2:00–3:00
Midweek tempo ride of 60–90 minutes
Active recovery ride of 20–30 minutes
Active recovery ride of 20–30 minutes (optional)
Total riding time: 2:20–5:30

Supplementary training:

Two midweek mental preparation sessions of 20–30 minutes analyzing last brevet and planning for the next brevet
Two core strength-training sessions of 10–20 minutes
Three stretching sessions of 10–20 minutes

WEEK 3—ENDURANCE

Riding:

Long ride—endurance ride of 5:00–8:00 ridden 0.5-1.0 km/h (0.25-0.5 mph) faster than the 200 km brevet in week 1
Midweek tempo ride of 60–90 minutes
Brisk ride of 60–90 minutes including 20–25 minutes of mixed intensity
Active recovery ride of 40–60 minutes
Second active recovery ride of 40–60 minutes (optional)
Total riding time: 7:40–13:00

Supplementary training:

Two midweek mental rehearsal sessions of 20–30 minutes practicing power words and visualizing the next brevet
Two core strength-training sessions of 10–20 minutes
Three stretching sessions of 10–20 minutes

WEEK 4—EVENT REHEARSAL AND TAPER

Riding:

Long ride—event rehearsal ride of 4:00–6:00
Midweek tempo ride of 45–75 minutes

(continued)

Brisk ride of 45–75 minutes including 15–20 minutes of mixed intensity
Active recovery ride of 40–60 minutes
Second active recovery ride of 40–60 minutes (optional)
Total riding time: 6:10–10:30

Supplementary training:

Two midweek mental rehearsal sessions of 20–30 minutes practicing power words and visualizing the next brevet
Two core strength-training sessions of 10–20 minutes
Three stretching sessions of 10–20 minutes

WEEK 5—300-KILOMETER BREVET

Riding:

Long ride—300 kilometers in 14:30-16:30
Midweek tempo ride of 30–40 minutes
Active recovery ride of 40–60 minutes
Active recovery ride of 40–60 minutes (optional)
Total riding time: 15:40–19:10

Supplementary training:

Two midweek mental sessions of 20–30 minutes relaxing and visualizing the brevet
Two core strength-training sessions of 10–20 minutes
Three stretching sessions of 10–20 minutes

WEEK 6—RECOVERY

Riding:

Long ride—recovery ride of 1:00–1:30 or endurance ride of 2:00–3:00
Midweek tempo ride of 60–90 minutes
Active recovery ride of 20–30 minutes
Active recovery ride of 20–30 minutes (optional)
Total riding time: 2:20–5:30

Supplementary training:

Two midweek mental preparation sessions of 20–30 minutes analyzing the last brevet and planning for the next brevet
Two core strength-training sessions of 10–20 minutes
Three stretching sessions of 10–20 minutes

WEEK 7—ENDURANCE

Riding:

Long ride—endurance ride of 7:00–10:00 ridden 0.5-1.0 km/h (0.25-0.5 mph) faster than the week 3 long ride
Midweek tempo ride of 60–90 minutes
Midweek brisk ride of 60–90 minutes including 15–20 minutes of mixed intensity
Active recovery ride of 40–60 minutes
Active recovery ride of 40–60 minutes (optional)
Total riding time: 9:40–15:00

Supplementary training:

Two midweek mental rehearsal sessions of 20–30 minutes practicing power words and visualizing the next brevet
Two core strength-training sessions of 10–20 minutes
Three stretching sessions of 10–20 minutes

WEEK 8—REHEARSAL AND TAPER

Riding:

Long ride—event rehearsal ride of 3:00–5:00 involving night riding, starting before dawn or finishing at night (to simulate the brevet)
Midweek tempo ride of 60–90 minutes
Midweek brisk ride of 60–90 minutes including 10–15 minutes of mixed intensity
Active recovery ride of 40–60 minutes
Active recovery ride of 40–60 minutes (optional)
Total riding time: 5:40–10:00

Supplementary training:

Two midweek mental rehearsal sessions of 20–30 minutes practicing power words and visualizing the next brevet
Two core strength-training sessions of 10–20 minutes
Three stretching sessions of 10–20 minutes

WEEK 9—400-KILOMETER BREVET

Riding:

Long ride—400 kilometers in 21:00-23:30
Midweek tempo ride of 40–60 minutes
Active recovery ride of 40–60 minutes
Active recovery ride of 40–60 minutes (optional)
Total riding time: 22:20–26:30

Supplementary training:

Two midweek mental rehearsal sessions of 20–30 minutes relaxing and visualizing the brevet
Two core strength-training sessions of 10–20 minutes
Three stretching sessions of 10–20 minutes

WEEK 10—RECOVERY

Riding:

Long ride—recovery ride of 1:00–1:30 or endurance ride of 2:00–3:00
Midweek tempo ride of 40–60 minutes
Active recovery ride of 60–90 minutes
Active recovery ride of 40–60 minutes (optional)
Total riding time: 2:40–6:30

Supplementary training:

Two midweek mental preparation sessions of 20–30 minutes analyzing the last brevet and planning for the next brevet
Two core strength-training sessions of 10–20 minutes
Three stretching sessions of 10–20 minutes

(continued)

WEEK 11—ENDURANCE

Riding:

Long ride—endurance ride of 6:30–10:00 ridden 0.5-1.0 km/h (0.25-0.5 mph) faster than the week 7 long ride. If you feel fine you could ride a few more hours or do back-to-back rides. You could ride a 200K on Saturday and then a 100K on Sunday. Or turn it into an overnight training ride with lights.
Midweek tempo ride of 60–90 minutes
Midweek brisk ride of 60–90 minutes including 10–15 minutes of mixed intensity
Active recovery ride of 40–60 minutes
Active recovery ride of 40–60 minutes (optional)
Total riding time: 9:10–15:00

Supplementary training:

Two midweek mental rehearsal sessions of 20–30 minutes practicing power words and visualizing the next brevet
Two core strength-training sessions of 10–20 minutes
Three stretching sessions of 10–20 minutes

WEEK 12—EVENT REHEARSAL AND TAPER

Riding:

Long ride—event rehearsal ride of 2:00–4:00
Midweek tempo ride of 60–90 minutes
Midweek brisk ride of 60–90 minutes including 10–15 minutes of mixed intensity
Active recovery ride of 40–60 minutes
Active recovery ride of 40–60 minutes (optional)
Total riding time: 4:40–9:00

Supplementary training:

Two midweek mental rehearsal sessions of 20–30 minutes practicing power words and visualizing the next brevet
Two core strength-training sessions of 10–20 minutes
Three stretching sessions of 10–20 minutes

EVENT WEEK—600-KILOMETER BREVET

Riding:

Long ride—600 kilometers in 34:00-37:30 (not including sleep break)
Midweek tempo ride of 40–60 minutes
Active recovery ride of 40–60 minutes
Second active recovery ride of 40–60 minutes (optional)
Total riding time: 35:20–40:30

Supplementary training:

Two midweek mental rehearsal sessions of 20–30 minutes relaxing and visualizing the brevet
Two core strength-training sessions of 10–20 minutes
Three stretching sessions of 10–20 minutes

Equipment

For ultradistance rides you might want a different bike and new ways to carry your gear. You probably need more clothes for a variety of conditions. For the longer brevets you need lights. You should test all of these thoroughly in training before the event.

Bike

The bike that you need for your tours or brevets depends on the types of events that you plan to do. If you will be participating in an organized tour, traveling light on a multiday credit-card tour, or riding a supported brevet, then the bike that you use for shorter events should work well. But many brevets and personal tours occur off the beaten path where access to bike shops is limited. For these events reliability becomes more important than high performance. Superlight components and fancy wheels are not the best choice for these rides. If you plan to camp, you probably want a bike designed specifically for touring, which would also serve for brevets and credit-card touring.

A touring bike, the two-wheeled equivalent of an RV, can take you and your gear on virtually any adventure. Some bikes are designed for road travel, whereas others feature robust mountain bike wheels that allow you to ride on rough roads and trails. Touring bikes differ from their racing counterparts in several ways:

- *Stronger frame.* Touring frames are designed to carry a lot of gear (riders may carry more than 40 pounds [18 kg] of gear on the bike) and usually are constructed of durable steel, aluminum, or titanium to withstand years of hard use with minimal maintenance.

- *Upright positioning.* At touring speeds you don't have much aerodynamic drag, so these frames provide a more upright, comfortable riding position to reduce fatigue and provide better visibility.

- *Longer chain stays.* The chain stays, which run from the bottom bracket to the rear dropouts, are longer on touring bikes to lengthen the wheelbase and make the bike more stable. Longer chain stays also provide greater heel clearance, which prevents your foot from hitting the rear pannier while pedaling.

- *More fork rake.* Rake in the fork refers to its forward bend near the wheel. Raking the fork farther forward helps absorb road vibrations and lengthens the wheelbase, promoting stability.

- *Strong wheels.* Hauling extra gear puts more stress on wheels. Touring bikes generally have conventional 36-spoke wheels laced to durable hubs and rims, and spokes that can be replaced in the field.

- *Shift levers.* Touring bikes usually have reliable bar-end, down-tube, or mountain bike thumb shifters instead of dual-control shift and brake levers. If a dual-control lever fails in the middle of nowhere, you probably won't be able to fix it. You can switch the other shifter types to the friction mode if the indexing mechanism fails, and you can easily replace a broken cable.

- *Frame eyelets.* Touring frames have attachment points for front and rear racks, extra water bottle cages, and fenders.

Depending on whether you plan to camp, take a credit-card tour, or ride brevets, some or all of these features may be desirable.

Bike Modifications

If you plan to ride your century bike on tours or longer brevets, several modifications can make it more comfortable. Your bike shop can advise you on the pros and cons of each option and the viability for your specific bike.

- *Lower gears.* With heavier touring loads, climbing is more difficult, and you need lower gears to protect your knees. Even if you're not riding a loaded bike, fatigue builds on multiday tours and longer brevets, and you can't spin the same gears. Consider these options:
  - *Compact crank set.* These have smaller chain rings that provide lower gearing at less weight than a triple crank set.
  - *Wider cassette.* Standard rear derailleurs handle a maximum range of rear cogs, typically 11 or 12 teeth to 25 or 27 teeth. If you put a touring or mountain bike derailleur on your bike, you can use a 12 to 32 or wider cassette.
  - *Triple chain rings.* Changing your double chain rings to a triple provides the maximum range of gears. Because your rear derailleur will need to maintain chain tension over a wider range of gears, you need to put on a touring or MTB derailleur.
- *Wider tires.* Most recreational riders use 20- to 25-millimeter-wide tires. Wider tires (28–32 mm) handle more weight and provide better cushioning, especially on rough roads. Some tires have a puncture-resistant tread. Although no tire is impenetrable, a puncture-resistant tire reduces the frequency of flats as long as the tire is inflated properly and inspected regularly.
- *Fenders.* Fenders help keep water off you and other riders, making riding in wet conditions more tolerable. They also protect your bike, especially the drive train and headset, from road spray and grit. Touring frames have eyelets to attach full-coverage fenders that provide the greatest protection. On racing frames small fenders that clip onto the seat tube can provide some protection. If you ride frequently in the rain in a group, add a mud flap to the bottom of the rear fender. Tape on a piece of cardboard or plastic and replace as needed. If you put on fenders, practice changing wheels. Fenders that fit close to the tire make installing wheels tricky, especially the rear wheel if you have a rack.

Carriers

When riding longer brevets and tours, you need to carry more stuff. Even on supported events, you want to carry some extra food, clothing, and other items to make your trip more comfortable. Review the simple ways to carry modest amounts of additional gear provided in chapter 9 (pages 181–184). For self-supported camping tours, you need to haul all your equipment using either panniers (see figure 10.1) or a trailer:

- *Panniers.* Panniers are pairs of bags that hang on racks over the wheels. The larger ones have pockets and hang over the rear wheel. Smaller ones hang over the front wheel. For events in which you don't need much gear, such as longer brevets, you could use the smaller front panniers on your rear rack. A heavily loaded bike handles quite differently, so some riders prefer trailers.
- *Trailer.* A trailer attaches to the rear with a quick release and carries quite a bit of gear. This setup keeps the weight low and off the bike, making handling easier. You can use a trailer with a bike that does not have rack attachment points. If you plan a multiday off-road tour, a trailer may be a good option because many mountain

FIGURE 10.1 **Properly loaded touring bike with handle bar bag and front and rear panniers.**

bike suspension systems do not accommodate racks. At home a trailer turns your bike into a grocery and cargo-hauling machine that makes running errands a breeze. If you are considering a trailer, do your research and try the various types before buying because they will affect bike handling.

Whichever system you choose, remember that gear expands to fill the available space! Even if you have room, don't take items that aren't essential. After a few days of pedaling with a load you'll be grateful that you didn't overpack.

If you use bags on the bike, it will handle better if you distribute the load over both wheels rather than place all of it on the rear. How much you can put on the front without affecting steering and stability depends on the fork rake—the greater the rake is, the more you can put on the front. Putting the weight relatively low by using panniers rather than just a rack trunk or handlebar bag keeps the center of gravity lower.

Whether you use panniers or a trailer, experiment on your training rides to figure out a packing system that protects your gear and helps you stay organized while on your trip. Just as you did on shorter trips, distribute items that you need during the day (snacks, maps, sunscreen, camera, and so on) among your jersey pockets, handlebar bag, small pack on the front of the top tube, or hydration pack. Put the heaviest items (tent, cookware, and so on) lowest to avoid crushing other items and to improve bike handling. Use plastic bags to organize and protect your gear. Label the bags if they are not see-through. Develop your system and stick to it. You should know exactly where and how to stow every item that you carry. The more of a habit this becomes, the less time you will spend searching for stuff, which is particularly important on brevets, and the less likely you will be to leave something behind. See the packing list for tours at http://tinyurl.com/49ha5wb.

Clothing

For a tour or brevet be prepared for all kinds of weather, including sun, rain, wind, and perhaps snow if you ride in the mountains. Quality rain gear (coat, pants, overmitts, and booties), wicking layers, insulating layers, and windproof fabrics will make your ride more enjoyable in inclement weather. The key is layering, which allows you to adjust clothing items to suit the conditions that you encounter.

- *Torso.* For a weekend tour or longer brevet, two wicking layers, one jersey, perhaps a thermal vest or heavy jersey, and a windbreaker or raincoat are sufficient. For longer events the chances of getting wet increase, and changing your wicking layer into a dry jersey feels great. Alternatively, you can wear a wool undershirt and wool jersey because wool stays warm even when wet. Wool clothing is particularly appropriate for longer brevets.

- *Legs.* For a weeklong tour or longer brevet, you may want better leg protection than you use for shorter rides. Take leg warmers or tights rather than knee warmers and consider taking rain or wind pants.

- *Extremities.* At a minimum take a thin balaclava, glove liners, toe covers, and a motel shower cap. A wind shell over your cycling gloves and liners or full-fingered gloves will keep your hands warmer. Lobster mitts, which keep the first two fingers in one bundle and the third and little fingers in another, are warmer than gloves. For your feet you may want full foot booties that fit over your shoes and up your ankles, but don't get tight booties for racers that impede circulation. To keep your hands and feet warm in extremely cold conditions, you can use small chemical packets that generate heat when opened. They heat up over 100 °F (38 °C), so do not put them directly on your skin because they may burn you.

Safety: Riding on Wet Roads

Even if you don't live in a rainy climate, you may have to ride in the rain, especially when you do longer events. These tips will help you ride safely:

- ▶ *Visibility*—Rain and fog make you less visible to drivers, so be sure to wear bright clothing. Also, remember that your own vision is affected by wet conditions.

- ▶ *Eyes*—Clear or yellow lenses for your cycling glasses protect your eyes.

- ▶ *Braking distance*—Even with the best brakes, water on the rims reduces the coefficient of friction and slowing down takes longer. Brake early. Squeeze lightly at first to skim surface water off the rims and then brake more firmly.

- ▶ *Traction*—Similarly, your tires don't grip as well when wet. If you brake hard you are more likely to skid.

- ▶ *Anticipate*—Poorer visibility, longer braking distance, and less traction make it more important to keep an eye peeled for traffic and obstacles.

- ▶ *Cornering*—In the previous chapter we recommended leaning the bike when you corner, which works well on dry roads. On wet roads lean your body into the corner while keeping the bike more upright.

- ▶ *Grit and glass*—Damp roads make grit and glass harder to see and more likely to adhere to your tires. Clean your tires frequently with your gloved hands to reduce the probability of flats.

- ▶ *Water-filled potholes*—Try to avoid riding into a water-filled pothole because you don't know how deep it is, what the bottom surface is like, or how sharp the edges are.

- ▶ *Stay warm and dry*—If you are caught without rain gear, improvise! A large garbage bag with holes torn for the arms and head will protect your torso. Plastic grocery bags over your socks but inside your shoes will keep your feet dry. Use tape or rubber bands to secure them around your ankles so they aren't caught in the chain. Extra-large dishwashing gloves over your regular gloves will keep your hands dry.

Your outer layers for your torso, legs, and extremities should be readily accessible if cold or rain is even a remote possibility. If you are riding in cold or wet conditions, keep your dry off-bike clothes accessible so you can get out of your wet clothes quickly.

Lighting

Ask 10 randonneur or touring cyclists which lighting system is best, and you'll get 10 different answers. You can start with simple lights that bolt onto your handlebars and seat stays. You can supplement these with redundant lights, more powerful units, or a front hub that generates powers for the lights, and perhaps a helmet lamp. Even if you don't plan to ride at night, get a good system. In inclement weather, lights improve your ability to see and attract the attention of motorists. On a tour you might have to ride late to reach a campsite or make a run at dusk to get supplies. You can use a battery-powered handlebar unit or helmet lamp around camp at night. Longer brevets require lights, and you probably will be training at night. Don't skimp.

In the United States, vehicle codes require lights and reflectors from before sunset until after sunrise. Check with your local jurisdiction to find out what specific laws apply. Sanctioning organizations and event organizers may have additional rules.

Consider the pros and cons of generator units and battery units presented in table 10.4. For more information on generators, see the article on testing the efficiency of generator hubs in the resources section.

TABLE 10.4 **Advantages and Disadvantages of Batteries and Generators**

Generator unit advantages	Generator unit disadvantages
Generally produce more light than battery units unless heavy batteries are used.	Low light output at slow speeds, such as when climbing, and thus less visible to motorists.
Amount of light increases as speed increases.	Works only when moving; not visible to motorists when stopped.
No batteries required; carrying spares isn't necessary.	Headlamp can't be used to illuminate bike for repairs.
	Generators drag, which is most noticeable at slow speeds.*
Battery unit advantages	**Battery unit disadvantages**
Headlights and taillights work when moving slowly or stopped.	Not as bright as generator sets at higher speeds.
Often lighter in weight.	Batteries run down; if not assured of easy resupply, need to carry extra batteries.
Can be used to illuminate bike for repairs and around camp.	

*Riding at 6 mph (10 km/h), a generator hub would slow you by about 1 mph (1.6 km/h). Riding at 15 mph (24 km/h), it would slow you by about .6 mph (.9 km/h).

When choosing and installing a lighting system from among the many options available, consider these factors:

- *Light output.* A headlight and taillight that meet legal requirements also meet the brevet rules, but a more powerful headlight allows you to see farther ahead to anticipate problems and makes you more visible. You can further increase your ability to see by using two headlamps, one aimed farther down the road as the high beam, which you turn on when riding fast.

- *Reliability.* Check the reliability of any system before buying it. Talk with other riders, use the Web, and visit bike shops to look at the options.

- *Lower headlights.* Light from a unit mounted on the fork crown or near the front hub makes it easier to see what's on the road surface compared with a light mounted on your handlebars or helmet.

- *Redundant lights.* If you break a derailleur or a wheel goes out of true, you can still finish, but if your lights fail your ride is over. In brevets you are not allowed to ride at night or in low-visibility conditions without working front and rear lights mounted on the bike. A pair of headlights and taillights double your visibility and provide backup in case a unit dies; however, they add weight. Or you could have a lightweight backup headlight in case your main unit fails.

- *Helmet-mounted light.* A hiking headlamp mounted on your helmet helps you read street signs, cue sheets, and electronics as well as search through your bags and work on your bike without a flashlight. Be careful to mount it in a way that does not compromise the integrity of the helmet or present a risk of injury in case of a crash. Headlamps also supplement your bike's lighting system and help you stay visible to other riders and motorists. Headlamps should be used with caution as supplemental lights, because they can distract, or even blind, fellow riders. Even with a helmet lamp, by law you still must have a front light mounted on the bike. Brevet rules allow helmet lights, but you must have a functioning headlight mounted on the bike.

- *Spare batteries and bulbs.* As batteries run down, light output decreases. The light may become so dim that brevet officials will not let you continue. Standard AAA, AA, or C batteries are available at minimarts and controls. If you use another kind of battery you may need to carry spares. Bulb models vary considerably, so even if you don't carry spare batteries take spare bulbs.

- *Rechargeable batteries.* Many units feature rechargeable batteries. In general, the brighter the light is, the heavier the battery is and the shorter the burn time is before recharging is needed. Commuters often use bright, rechargeable lights, which typically have only enough power for one to six hours, making these lights unsuitable for touring and longer brevets.

- *Aim your taillight.* If you mount the light parallel to the seat stays, it may be pointing at the sky! If you hang it from your seat pack, it may be shining on the ground. Can cars really see you?

- *Flashing taillight.* It may be more visible to cars but obnoxious to other riders. Check your state laws and use flashing lights with caution. For brevets at least one taillight must be in the steady state mode.

- *It's not just lights.* Use reflective tape, wear reflective clothing, and put reflectors on your bike. Reflective material is best on moving parts—wheels, spokes, cranks, ankle bands, heels of shoes. Brevets require a reflective vest or sash.

You can never be too bright at night—light up like a Christmas tree!

Coach John's Lighting System

John has been enjoying night riding for over 30 years. As the technology has evolved so have his equipment choices. He now uses this system:

▶ A front generator hub to power two headlights. He aims one farther down the road to provide a high beam and switches it on when needed.

▶ In case the generator fails, a small battery light on the handlebars, which uses AA batteries.

▶ A mountaineering headlamp on his helmet with a separate battery pack and a wire long enough to put the batteries in a jersey pocket to reduce the weight on his head. The unit uses the same AA batteries as the handlebar light.

▶ A pair of taillights on the seat stays, which use AAA batteries and can be set for flashing or steady light output.

▶ Reflective Velcro ankle bands and a reflective triangle hanging from his seat pack or hydration pack.

▶ Reflective red tape on all four sides of his helmet.

▶ Reflective red tape around the cranks and on the sides and rear of the seat stays.

▶ Reflective white tape on the sides and front of the forks.

▶ Reflective red tape across pairs of spokes.

Nutrition

During your shorter events and long training workouts, you ironed out the details of your nutrition. Remember to use nothing new for your big events. Test your food and drink choices beforehand. Find out from the organizers whether they provide food. If they do, learn what kinds of food they will provide at rest stops, at brevet controls, and at tour meals. For an unsupported brevet or multiday tour, research the availability of stores en route and prepare accordingly.

Three or four days before your event, increase your intake of carbohydrate and reduce the amount of fat. As described in chapter 7, elevate your glycogen stores by getting 70 to 75 percent of your total calories from carbohydrate, 15 to 20 percent from fat, and the remaining 10 percent from protein.

Final Preparation

Leading up to your event or tour, you should practice every aspect of the event to gain confidence and work out any last-minute details.

Train with anticipated loads because your bike will handle differently loaded with gear. Climbing, pedaling while standing, braking, cornering, and descending will all be different, so on training rides load your bags or trailer and get used to it.

Ride at night to prepare for a long brevet. Night riding can feel quite peaceful with the stars and moon and fewer cars, but it takes practice to become comfortable. To test your lights and your ability to see and navigate at night, plan some of your training rides so you either start or finish in the dark. You may want to take your first few rides on familiar roads close to home in case you run into problems.

Practice after-dark repairs. Because you can't see as well at night, a puncture from invisible glass becomes more likely. Sit in your backyard some evening and practice fixing a flat by the light of your bike headlamp or helmet lamp.

Simulate your event on the weekend rides in each of the training programs. Take these opportunities to practice pacing, eating and drinking the right amounts, and managing your off-bike time. Avoid the temptation to postpone a training ride because of the weather. Instead, relish the opportunity to test your gear. Unless the weather is downright dangerous, events usually proceed as scheduled.

Two weeks before the start of an event you should either inspect your bike yourself or have a shop check it to make sure that everything is operating correctly. If you have a shop do this, explain what kind of an event you plan to do. Refer back to Table 7.1 (page 137) for specifics on what to check on the bike or go online to http://tinyurl.com/49ha5wb.

On the Road

While training for Paris–Brest–Paris years ago, John and his friend Warren discovered that if one of them wasn't having fun, he probably hadn't eaten recently! They were developing athletic maturity.

Cyclists who have acquired a good degree of mastery of their training, equipment, and cycling technique often find that nutrition and mental skills become more important factors in their ability to complete and enjoy their events.

Nutrition

On the morning of the start, have the same preride breakfast that you eat before your weekly long rides, even if you feel nervous, at least an hour before the start. Avoid starting on an empty stomach because making up those calories will be difficult.

Then, start eating in the first hour of the event. We recommend eating a mix of carbohydrate totaling 240 to 360 calories every hour plus a bit of protein and fat. If you get behind on your eating schedule, you could run into trouble later in the day. If necessary, set your watch to remind you. Stick to familiar foods while riding and at rest stops. Fresh baked cookies, brownies, and other treats may seem appetizing, but if your system is not used to them, you may have some digestive distress. Drink to satisfy your thirst but don't overdrink. Be alert for signs of bloating. Follow the same nutrition routine that you have been using for your long rides; if it worked in training, it probably will work during the event. But if a particular food becomes unappetizing or upsets your stomach, try something different. Remember that you want foods that are high in carbohydrate. Although foods with a lot of fat and protein may taste good, they also take longer to digest.

If you neglect your nutrition in the first few hours of brevets, the rest of the event will be tough or may be impossible. If you don't pay attention to your daily intake during the first couple days of a tour, you may develop chronic glycogen depletion and have trouble getting through the rest of the trip. On brevets or extended tours, you will have many hours (or days) of riding. You must support that effort with solid daily nutrition on and off the bike. Remember, calories taken in should equal calories expended over each 24-hour period.

On longer tours, postride recovery nutrition becomes more important. When you get off the bike each day, immediately start drinking and within the next several hours eat 500 to 1,000 calories of a moderate- to high-glycemic-index carbohydrate along with

Before a tour, brevet, or other long event I develop the three ride plans: good ride, great day, and struggling some. From the scenario for the good ride I know about how long the event will take and my projected time on and off the bike. I then estimate my caloric needs based on my weight of 190 pounds (86 kg):

On a multiday supported tour I'll ride six hours at 15 miles per hour (24 km/h), burning 4.5 calories per pound per hour, and spend the rest of each day relaxing, eating, or sleeping.

Basal metabolism rate (BMR)	190 lb × 10	1,900 calories
Light activities of daily living	30% of BMR	600 calories
6 h of riding at 15 mph	190 lb × 4.5 × 6 h	5,100 calories
		Total 7,600 calories

Assumptions for brevets of 400 kilometers or longer:

▶ 400-kilometer finish in 20:30; 600-kilometer finish in 36:00

▶ Average 21.5 km/h (13.5 mph) on the bike, burning 3.7 calories per pound per hour

▶ Stop every 2 hours at a minimart for quick resupply; stop every 4 hours at a control; 2 hours total off-the-bike time per 24 hours

▶ For brevets of 600 kilometers or longer add 4:30 off the bike every 24 hours for a sleep break (3 hours of actual sleep)

Basal metabolism rate	190 lb × 10	1,900 calories
Very light activities of daily living (almost always riding)	10% of BMR	200 calories
During first 24 h of 600-kilometer brevet, ride 17.5 h at 21.5 km/h	190 lb × 3.7 × 17.5 h	12,300 calories
		Total 14,400 calories

Some argue that the human body can digest a maximum of 300 calories per hour, but recent research indicates one can digest up to 360 calories of carbohydrate per hour if the carbohydrate includes a mix of types, e.g., glucose and fructose (Jeukendrup, 2010). I ate up to 500 calories per hour including some protein and fat when I raced RAAM, and I have coached RAAM riders who did the same. On your long rides you can accustom your digestive system to process more food per hour, especially if you nibble frequently during each hour. I base my nutrition plans on eating 350 to 450 calories per hour on the bike.

On the tour I burn about 850 calories per hour. Every hour on the bike I try to consume about 400 calories, although I eat less if I'm climbing or it's hot and more if I'm descending or it's cool. I run a deficit of 450 calories per hour over six hours for a total deficit of 2,700 calories while riding. I also need 2,500 calories for the rest of the 24 hours, so I need to consume 5,200 calories when not riding during each day.

On the 600-kilometer brevet, while pedaling I use about 700 calories and consume about 450 calories every hour. So my deficit is 250 calories per hour, or 4,400 for 17:30 of riding. Add 2,100 calories for my BMR and minimal off-the-bike activities, and I need a whopping 6,500 calories

(continued)

in addition to what I eat on the bike. On either a tour or brevet I get enough calories by grazing all day. Here's how I do it:

▶ *Breakfast.* 750 to 1,000 calories consisting of a muffin or bagel with jam or cereal or pancakes, juice, milk or yogurt, and fruit on a tour. To save time on a brevet I have several servings of a meal replacement drink and sports gel supplemented by a piece of fruit or bagel.

▶ *Hourly on the bike.* 400 calories (tour) to 450 calories (brevet). On both a tour and a brevet, I ride with two 24-ounce (750 ml) bottles. One has Gatorade; the full bottle contains 180 calories. The other has water. I drink at least half of each bottle every hour (90 calories) and eat another 350 to 400 calories. I like fruit, crackers, pretzels, granola bars, and fruit Newtons. I also carry sports gel for times when I need a boost or when I'm climbing and chewing real food is hard.

▶ *Rest stop or minimart.* 250 to 500 calories (tour) or 500 to 750 calories (brevet). I eat the same kinds of things that I do on the bike: fruit, crackers, pretzels, granola bars, and fruit Newtons. But I eat variations. If I've been eating granola bars on the bike, I get some Wheat Thins, another favorite. On a brevet I have a high-calorie, easily digestible drink such as a Frappuccino (for the caffeine), chocolate milk, or fruit juice.

▶ *Lunch.* 1,000 calories (tour) to 750 calories (brevet). On a tour I chose the high-carbohydrate options: a sandwich on multigrain bread, pasta salad, fruit, and dessert. For lunch on a brevet, I buy and drink another high-calorie beverage at a store and get a sandwich and cookies to eat on the bike. If I eat more than 500 calories at a rest stop or lunch, I ride at an easy pace for a while to allow the food to digest and my legs to warm up again.

▶ *Recovery.* 500 to 1,000 calories. On a tour I start eating even before I take off my bike shoes. I start with V-8 and chips, both of which provide calories and sodium, and then continue with pretzels (less fat than chips) and water (I'm usually tired of Gatorade).

▶ *Dinner.* 1,000 calories (tour) to 750 calories (brevet). Even on a strenuous tour, I don't need a lot of protein. I get a fresh salad, a nice change from all the grain products that I've been eating, and a pasta dish. On a brevet I buy dinner at a minimart to eat while pedaling onward, again trying for variety and emphasizing carbohydrate. I eat smaller meals on brevets than on tours because they are on the run.

▶ *Prebed snack.* 250 calories (tour) to 1,000 calories (brevet). On a tour I enjoy walking to get ice cream with friends, which offers a chance to stretch my legs and eat more! On a brevet I eat a lot before my sleep break so I can digest while sleeping. I may eat a quick meal in a control, a meal replacement drink from my drop bag, cereal from the motel's breakfast bar, or delivery pizza.

▶ *Midnight snack.* I also keep something by the bed in case I wake up with the munchies.

Riders often say, "But I don't feel like eating." Sometimes I don't feel like pedaling, but I keep pedaling if I want to finish the event. I keep eating and drinking with the same consistency. Consuming all the calories that I burn on a brevet is difficult, but I don't worry if I'm a little short because I can also burn body fat. Remember, however, that fat burns in the flame of glycogen, so you still need plenty of carbohydrate.

a bit of protein to help you recover. Don't wait to start replenishing your fuel stores. If solid food seems unappealing, have a smoothie-type shake or a recovery drink. Then eat a good dinner, still emphasizing carbohydrate, and perhaps have a snack before bed. Keep some food and water handy at night in case you wake up and are hungry. Start the next day with a good breakfast.

On brevets of 400 kilometers and longer, you'll ride better if your three event scenarios include a specific quantified plan of how much to consume and when so that you take in enough calories. Plan on 240 to 360 calories from carbohydrate plus a little protein and fat every hour on the bike and somewhat more at controls. Some riders eat sit-down meals at controls, but remember that this practice cuts into your time for a sleep break. Before a sleep break eat 500-1,000 calories primarily of carbohydrate and drink some fluid. This is the only recovery break you get. Then consume 300-500 calories primarily of carbohydrate before getting back on the bike. If your event has a drop bag service, consider sending ahead easy-to-digest meal replacement drinks such as Ensure Plus, which has 350 calories per serving, for your prebed meal and breakfast. Some meal replacement drinks are also available in powdered form, which you can send ahead or carry.

Mental Management

You've developed your ride scenarios, visualized the event, and practiced your power words. Have confidence in your ride plan and your preparations; you have trained to deal with whatever comes your way. Ride your ride following your plan. As you pedal onward periodically assess what type of ride you are having and adjust if necessary.

If you run into problems while on the road, don't panic. Draw on the problem-solving skills that you have practiced. Take a minute to relax and then diagnose the issue. Think the situation through. You can solve almost any problem. If you can't solve it, you probably can adapt to ride in spite of it.

Keep a good mental attitude while riding through the inevitable tough times. You may pedal alone in the dark, get wet or cold, and encounter problems. Use your relaxation skills and power words to help you focus on what you can control. Ignore the rest. Try to find something positive about the current situation or think about better times to come.

Follow your overnight routine. Whether on a tour or brevet, you will feel more in control if you follow a plan for your off-the-bike time: your recovery, meals, hygiene, sleeping arrangements, gear organization, and so on. Your plan ensures that nothing is overlooked and allows more time for relaxation and sleep.

Putting the Pieces Together

You feel excited, and perhaps nervous, at the start of any cycling event. Try to relax. You have practiced each piece of the ride first; now you just put them together. In chapter 8 you learned how to train for and ride all-day events. In chapter 9 you took those skills and learned how to pace yourself through and manage events that include overnight stops. Now just apply those same skills to longer events.

- *Watch your pace.* As we keep emphasizing, ride at a comfortable pace. These events have no awards for coming in first, so relax and enjoy your ride. Use heart rate, watts, or RPE purposefully to keep the pace down and conserve your energy because you will be riding for many hours (or days). Start at the same pace that you rode your long training rides, or slower.

- *Enjoy a group.* Find a group and chat. The time usually goes by a lot faster when riding with others, and you might make new friends. If you can ride and maintain a normal conversation, you're at the right pace. If you struggle to talk, the group is probably too fast, so drop back and find another group. In a group remember the safety tips for group riding from chapter 3 (see page 24).

- *Riding at night or while fatigued.* Be extra careful with group riding when you are fatigued, especially at night. At night, the distance from other riders may be more difficult to judge and fatigue increases your reaction time.

- *Manage time off the bike.* At rest stops, grab some food, refill your bottles, use the restroom if you need to, and get back on the road fairly quickly to keep your mental and physical rhythm. At the end of the day, stick to your overnight routine.

- *Sleep considerations.* On brevets the shorter you keep the stops, the more time you'll have for a sleep break. You can't train physiologically to need less sleep, but you can learn to manage with less sleep. How much sleep deprivation can be tolerated and which time of night is most troublesome varies from person to person. Some riders do better if they ride until the wee hours and then sleep until dawn. Others do better if they take a sleep break in the middle of the night and then start to ride again a few hours before sunrise. The brain cycles from light to deep sleep, typically in about 90 minutes. If you try to wake up during a sleep cycle, you will be groggy. You can estimate your sleep cycle by noticing when you wake up during the night. If you wake up after five hours of sleep to use the bathroom, then your sleep cycle is probably 300 minutes (5 hours) divided by 3, or 100 minutes. Plan your sleep breaks so that they are one or more full sleep cycles.

- *Equipment.* Perform the rest stop checks and nightly bike checks described in chapter 9 (pages 192–193). On a tour with mechanical support get help for any problems you may have.

After the Event

First off—congratulations! Riding a tour or brevet is no easy task. When all the good-byes have been said and you've had time to relax, reflect on the experience. What did you like? Would you have done anything differently either in preparation or during the event itself? Keep records of your events, both objective (distance, average speed, amount of climbing, and so on) and subjective (emotions and feelings). The more rides you do, the more knowledge you can apply to future events.

After an extended tour or series of brevets, take time to allow your body to recover before resuming any significant riding. Recovery needs vary, but as a rule take one week of recovery for every week of a tour. If you have completed a two-week tour, allow two weeks of active recovery before resuming normal training. After a brevet series give yourself at least a couple of weeks of easy riding after the 600-kilometer event. Don't force yourself to get back on the bike; you should want to start riding again before you begin working out. Until then play with family or friends, go hiking, do some cross-training, or try something new. You will know when the time comes to train again; don't force it. Don't lose sight of the big picture. Whether you're riding in one-day events or riding across your country, keep it fun!

In this chapter we discussed preparing and training for long-distance multiday events, both tours and brevets. Whether you ride a single-day event, a weekend tour, a longer brevet, or a multiday tour, the concepts remain the same. By applying our six factors of success—goal setting and planning, training, equipment, nutrition, technique, and mental skills—you can prepare for and master virtually any cycling challenge.

Lots of distance in the saddle puts a smile on the face, but aches and pains may also result. No one plans to get injured, but that may happen. In the next chapter we look at some of the common cycling problems and what to do if you encounter them. More important, we discuss some preventive measures to keep you riding happily.

CHAPTER 11

Preventing Injury

No one likes to think about getting hurt. Cycling is easy on the joints and suitable for nearly everybody, but distance cycling requires a lot of training, and the more you ride, the greater the chance you have of being injured. Cycling injuries range in severity from relatively minor problems such as sunburn to potentially life-threatening traumatic injuries. In this chapter we discuss three common injury types—overuse injuries, environmental problems, and accidents— as well as steps you can take to reduce the probability and severity of injuries including key concepts regarding bike fit, training, and recovery. We also offer information to help you identify possible causes for the complaints most often cited by cyclists.

Although we offer suggestions for preventing and alleviating common problems, you should consult a health care professional soon after an injury or accident to ensure proper treatment, prevent further damage, and reduce your time off the bike. A truck made a sudden left turn and hit a good friend of John's last year, an experienced, safe rider. Mike had bruises and road rash, but because nothing was broken, he finished the full brevet series and rode the rest of the season. When he finally had MRIs done and consulted an orthopedic surgeon, he found that he needed wrist and hip surgery and would be off the bike for six months to a year.

Overuse Injuries

Overuse injuries result from repetitive submaximal loading of a particular musculoskeletal part, creating fatigue of the tendons or inflammation of surrounding tissues. Endurance athletes are particularly vulnerable. During a four-hour ride averaging 85 revolutions per minute, each of your legs will go through 20,400 flexion and extension cycles! If you have any biomechanical abnormalities, muscle imbalances, or bike fit imperfections or if you push too big a gear, over time this repetitive stress could cause damage resulting in pain. Overuse injuries can result from intrinsic factors or extrinsic factors (see table 11.1 on page 226) and result in pain, dysfunction, or both.

The severity of these injuries progresses in four stages:

Stage 1: Pain after activity only

Stage 2: Pain during activity but does not restrict performance

Stage 3: Pain during activity that restricts performance

Stage 4: Chronic, unremitting pain, even at rest

TABLE 11.1 **Intrinsic and Extrinsic Factors in Overuse Injuries**

Intrinsic factors in overuse injuries	Extrinsic factors in overuse injuries
Malalignment of limbs or problematic foot structure (high or low arch)	Improper bike fit
Muscular imbalances	Training errors
Body weight	Incorrect equipment
Previous injuries	Poor technique

This overview, drawn from our years of experience as coaches, lists overuse injuries common among cyclists by body part. We discuss ways that you can prevent these problems by adjusting your training, technique, bike, equipment, and clothing. But if you suspect that you have an injury (a persistent stage 1 or stage 2 condition), or feel one developing, seek medical care as soon as you can so that the injury doesn't worsen. Your health care provider may refer you to an orthopedic specialist, physical therapist, or a licensed athletic trainer, depending on the type and severity of the injury. For detailed information on these and other conditions, we recommend that you consult *Andy Pruitt's Medical Guide for Cyclists* (Pruitt & Matheny, 2006).

Butt Injuries

- Saddle sores result from excess pressure, shear force, moisture, or temperature. The pain could be because of pressure on the ischial tuberosities (sitz bones), chafing, infected hair follicles, skin ulcerations, or numbness (Pruitt & Matheny, 2006).

If you carry extra weight, you are putting excessive pressure on your buttocks. Women have a different pelvic structure than men do and generally need a different saddle. If you have a leg-length discrepancy, your shorter leg may be overreaching for the pedal, causing chafing on that side of the crotch against the saddle. Look for unusual wear on the saddle.

Conditioning   You shouldn't sit on a saddle; you should straddle it. Your legs should be strong enough to support your pedaling motion, so most of your weight doesn't rest on the saddle. If you have a weak core your weight won't be distributed properly between the saddle and handlebars. If you aren't flexible enough to bend forward comfortably, too much weight will be on your butt.

Technique   Sitting all the time puts more pressure on your buttocks. Even on a flat road get out of the saddle every 10 to 15 minutes to relieve the pressure and restore circulation. If you pedal with a flat foot throughout the stroke but your saddle height is set for an ankling motion, you are putting extra pressure on the buttocks.

Saddle choice   Saddles range from light, narrow, racing models to leather touring models with suspension springs. Buttocks are as individual as faces. Try various saddles to find one that fits you. The correct saddle for you has a width that supports your weight on your sitz bones rather than your crotch. Don't get a saddle that is too soft; when your sitz bones sink into it, the saddle will put pressure on your crotch. You should slide smoothly on the saddle; a soft saddle causes more friction than a firm saddle. If you get a leather saddle, follow the manufacturer's guidelines to break it in.

Saddle position Saddle sores often result from improper bike fit. A saddle that is too high will cause you to rock excessively as your legs reach for the pedals on each stroke. If the saddle tip is tilted down too much, you'll constantly slide forward and push yourself back up. A nose that is too high puts pressure on the crotch.

Handlebar position If the handlebars are too high or too close to the saddle, you will sit too upright, which puts more weight on your buttocks. If you have a touring style frame, pay particular attention because these frames are designed for a more upright posture.

Clothing Bike shorts can cause discomfort and saddle sores. Like saddles, shorts should fit your anatomy. Shorts that bunch up easily, have the wrong chamois cut or uncomfortable seams, or don't allow freedom of movement will cause problems. Don't skimp on shorts. Quality shorts may be more expensive but will outlast other shorts and be cheaper in the long run. Use petroleum jelly to prevent chafing between the chamois and your skin. Although more expensive preparations are available, petroleum jelly is inexpensive, works well, and unlike other lubricants contains no additives that might irritate sensitive skin.

Knee Injuries

- *Chrondomalacia*. A degenerative condition of the patella (kneecap) resulting from excessive compressive or shear forces on the knee. You will feel pain or a grinding sensation or sound when squatting or pushing big gears. Abnormal foot mechanics may be a contributing factor.
- *Tendinitis*. Inflammation of the tendon (tendons connect muscle tissue to bone) or tendon sheath, characterized by pain and swelling with tendon movement in the hip, knee, or ankle. Prolonged chronic inflammation may result in the accumulation of mineral deposits. Tendinitis results from doing too much too soon as you ramp up your weekly volume, add resistance in the weight room, or increase intensity.
- *Spring knee*. A type of tendinitis characterized by pain above the kneecap, the result of too much too soon in the spring.
- *Iliotibial band friction syndrome*. The iliotibial band (IT band) is a thick, fibrous tissue that runs along the outside of the thigh from the top of the hip joint to just below the knee. The IT band provides lateral (side-to-side) stability for the knee. While riding, the IT band passes over the protrusion on the outside of the lower thigh bone. The resulting friction can lead to pain if the IT band is tight or malalignment is present.
- *Pes anserine bursitis*. An inflammation of bursae, the fluid-filled sacs that reduce friction in the tissues surrounding joints. Cyclists who have tight hamstrings and calves are susceptible to bursitis in the knee, which results in local swelling that may be point tender and warm to the touch.

Abnormal mechanics related to leg-length discrepancies, bow legs, knock knees, or muscle imbalance could lead to knee pain. Women have a wider pelvic structure, which affects the angle at which the femur meets the tibia. Pedals too close to the centerline of the bike can contribute to knee stress. You need a trained eye to spot and correct biomechanical issues. If you know or suspect that you have one, seek the advice of a health care professional.

Conditioning Pedaling higher gears takes more muscle strength. If you lack sufficient strength, you put more stress on the knees. Muscle imbalance also puts strain on the knees. Cycling develops the quadriceps more than it does the gluteus and hamstring muscles. The gluteus and hamstring muscles wrap around the knees and help to stabilize them. By strength training regularly with the exercises in chapter 3 and following the in-season maintenance training described in chapter 6, you strengthen the muscles that promote optimal joint stability.

Training Ramping up too quickly can overload your knee joint and cause spring knee, tendinitis, bursitis, chondromalacia, or ITB friction syndrome. Gradually increase your training volume and intensity by following our recommended programs.

Technique While riding, concentrate on good form. Pedaling in smooth circles (think spin rather than stomp) reduces the stress on your knees. Maintaining a higher cadence in a lower gear (particularly while climbing) puts less strain on your knees.

Bike fit. A saddle that is too low or too far forward increases compressive forces on the patella (kneecap). A saddle that is too high can cause pain behind the knee and strain the hamstring tendons. A pedal with no rotation doesn't allow the knee to move laterally during the pedal stroke, and a pedal with too much rotation causes the muscles and tendons to work too hard trying to stabilize the knee. Your cleats need to be positioned properly, especially if you have any leg-length or anatomical issues. A crank arm that is too long or too short will affect your pedaling mechanics. When you get a new bike or new piece of equipment or change your riding style, get your bike properly fitted to you. If you have any injury problems or biomechanical abnormalities, a fitting with a medical specialist familiar with cyclists may be best.

Clothing The knees have poor circulation, so they chill easily, which increases the risk of injury. Wear warmers until it is at least 60 °F (16 °C).

Foot and Ankle Injuries

- *Tendinitis*. The Achilles tendon at the back of the ankle may become inflamed.
- *Hot feet*. Compression of the nerves in the foot results in a sensation of heat, which may become searing pain.
- *Blisters*. Caused by friction, a blister can escalate from a minor annoyance to a broken, open sore if untreated.

Feet are like fingerprints—everyone's are different. Yours may have high or low arches, or be wide or narrow. The mechanics of your foot have a direct effect on the joints above, and injuries to the knee or hip may result from abnormal foot mechanics. If you have foot problems, your health care provider may recommend a visit to a podiatrist.

Conditioning Weak ankle muscles put more stress on the foot and ankle. General lower-body strengthening exercises such as lunges and wall squats along with exercises that target the feet and ankles such as standing and seated heel raises increase the overall integrity of your ankle joints.

Technique Good pedaling mechanics reduce the stress on your feet and ankles, but if you develop Achilles tendinitis, then pedaling with a flat foot rather than ankling will reduce the irritation during the flare-up. If you start to ride with a flat foot, lower your saddle to compensate.

Bike fit A saddle that is too high causes you to ankle excessively to reach the pedals, which puts more stress on the foot and ankle. Cleat position has a big effect on your foot and ankle, so have a knowledgeable specialist help you position your cleats properly. A cleat that is too far forward puts stress on your Achilles tendon.

Clothing   A cleat that is too small may put too much pressure on the bottom of your foot, causing hot feet. Tight shoes may also cause hot feet. Shop for shoes at the end of the day because feet tend to swell as the day progresses. If you wear orthotics, take them with you to check the fit. Note that European road cycling shoes tend to be narrow. Thick socks also cause pressure and friction, resulting in blisters. Try on shoes with the type of socks you normally wear while riding. If you ride a lot in winter, consider getting shoes that are slightly larger to accommodate thicker socks. For ultra endurance events such as longer brevets consider getting a larger pair of shoes to accommodate more swelling.

Low Back Injuries

- *Muscle strain.* Damage to the muscle or surrounding tendons causes a lower-back strain. This condition can result from activities of daily living, poor biomechanics, or sports activities. Symptoms of a muscle strain include swelling, bruising (in more severe instances) or redness at the site of injury, sharp pain, limited range of motion, and weakness.

Muscle tightness or weakness can predispose you to lower-back pain. A weak core or tight hamstrings put unnecessary stress on your lower back. Leg-length discrepancies and other anatomical differences can cause low-back problems. If you have any issues, your health care provider may refer you to a physical therapist.

Conditioning   Throughout the book we emphasize strengthening your core and improving your flexibility. Doing these exercises won't take much of your time and will protect your lower back, so be consistent.

Training   Gradually increase your training volume and intensity to allow the muscles of your lower back to adapt to the additional load.

Technique   While riding, avoid staying in one position too long. Move around in the saddle, stand up, and use different positions on the handlebars. Try to relax while you are riding because relaxing reduces tension in all your muscles. On the bike, you can do a modified version of the cat stretch, as described in chapter 3. The activities of daily living can also cause back pain. Practice good posture while sitting and standing. If you have a job that requires a lot of sitting, concentrate on your posture. Get up and walk around frequently. If you have to lift something, don't bend at the waist. Instead, squat and use the powerful muscles of your hips and legs to do the lifting.

Bike fit   A saddle that is too high forces you to reach excessively at the bottom of each pedal stroke, causing your pelvis to rock. Your lower back will try to stabilize the action. Handlebars or aerobars that are too low or too far forward result in increased tension in your lower back. With your hands on the brake hoods you should be able to ride with a fairly flat back rather than hunched over.

Neck and Shoulder Injuries

- *Muscle strain.* If you have strained one of your neck or shoulder muscles, you may notice pain, stiffness, or limited range of motion. This pain may be noticeable right away or develop over the course of a ride, and it can be constant or intermittent. For example, you may notice pain only when you turn your head to look for traffic behind you or while you are in the drops.

Muscle weakness or tightness can cause neck and shoulder problems. Your helmeted head is heavy, so all the muscles of your neck and shoulder have to work hard while riding. Long rides can be a literal pain in the neck.

Conditioning The upper-body strength exercises described in chapter 3 develop shoulder and neck strength for riding, which can be maintained with the in-season exercises described in chapter 6.

Training Gradually increase the duration of your training to allow the muscles of your neck and shoulder to adapt.

Technique Varying your position while riding will help your neck and shoulders as well as your lower back. You've learned to drink and eat frequently; change your position at the same time. Learn to ride with slightly bent elbows. Many riders unknowingly make a shrugging motion when riding into a headwind, climbing, or performing hard efforts; consciously let your shoulders fall. As with low-back problems, activities of daily living and poor posture can result in neck pain, so the problem may not be the bike.

Bike fit If your saddle and handlebars are too far apart, you have to reach excessively, putting more stress on your shoulders. If your bars are too low, pain may result. Experiment with different stem adjustments, the position of your brake hoods and try handlebars of various widths.

Hand and Wrist Injuries

- *Cyclist's palsy*. Compression of the ulnar nerve resulting in a tingling feeling, numbness, or pain in the ring and little finger, sometimes extending up the hand and forearm.
- *Carpal tunnel syndrome*. Compression of the median nerve causing pain, weakness, or numbness in the thumb and forefinger, sometimes radiating up the hand and the forearm.

Compression of the nerve may come from the pressure of the handlebars on your hands or from riding with cocked rather than straight wrists. Few identifiable intrinsic factors are associated with hand and wrist pain, but some people seem to be more prone to ulnar nerve irritation than others.

Conditioning Your core should be strong enough that your hands rest lightly on the handlebars, as if you were playing the piano or typing. Your resistance-training program also strengthens your wrists. Every time you hold a weight in your hands, you exercise all the flexor and extensor muscles of your wrists. If you have a job that requires a lot of typing or manual dexterity, you may be more prone to hand and wrist conditions.

Technique Vary your hand position while riding. Move your hands frequently among five different positions on the handlebars:

The flats, the top of the bars nearest you, with your fingers in front of the bars and your wrists straight, not flexed

The bends at the top, with your thumbs on the inside and your wrists straight

The brake hoods, either with the thumbs on the inside and all four fingers on the outside or the index fingers and thumbs on the inside, again with your wrists straight

The hooks behind the brake levers, although this position will cause you to flex
your wrists

The drops at the bottom of the bars with your wrists straight

Changing hand positions frequently also provides variety for your neck, shoulder, and
back muscles. You can use padded gloves, although too much padding may cause compression or friction.

Bike fit   Bikes with more fork rake or wider tires don't transmit as much road shock.
If you have a racing frame with a straight fork, you might install a fork with some rake.
Racing-style handlebars that are too low cause you to put excessive weight on your
hands and wrists. Newer anatomical handlebars disperse the pressure better. You can
also pad the bars to help cushion you from road shock and vibrations:

Wrap with two layers of handlebar tape.

Use tape with gel inside.

Put a layer of wetsuit material under the bar tape on the upper surfaces of the bars
where your hands rest.

Although you can't prevent all overuse injuries, you have a great deal of control
over the extrinsic factors of training, equipment, and technique. The intrinsic factors
can be addressed with proper medical help. Most overuse injuries result from training
errors, so adhere to the principles described in the book to stay healthy and enjoy the
time on your bike. Table 11.2 outlines strategies that you can use to reduce your risk of
developing an overuse injury.

TABLE 11.2   **Strategies for Avoiding Overuse Injuries**

- *Ramping.* Avoid doing too much, too soon; gradually increase training volume and intensity.
- *Bike fit.* Have your bike properly fitted and see a specialist if you have any biomechanical abnormalities. Get the fit rechecked periodically—aging, changes in strength or flexibility, injuries, and changes in cycling goals may warrant a different position.
- *Gear selection and use.* Get gears appropriate to your terrain and riding and avoid pushing gears that are too high.
- *Strength train.* Stronger muscles, ligaments, and tendons can withstand more force and can help reduce the risk of injury as well as help correct muscular imbalances.
- *Maintain flexibility.* When we ride we tend to sit in one position, and our legs move in one dimension with a limited range of motion. Inevitably, muscles get tight.
- *Cross-training.* Activities other than cycling strengthen the muscles in different ways and can make you a healthier person overall.
- *Protect your extremities.* The knees have poor circulation. If the temperature is below 60 °F (16 °C), wear tights or leg warmers. Some people are more susceptible to tendinitis in cold weather.
- *Select proper equipment.* Get a saddle, shoes, gloves, and bike components that fit your anatomy and replace them when worn out.
- *Alter your position.* Move around while riding.
- *Take breaks.* Walking around for a couple of minutes each hour or two can help.

By Michelle Grainger

Grainger took third in the 1990 Race Across America. She competed for over 10 years as a pro mountain bike racer. On her MTB she won Montezuma's Revenge 24-Hour (2001) and 24 Hours of Finale, Italy (2001, 2002, 2003), held course records at the Vail Ultra 100 (1999, 2001, 2002), and placed top seven at the Cape Epic (South Africa) seven-day stage race (2004). She is now an active randonneur. Grainger has 20 years of coaching experience, including training John. For more information visit www.athleticexcellence.net.

Cumulative fatigue is inevitable on a 200-kilometer or longer event. Even a multiday tour will bring on muscle and mental fatigue. It seeps into our legs and convinces us to check for rubbing brakes or the inevitable flat tire that isn't there. You can defer the onset of fatigue by staying in good physical shape all year including aerobic conditioning and muscular strength.

▶ Train sensibly with a gradual buildup of volume and intensity.

▶ Follow a plan that includes long, slower rides and sessions of intensity training.

▶ Include year round strength training.

Some of this painful feeling is delayed onset muscle soreness (DOMS). DOMS is caused by stress on your muscles, which results in deep-tissue muscle fatigue and fiber tears. After a strenuous ride or other intense workout the body works to repair mild muscle damage with increased blood flow to those muscles and the release of chemical irritants, which cause pain receptors to fire and the nerves in the muscle to send pain signals to the brain.

Continued muscle movement of less intensity will aid the process of repairing the muscles—hence the importance of active recovery. Age greatly influences how we recover daily, and throughout the season. The older we get, the less muscle tissue elasticity we have. Staying in good physical shape year round will improve your recovery.

After you accept the reality of DOMS and have taken steps to minimize it, you are more prepared for the challenge of longer multiday riding. Here are some tips on preparing for and addressing fatigue:

▶ Eat before your ride, during your ride, and especially as soon as your ride ends. Drink when you are thirsty.

▶ Stretch regularly before and during rides.

▶ If you know your route and the difficulty of the terrain, you can plan for rest stops and mental breaks.

▶ Focus on small goals such as riding to the next control or rest stop rather than thinking about the whole thing.

▶ Each ride builds on the prior one. If you have completed several 200-kilometer rides, you have the physical and mental foundation to break down a longer distance into smaller increments with the certainty that you can finish it section by section until the end.

▶ For longer brevets learn what happens to you when you get little sleep. You may never be able to ride 24 hours nonstop, but you should know your limits. You learn by incrementally increasing the length of your rides and testing your ability to stay focused on little sleep.

▶ We inevitably slow down with fatigue. We can't ride a 600-kilometer event with the same speed that we can achieve on shorter rides, and we can't ride 100 miles (160 km) on day 7 of a tour as fast as we can a single century. Recognize and accept this.

▶ To continue riding through muscle soreness stretch and massage the sore muscles, apply analgesic sports balms, and apply ice or soak in cold or hot tubs.

▶ Use over-the-counter anti-inflammatory aids (NSAIDs) with a doctor's guidance.

As fatigue builds, remember that performance degrades but then just levels off. Your legs will be tired but you can keep moving!

If you start to develop an overuse injury, don't try to ride through it because doing so may end your season. Take a few days off the bike to recover. To alleviate the immediate symptoms, use ice, stretch gently, and massage the affected part. To relieve inflammation, take NSAIDs following the instructions on the bottle. While you recover diagnose and address the underlying cause: improper training, poor bike fit, anatomical abnormality, faulty technique, and so on. You may need a medical, bike fit, or other expert to help you with the diagnosis and to recommend specific treatment.

Environmental Injuries

Long-distance cyclists often train and compete in conditions that have the potential for various environmental problems. Environmental injuries range from mild but annoying to serious and potentially life threatening. Heat-related problems range from cramping to heat exhaustion to heat stroke. Cold-related problems range from mild to severe hypothermia. Altitude-related problems range from discomfort to cerebral or pulmonary edema. In each case the key indicator is change in mental status. If someone is confused or disoriented, or has slurred speech or difficulty coordinating limbs, then the central nervous system is affected—a life-threatening emergency. Call 911. Even if you don't exercise in an extreme environment, problems can develop in relatively mild conditions. You should know how to protect yourself, assess risks, evaluate symptoms, and be prepared to take emergency action.

Heat-Related Injuries

- *Sunburn.* Sunburn can result from as little as 30 minutes of exposure to UV rays, and the risk increases as you gain altitude or cycle in an environment with bright, reflective surfaces. Use plenty of sunscreen (SPF greater than 15) on your exposed skin and lips, even on cloudy days, and reapply frequently. Fair-skinned and sun-sensitive riders should wear light-colored clothing and minimize the amount of exposed skin. Although most clothing reduces UV exposure it does not completely block UV rays; John once got sunburn through his cycling shorts after a day riding at altitude! Some companies now make SPF-rated cycling clothing from UV-resistant fabric.

- *Skin cancer.* This abnormal growth of skin cells most often occurs on areas of the skin exposed to the sun. Although on the rise, most skin cancers can be prevented by limiting exposure to UV radiation and monitoring any suspicious changes in the skin.

- *Eye injuries.* Excessive exposure to the sun over time causes cataracts to develop, a clouding of the lens that prevents you from seeing clearly. When riding, wear glasses with UV protection. Wraparound glasses also help keep airborne particles out of your eyes. Yellow lenses are available for cloudy days and clear lenses for night riding.

- *Cramps.* Cramping occurs when a muscle goes into involuntary spasm. This condition is caused by muscle fatigue and contracting an already shortened muscle. Cycling involves repetitive motions without full extension of the muscles unless you are standing, so as you fatigue you are prone to cramping, especially in the heat. Stretching at stops will help prevent cramps; see chapter 7, pages 142–143. Although not direct causes, dehydration and electrolyte depletion or imbalance may contribute to cramps. Pay close attention to your diet so that you start rides with your electrolytes in balance. While riding, you should drink to satisfy thirst, but not more.

● *Heat exhaustion.* You may suddenly feel more tired than usual when exercising in the heat. Exercising hard in a hot environment, particularly a humid one, makes you more prone to heat exhaustion. The signs and symptoms include the following:

Fatigue

Headache

Dizziness

Nausea

Profuse sweating

Cool, clammy skin

Ashen or gray skin

Slightly elevated body temperature

Rapid, weak pulse

If you suspect heat exhaustion, take these steps:

1. Stop exercising.
2. Get out of the sun and into a shady or air-conditioned location, if possible.
3. Lie down and elevate your legs and feet slightly.
4. Loosen or remove clothing.
5. Drink cool water or other nonalcoholic beverages without caffeine.
6. Spray or sponge your body with cool water. If someone else shows symptoms of heat exhaustion fan him or her and apply cool water.
7. Monitor the situation carefully. Heat exhaustion can quickly become heatstroke. If you don't start to feel better within an hour, get prompt medical attention (Mayo Clinic, *Heat Exhaustion*, n.d.).

Because the recommendations for preventing heat exhaustion are similar to those for preventing heat stroke, we provide them after describing heat stroke.

● *Heat stroke.* Heat stroke is the least common but most serious heat-related condition. It results from strenuous exercise in a hot environment combined with inadequate fluid intake. The body's cooling mechanisms fail to dissipate the rising core temperatures. As body temperature rises, the brain may be affected, resulting in loss of consciousness followed by brain damage. If untreated, death is imminent. Because of the effect on the brain, the key danger sign is change in mental status; if this occurs, immediately call 911. Heat stroke is a medical emergency. The symptoms include the following (Mayo Clinic, *Heat Stroke*, n.d.):

Disoriented, irritable, confused

Unconscious

Feeling dizzy or lightheaded, fainting

Initially heavy sweating; no profuse sweating in later stages

Hot, dry skin; may be moist if caused by exercise

Reddish skin

Body temperature increased markedly

Rapid heartbeat

> Rapid, shallow breathing
>
> Headache
>
> Nausea

You can reduce considerably the risk of heat exhaustion and heat stroke by taking these steps:

Acclimatization. As you acclimate, your body adapts to exercising in hot conditions, and physiological changes occur to help dissipate the heat generated by exercise. Adaptation results from the duration of exposure to heat, not the activity level, and it takes several weeks. Passive exposure is almost as effective as active exposure, so turn off the AC, open the windows, and get used to it!

Pacing. Unfortunately, our muscles aren't completely efficient and much of the energy consumed produces heat rather than forward motion. The hotter the day is, the more difficult it is to dissipate that heat, and in extremely hot conditions you may gain heat from the environment. Slow down!

Hydration. Your body disperses heat by sweating, so if you are thirsty, drink. Besides putting ice in your hydration pack or bottles, you can keep your fluids cooler by freezing your bottles the night before or wrapping them in wet socks.

Judgment. You always should assess when, or even whether, to ride. If the day will be hot, ride before breakfast. If you plan a long endurance ride, break it into two slightly faster tempo rides, one before breakfast and one after dinner, totaling less time.

Protection. Wear light-colored, breathable clothing.

Moderation. Limit caffeine and alcohol intake.

Monitor. As noted previously, the effects of heat exposure can be cumulative. To ensure that you are not developing heat exhaustion, note your weight before and after long rides. For every pound lost, replace with 16 fluid ounces of liquid (for every kilogram lost, replace with 1 liter of fluid).

Cold-Related Injuries

- *Exercise induced bronchospasm* (*EIB*). Formerly known as exercise-induced asthma, EIB affects many people when they exercise in cold, dry conditions. They have difficulty breathing, shortness of breath, coughing, chest tightness, and wheezing. If you are prone to EIB, covering your mouth and nose with a balaclava or something similar can help warm and humidify the air and potentially lessen the onset of symptoms. If that practice fails to provide relief, seek medical attention.

  Wind chill, the temperature that you feel, drops dramatically as the ambient temperature falls, the wind speed picks up, or both as evidenced by the data in table 11.3 on page 236.

- *Hypothermia*. If your body loses heat faster than it produces heat, your core starts to cool and hypothermia results. Most cases of hypothermia, a potentially fatal condition, happen when the temperature is around 40 °F (4 °C), not in the arctic or mountains. A little rain and the wind chill from your moving speed create potentially risky conditions if you aren't prepared. The causes of hypothermia include not wearing warm enough clothes, staying out in cold conditions too long, and not changing out of wet clothes. The symptoms of mild hypothermia are shivering and then loss of fine motor control, indicated by difficulty with tasks like zipping a

TABLE 11.3 Wind Chill While Riding

Ambient temperature	Riding at 15 mph (24 km/h) when there is	Wind chill
40 °F (4 °C)	no wind	32 °F (0 °C)
30 °F (–1 °C)	5 mph (8 km/h) head wind	17 °F (–8 °C)
20 °F (–7 °C)	15 mph (24 km/h) head wind	1° F (–17 °C)

From NOAA. Available: www.nws.noaa.gov/os/windchill/index.shtml

zipper. If not treated immediately, you chill further and progress into moderate and then severe hypothermia. With severe hypothermia, the brain is affected, speech becomes slurred, and you are disoriented. Then you become unconscious and finally die. To prevent hypothermia, wear the right clothing, limit your exposure to wet and cold conditions, and use good judgment. If you lose fine motor control, treat the condition immediately:

Reduce exposure. If possible, get inside. If exposed to the wind (but not the rain), stop riding and crouch down (to reduce the exposed area) with your back to the wind.

Put on clothing. Put on everything you have with you.

Improvise. Dry newspapers or scrap paper under your jersey will provide more insulation. Garbage bags can serve as raincoats and gaiters.

Remove wet clothing. Wool clothing insulates when wet, but cotton and some synthetics pull warmth from the body.

Drink warm liquids. Drink warm, noncaffeinated, nonalcoholic beverages.

Buddy up. Body heat from someone not suffering from hypothermia provides a lot of warmth.

Any change in mental status such as confusion or slurred speech indicates a medical emergency. Call 911 immediately.

• *Frostnip or frostbite.* Frostnip occurs when the outer layer of skin becomes frozen from exposure to severe wind chill or contact with cold surfaces and is the first stage of frostbite. Superficial frostbite injures the outer layer of skin and some underlying tissue. Blistering usually occurs within 24 hours. Severe frostbite involves complete crystallization of the fluids in the skin and may result in destruction of the injured tissue. To prevent frostnip and frostbite, wear good clothing (not too tight), particularly on your extremities, and use good judgment about when and whether to ride outside.

Dan lived in Alaska, and John lives in Colorado, so we are familiar with cold-related injuries and offer these recommendations for preventing them:

Clothing. Wear dry, windproof, well-insulated clothing that allows water to evaporate. We discussed clothing for inclement conditions in chapters 8 and 10 (see pages 167–169 and 215–216). Dress in layers and carry extra dry clothes adequate for all possible conditions. Pay close attention to your extremities. In cold conditions your body will reduce blood flow to your extremities to keep your core warm.

Helmet. Use a helmet cover in addition to a balaclava or head cover. Many riders in Alaska have a winter helmet that has the vents covered with reflective duct tape.

Nutrition. During cold weather you need calories both to provide energy to cycle and to keep warm, so eat more than you do during a summer ride. You also need fluid. Even when the temperature is above freezing, you may not be motivated to reach for food or fluid, so you may need to stop for just a minute to eat and drink every 20 to 30 minutes. In conditions below freezing, you need to keep your fluids liquid. John uses a small hydration pack that fits under his outer layers.

Plan your ride. For safety's sake adjust where and how you ride. Rather than riding a four-hour loop, ride a one-hour loop four times. That way you can always stop at home for hot chocolate! In snowy conditions ride your mountain bike on the road for better traction and reduced risk of flats; you'll also go more slowly, thus reducing wind chill. In extreme cold avoid touching metal on your bike. Finally, use good judgment and ride the trainer if it is too cold.

Altitude Sickness

At higher elevations reduced air pressure and less oxygen concentration affect how you perform on the bike and how you feel on and off the bike. You may notice the effects of altitude as low as 5,000 feet (1,500 m) and may develop symptoms of mountain sickness above 8,000 feet (2,400 m).

The early symptoms of altitude sickness include the following:

Headache	Shortness of breath with exertion
Less appetite	Difficulty sleeping
Higher pulse	Dizziness or light-headedness
Fatigue with exercise and at rest	Nausea or vomiting

Mount Evans in Colorado has the highest paved road in the United States at 14,130 feet (4,307 m). John lives at 6,000 feet (1,800 m), but in a good season he climbs Mount Evans. He has learned to do the following:

Adjust pacing and gearing. At altitude the limitation is the amount of oxygen available. Accept this fact and slow down.

Weight. The more weight that you carry, the harder your body has to work.

Eat and drink. When breathing hard you may find it impossible both to pedal and to eat or drink. So stop for a minute, replenish, and get back on the bike.

Even if you don't live in Colorado, you can enjoy riding in the mountains. Acclimating takes time. When you arrive at altitude, for example Denver at 5,000 feet (1,500 m), your body starts to adapt, but you may need up to a week until you adjust to the altitude. For the first several days at altitude, your performance may actually decline. If you want to climb Mount Evans, for example, either come to Colorado at least a week beforehand or fly into Denver the night before. Altitude often affects how well you sleep. John led many tours in Colorado and planned the routes so that for the first week participants would sleep at relatively low elevations to allow time to acclimate while climbing progressively higher passes during the day. The faster you ascend from night to night, the more likely you are to develop altitude-related symptoms.

As with other environmental problems, altitude-related problems range from mild to severe. Again, pay attention to mental status. If a person is confused, disoriented, or staggers, then the central nervous system is affected and the condition is life threatening. Descend to lower elevation as quickly and safely as possible.

Safety: Dealing With Dogs

On a credit-card tour in California, a dog chased and bit John. When the county officials were unable to locate the dog, John had to undergo the painful series of antirabies shots. We hope that you never have to deal with a vicious dog, but you probably will encounter overfriendly to aggressive animals. Here are some suggestions:

▶ *Be aware.* Awareness of your surroundings is the key to safety. Keep an eye and ear out for dogs just as you watch for traffic and other riders.

▶ *Anticipate.* If you see a dog, judge the situation. Is it tied up? Is it just barking, or is it moving toward you? How fast? By the time it gets to you, will it be closing from the front or chasing after you?

▶ *Warn.* Alert your riding companions.

▶ *Stay calm.* Don't hit the dog, lest you crash or kill the dog. Don't panic—keep control of your bike.

▶ *Assess whether the dog is friendly.* Dogs like to chase moving objects and get more enjoyment chasing faster things. If the dog is playing, slow down and talk to the dog in a friendly voice. You may be able just to ride by. If the dog still wants to play, get off your bike and walk past the area, keeping the bike between you and the dog.

▶ *Give a command.* Many dogs obey commands issued in a firm voice. Try "Stop!" "Sit!" or "No!"

▶ *Evade.* If you have the speed, you can try to outrun the dog, but remember that the dog enjoys chasing moving objects.

▶ *Discourage.* If the dog doesn't respond to voice commands and seems aggressive, squirt it with your water bottle.

▶ *Protect yourself if you must.* Pepper spray or physical violence should be used only in dangerous cases.

▶ *Anticipate a collision.* Even a playful dog might run in front of you and cause a collision. If you try to swerve to avoid the dog, you may lose control of the bike. If you anticipate a collision, get your butt back off the saddle to reduce the risk of going over the handlebars and take a firm grip on the bars to reduce the risk of having the front wheel twist out from under you.

▶ *Ride the bike down.* Even a minor crash can result in a broken collarbone. If you are about to fall to the right and stick out your right arm to absorb the crash, the shock is transmitted up the arm and snaps the relatively weak collarbone. In the event of a crash, whether from a dog or other obstacle, hang on to the handlebars. You may lose a little skin on your hand and forearm, but that heals in a few days, whereas a collarbone may take six weeks to heal.

Consider contacting your local animal control office if you have trouble with a dog on your training route.

Traumatic Injuries

You are pedaling along enjoying your long ride when a car cuts you off, causing you to veer off the road and go down. Or worse, a vehicle hits a rider just ahead of you and she lies motionless in the road. Bike accidents are scary. Accidents involving falls, other riders, pedestrians, motor vehicles, and dogs, account for hundreds of thousands of emergency room visits each year.

Accident Prevention

Although not all accidents can be prevented, you can ride defensively to reduce the risks. Maturing as an athlete includes making defensive riding second nature. Just as you reviewed your nutrition plan and training program as you progressed, take a few moments to review these key safety points:

- *Wear your helmet.* Head injuries are one of the leading causes of cycling fatalities. Wear your helmet every time you get on your bike, even for a simple test ride.
- *Be aware.* Continually look around and behind you (a mirror may make this easier) and pay attention to other riders, pedestrians, cars, and road hazards.
- *Be visible.* Wear bright colors or reflective clothing. If you ride at dusk or night, use bright lights and reflective clothing and equipment.
- *Observe all traffic laws.* As a cyclist, you operate a vehicle and must obey the same laws that motorists do.
- *Ride predictably.* Act like a car. At an intersection stay in the straight-ahead lane. Don't get in the right-turn lane unless you are turning right. Get in the left-turn lane if you are turning left. Signal turns with your arm. Don't ride on sidewalks, which are for pedestrians. Drivers don't expect riders to appear at cycling speed from sidewalks.
- *Groups.* While enjoying the sociability, stay aware, move predictably, and protect your front wheel.
- *Choose your routes.* Try to pick relatively quiet roads and avoid the busiest streets.
- *Minimize distractions.* Be careful when fiddling with your bike computer, heart rate monitor, or power meter. Never ride with earphones.

Emergency Response

You see an accident and rush to it. What should you do? Follow these steps if you are first on the scene. (The procedures to move an injured person, apply CPR, and administer first aid are outside the scope of this book.)

1. *Think.* Don't just do something; stand there. Before you take any action, think for a minute about what happened and how to proceed.
2. *Scene safety.* One down rider is enough. Before attending to the rider, get other riders and drivers to direct traffic around the accident. It may be necessary to move the rider, but do this very carefully if there is any possibility of head or spinal injuries.

3. *Assess condition.* Is the injured person's condition life threatening? Check the following:

   ▪ *Responsiveness.* Shout, "Are you OK?" If the person doesn't answer, tap him or her on the chest bone to check for a response.

   ▪ *Airway.* If the person responds, have the rider open her or his mouth. If the rider is unresponsive, pull the jaw down and forward. Then use your fingers to remove any broken teeth or other foreign objects. Because head and spinal injuries are common in cycling, do not lift or tilt the head.

   ▪ *Breathing.* Put your ear close to the person's mouth and nose and watch the person's chest. Is the rider breathing? If not, and you are trained, start CPR.

   ▪ *Circulation.* If you are a medical professional, check the pulse. If not, skip this step because the results are often unreliable for lay people.

4. *EMTs.* Call for help. If you are alone, take care of all the previous steps before calling the EMTs. If others are on the scene, have them call while you do the assessment.

Although we can't teach you first aid, we recommend that you take a first aid class and carry a small first aid kit for minor injuries (see table 11.4).

TABLE 11.4 **First Aid Kit**

• Several 3 in. (7.5 cm) sterile gauze pads
• Several feet of 1 in. (2.5 cm) adhesive tape rolled into a small roll
• Half-dozen Band-Aids
• Double antibiotic ointment (triple antibiotic ointment may cause skin allergic reaction)
• Six cleansing wipes with alcohol
• Tweezers (which are also useful for removing small objects from tires)
• Ibuprofen
• Several pair of latex gloves to protect your hands from pathogens
• Hand sanitizer

Medical Treatment

Any abrasion or other open wound needs to be cleaned and disinfected properly. Because cleaning may be painful and your supplies will be limited, you probably won't do a thorough job at home. Your tetanus shot should be current. You also may have underlying musculoskeletal problems, which aren't immediately apparent. Your health care practitioner will clean up the injuries, provide any necessary shots, perform a physical exam to assess possible underlying problems, and order further tests if appropriate. Although a trip to the doctor or emergency room takes time and often money, prompt action may reduce considerably the risk and severity of future complications.

Documentation

No matter how innocent a crash with a vehicle or other rider may be, take time to document everything. If you are in an accident and hurt seriously, do not move. Wait for medical help to arrive. If you are OK, take the following steps:

- Notify police or emergency services.
- Get your version of the events into the accident report.
- Obtain driver and witness contact information.
- Document what happened.
- Document your injuries.
- Preserve evidence—don't fix your bike or clean your clothes. Take pictures of the scene.
- Consult legal counsel.

If you are in an accident with a pedestrian or another cyclist, a police report may not be necessary, but you should cover your bases and follow the same course of action.

Overuse, environmental, and traumatic injuries are not completely avoidable, but you can take steps to minimize the possibility of their occurrence. Keep these points in mind to help prevent injuries:

- *Bike fit.* Have your bike set up properly. Refer to chapter 5 and remember that your positioning may change periodically because of age, changes in strength or flexibility, or changes in cycling goals.
- *Training progression.* Overuse injuries often result from improper training. Use our training programs to ensure that you gradually increase volume and intensity.
- *Rest and recovery.* When you train, you must also rest because that's when your body recovers. Remember that stress is cumulative. Family or work issues affect your capacity to train and recover. Allow time for your body to rebuild by incorporating rest days, recovery weeks, and taper periods.
- *Seek medical advice early.* If you feel any unusual pain or persistent discomfort or have an accident, get it checked out. The earlier you catch a possible injury, the better the outcome will be. Heed the advice of doctors or therapists; don't force the recovery.
- *Good nutrition.* Performance and recovery depend on your nutrition at home and on the bike.
- *Use safety equipment.* Wear your helmet, use bright or reflective clothing, and equip your bike with lights and reflectors for riding at night.
- *Assess conditions.* Before a ride look at the weather and use good judgment about riding and clothing.
- *Ride defensively.* Always be aware of your surroundings and use extra caution in traffic.

By following these guidelines and using good judgment, you can reduce the risk of common cycling injuries and enjoy your riding for years to come. Get out there, ride smart, ride safe, and above all have fun!

RESOURCES

Organizations With Century Challenges

Randonneurs USA R-12, www.rusa.org

Ultra Midwest Century Challenge, www.ultramidwest.net/main/bdmain.aspx

UltraMarathon Cycling Association Year-Rounder, www.ultracycling.com

Organizations With Club Lists

League of American Bicyclists, www.bikeleague.org

Randonneurs Mondiaux, www.lesrandonneursmondiaux.org

Randonneurs USA, www.rusa.org

Organizations With Ride Calendars

Active, www.active.com

Adventure Cycling Association, www.adventurecycling.org

BikeRide.com, www.bikeride.com

Double century information: California Triple Crown, www.caltriplecrown.com

League of American Bicyclists, www.bikeleague.org

Leukemia Society, www.teamintraining.org

National MS Society's MS-150 rides, www.nationalmssociety.org

Perimeter Bicycling Association of America, www.pbaa.com

Planet Ultra, www.planetultra.com

Randonneurs Mondiaux, www.lesrandonneursmondiaux.org

Randonneurs USA, www.rusa.org

Ultra Midwest, www.ultramidwest.net/main/bdmain.aspx

Ultra Marathon Cycling Association, www.ultracycling.com

Randonneuring Organizations

Country	Organization	Website/Contact
Australia	Audax Australia	www.audax.org.au
Austria	Audax Randonneurs Austria	http://members.liwest.at/jungferdinand/
Belgium	Randonneurs Belgium	www.randonneurs.be

(continued)

Country	Organization	Website/Contact
Brazil	Audax Randonneurs Brazil	www.randonneursbrasil.com.br
Bulgaria	Audax Bulgaria	www.sv-cycling.s5.com
Canada-Alberta	Alberta Randonneurs	www.albertarandonneurs.com
Canada-British Columbia	British Columbia Randonneurs	www.randonneurs.bc.ca
Canada-Montreal	Randonneurs Montreal	http://pages.videotron.com/cvrm
Canada-Manitoba	Manitoba Randonneurs	e-mail:leir@mts.net
Canada-Nova Scotia	Randonneurs Nova Scotia	www.randonneurs.ns.ca
Canada-Ontario	Randonneurs Ontario	www.randonneursontario.ca
Canada – Saskatchewan	Prairie Randonneurs, Inc.	www.saskcycling.ca/~pri/index.htm
Chile	Randonneurs Chile	e-mail:Daniel@bicicletaspublicas.cl
China	Randonneurs China	e-mail: hans.ngo@bikechina.org
Croatia	Randonneurs Croatia	www.bksvn.hr
Denmark	Audax Randonneurs Denmark	www.audax-club.dk
Finland		e-mail: paavo.nurminen@kymp.net
Germany	Audax Randonneurs Germany	www.ara.randonneure.de
Greece	Audax Randonneurs Greece P.E.P.A.	www.pepa.gr
Hungary	Randonneurs Hungary	e-mail: simon_hursthouse@hotmail.com
India	Randonneurs India	e-mail: dongarmaltroll@gmail.com
Ireland	Audax Club Randonneurs Ireland	www.sorrentocyclingclub.com
Israel	Israeli Randonneurs	e-mail:israeli.randonneurs@gmail.com
Italy	Bicitaliaudax	www.audaxitalia.it
Japan	Audax Randonneurs Japan	www.audax-japan.org
Luxembourg	Audax Randonneurs Luxembourg	www.sunshinebikers.eu
Netherlands	Lowlands Randonneurs	www.lowlands1000.nl
New Zealand	Audax Australia	www.audax.org.au
Norway		e-mail: oystein.rohlff@getmail.no
Poland	Randonneurs Poland	e-mail: irek.koziol.cfteurope.pl
Russia	Russian Randonneurs	http://russianrandonneur.ru
Singapore	Audax Randonneurs Singapore	www.audaxsingapore.com
Slovenia	Slovenia Randonneurs	e-mail: marko@markobaloh.com
South Africa	Audax South Africa	www.audaxsa.co.za
South Korea	Randonneurs Korea	e-mail: vze79pi7@verizon.net
Switzerland	Radmarathon	www.radmarathon.ch
Taiwan	Randonneurs Taiwan	www.acp-randonneurs-taiwan.org.tw
Ukraine	Audax Randonneurs Ukraine	e-mail: levkovsk@sat.poltava.ua
United Kingdom	Audax UK	www.audax.uk.net
United States	Randonneurs USA	www.rusa.org

Touring Companies

Adventure Cycling Association, www.adv-cycling.org

Backroads, www.backroads.com

Bicycle Adventures, www.bicycleadventures.com

Breaking Away Tours, www.breakingaway.com

International Bicycle Fund, www.ibike.org

PAC Tour, www.pactour.com

Second Summer Tours, www.secondsummertours.com

Trek Travel Bike Tours, www.trektravel.com

Vermont Bicycle Tours, www.vbt.com

Equipment

Adventure Cycling, *Packing Your Bike*,
www.adventurecycling.org/features/boxingbike.cfm

Ball Dynamics, www.balldynamics.com

Bicycle Helmet Safety Institute, www.bhsi.org

Bicycle Quarterly bike tests, www.bikequarterly.com/biketests.html

Gym and Fitness, Australia, www.gymandfitness.com.au

Heine, J., and Oehler, A., *Testing the Efficiency of Generator Hubs*,
www.vintagebicyclepress.com/VBQgenerator.pdf

Heine, J., *What Makes a Good Randonneur Bike*,
www.vintagebicyclepress.com/images/BQRandonneurBike.pdf

Heroes Fitness, United Kingdom, www.heroesfitness.co.uk

Jones, C. C., *The Big Blue Book of Bicycle Repair*, 2005, Park Tool Company, St.
Paul, MN.

McNaughton, W., and Hughes, J., *Testing Equipment for Long Rides*,
www.coach-hughes.com/resources/equipment_showstoppers.html

Perform Better, www.performbetter.com

Power Systems, www.power-systems.com

RBR Publishing Company, Kutztown, PA, www.roadbikerider.com

Vande Kamp, M., Heine, J., and Wetmore, A., *A Survey of Equipment in PBP 2007*,
www.vintagebicyclepress.com/BQPBPEquipsurvey.pdf

Events and Tours

For a representative but not all-inclusive list of the most popular events and tours,
go to http://tinyurl.com49ha5wb

Fit

Bike Fit Systems LLC, www.bikefit.com

Specialized Bicycles,
www.specialized.com/us/en/bc/SBCGlobalPages.jsp?pageName=BGFIT

Injury Prevention

Kortebein, P., *Saddle Sores: The What and Why, as Well as Tips on Prevention and Treatment*,
www.liquicell.com/assets/pdf/Saddle%20Sores%20(P.%20Kortebein).pdf

Mayo Clinic, www.mayoclinic.org

NOAA, National Weather Service, www.nws.noaa.gov/os/windchill/index.shtml

Pruitt, A. L., and Matheny, F., *Andy Pruitt's Medical Guide for Cyclists*, 2006, RBR, Kutztown, PA, www.roadbikerider.com

Mental Preparation

Hughes, J., *Mental Training Techniques*, a five-part article,
www.coach-hughes.com/resources/breathing1.html

Hughes, J., (2010) *Stop Cycling's Showstoppers*, RoadBikeRider, Atlanta, GA,
www.roadbikerider.com/e-books/stop-cyclings-showstoppers-ebook

Lynch, J., and Huang, C. A., *Working Out, Working Within*, 1998, Tarcher/Putnam, New York, NY.

Miller, S., and Maass Hill, P., *Sport Psychology for Cyclists*, 1999, VeloPress, Boulder, CO.

Nutrition

American College of Sports Medicine. (2007). Exercise and fluid replacement position stand, pp 384-386.

Barr, S. I., and Hughes, J., Eating for Events,
www.coach-hughes.com/resources/calories.html

Calorie data: Calorie King, www.calorieking.com

Calorie free phone app: LoseIt!, http://loseit.com

Carew, L., *Musings of a Vermont Nutritionist,* 2010, Wind Ridge Publishing, Shelburne VT

Clark, N., and Hegmann, J., *The Cyclist's Food Guide*, 2005, Sports Nutrition, West Newton, MA.

Clark, N., *Nancy Clark's Sports Nutrition Guide*, 1990, Leisure Press, Champaign, IL.

http://foodpyramid.com/wp-content/uploads/2009/09/MyPyramid2.jpg

Hughes, J., (2011). Nutrition for 100K and beyond, RoadBikeRider, Atlanta, GA,
www.roadbikerider.com/e-articles/nutrition-100K-and-beyond-earticle

Hughes, J., commentary by Barr, S. I., Experiment of One, Applying Nutrition Principles, www.coach-hughes.com/resources/nutrition_mantras.html

Institute of Medicine, http://iom.edu/Home/Global/News%20Announcements/DRI

Jeukendrup, A. E., (2010). Carbohydrate and exercise performance: the role of multiple transportable carbohydrates. *Curr Opin Clin Nutr Metab Care.* Jul;13(4):452-7.

Mayo Clinic, www.mayoclinic.com

United States Department of Agriculture, (n.d.), MyPyramid, www.mypyramid.gov

Weschler, L., *Drinking Too Much*,
www.ultracycling.com/nutrition/drinking_too_much.html

www.glycemicindex.com

www.mayoclinic.com/health/mediterranean-diet/CL00011

www.mediterraneandiet.com/

www.oldwayspt.org/mediterranean-diet-pyramid

www.sfsn.ethz.ch/index_EN

www.sfsn.ethz.ch/PDF/pyramide/IJSNEM_2009.pdf

www.sge-ssn.ch/fileadmin/pdf/100-ernaehrungsthemen/10-gesundes_essen_
trinken/Food_Pyramid.pdf

www.webmd.com/diet/features/the-mediterranean-diet

Publications

Magazine	Organization	Contact
Adventure Cyclist	Adventure Cycling Association	www.adventurecycling.org/
American Bicyclist	League of American Bicyclists	www.bikeleague.org/
American Randonneur	Randonneurs USA	www.rusa.org/
Arivée	Audax UK	www.aukweb.net/index.htm
Bicycle Times	Bicycle Times	www.bicycletimesmag.com/
Bicycling	Rodale Press	http://bicycling.com/
Checkpoint	Audax Australia	http://audax.org.au/public/
Tailwinds	Perimeter Bicycling Association	www.pbaa.com/
Ultra Cycling	Ultramarathon Cycling Association	www.ultracycling.com
Velo News	Competitor Network	http://velonews.competitor.com/

Randonneuring

Heine, J., et al., Randonneuring Basics, a series of 15 articles in *Bicycle Quarterly*,
www.bikequarterly.com/RandoBasics.html

Hughes, J., (2011), Beyond the century: How to train for and ride 200 km to 1200 km
brevets, RoadBikeRider, Atlanta, GA,
www.roadbikerider.com/e-articles/beyond-century

Ride Planning

Adventure Cycling Association, www.adventurecycling.org

Google Maps, maps.google.com/biking

League of American Bicyclists, www.bikeleague.org

Map My Ride, www.mapmyride.com/

Safety

Allen, J., Bicycling Street Smarts on-line tutorial, www.bikexprt.com

Bicycling Life, www.bicyclinglife.com

Forester, J., *Effective Cycling*, 6th ed., 1993, MIT Press, Cambridge, MA, and London, England.

League of American Bicyclists, www.bikeleague.org

Pedestrian & Bicycle Information Center, www.bicyclinginfo.org

Training

Allen, H., and Coggan, A., *Training and Racing with a Power Meter*, 2006, VeloPress, Boulder, CO.

Burke, E., *Serious Cycling*, 2nd ed., 2002, Human Kinetics, Champaign, IL.

Meagher, J., and Boughton, P., *Sports Massage*, 1990, Stanton Hill Press, Barrytown, NY.

Concept 2, www.concept2.com

Friel, J., *The Cyclist's Training Bible*, 4th ed., 2009, VeloPress, Boulder, CO.

Hughes, J., and Kehlenbach, D., *Resistance Training for Endurance Cyclists, Part 1 & Part 2*, www.coach-hughes.com/resources/resistance_training1.html, www.coach-hughes.com/resources/resistance_training2.html

Hughes, J., (2010) Intensity: How to plan and gauge your most effective training efforts, RoadBikeRider, Atlanta, GA, www.roadbikerider.com/e-articles/beyond-century

Matheny, F., *Fred Matheny's Complete Book of Road Bike Training*, 2002, RoadBikeRider, Atlanta, GA, www.roadbikerider.com

Stretching

Anderson, B., *Stretching*, 1980, Shelter, Bolinas, CA.

Clark, M., and Russell, A., *Self Myofacial Release Techniques*, www.performbetter.com/catalog/matriarch/PrintPage.asp?PageID=91&PageName=ArticleMyofacialRelease

M-F Athletic Company, *Multiple Uses of Biofoam Rollers*, www.performbetter.com/catalog/assets/Exercisesheets/PDF/FoamRoller.pdf

Training Log Examples

Garmin, www.garmin.com/garmin/cms/us/intosports/training_center#fragment-1 (if using Garmin GPS units)

Training Peaks, http://home.trainingpeaks.com/personal-edition/training-log-and-food-diary.aspx

Ultra Midwest, www.ultramidwest.net/main/bdmain.aspx

WORKS CONSULTED

Allen, H., & Coggan, A. (2006). *Training and racing with a power meter*. Boulder, CO: VeloPress.

American College of Sports Medicine. (2007). Exercise and fluid replacement position stand. *Medicine and Science in Sports & Exercise*, 39, 377–390.

Anderson, M.K., Hall, S.J., & Martin, M. (2000). *Sports injury management*. Baltimore: Lippincott Williams & Wilkins.

Armstrong, L.E. (2000). *Performing in extreme environments*. Champaign, IL: Human Kinetics.

Bicycle Helmet Safety Institute. (n.d.). www.bhsi.org

Burke, E. (2002). *Serious cycling* (2nd ed.). Champaign, IL: Human Kinetics.

Clark, N., & Hegmann, J. (2005). *The cyclist's food guide*. West Newton, MA: Sports Nutrition.

Clark, N. (1990). *Nancy Clark's sports nutrition guidebook*. Champaign, IL: Leisure Press.

Hew-Butler, T., et al. (2008). Practical management of exercise-associated hyponatremic encephalopathy, *Clinical Journal of Sport Medicine*, 18(4).

Jeukendrup, A. E. (2010). Carbohydrate and exercise performance: the role of multiple transportable carbohydrates. *Curr Opin Clin Nutr Metab Care*. Jul;13(4):452-7.

Kortebein, P. (n.d.). *Saddle sores: The what and why, as well as tips on prevention and treatment*. www.liquicell.com/assets/pdf/Saddle%20Sores%20(P.%20Kortebein).pdf

League of American Bicyclists. (n.d.). www.bikeleague.org/resources/

Mayo Clinic. (n.d.). *Health information*. www.mayoclinic.com/health-information

Mayo Clinic. (n.d.). *Heat stroke*. www.mayoclinic.com/health/first-aid-heatstroke/FA00019

Mayo Clinic. (n.d.). *Heart disease*. www.mayoclinic.com/health/heart-disease/DS01120

Mayo Clinic. (n.d.). *Heat exhaustion*. www.mayoclinic.com/health/heat-exhaustion/DS01046

Mayo Clinic. (n.d.). *Muscle cramp*.www.mayoclinic.com/health/muscle-cramp/DS00311

Mayo Clinic. (n.d.). *Sodium: How to tame your salt habit now*. www.mayoclinic.com/health/sodium/NU00284

Mionske, B. (2007). *Bicycling and the law*. Boulder, CO: VeloPress.

NOAA National Weather Service. (n.d.). *Wind chill*. www.nws.noaa.gov/os/windchill/index.shtml

NSCA. (2008). Nutritional factors in health and performance. by K. Reimers. In *Essentials of strength training and conditioning* (3rd ed.), edited by T.R. Baechle and R.W. Earle. Champaign, IL: Human Kinetics, 210.

Outdoor Foundation. (2008). *Outdoor recreation participation report 2008*. http://www.outdoorfoundation.org/pdf/ResearchParticipation2008.pdf

Pruitt, A. L., & Matheny, F. (2006). *Andy Pruitt's medical guide for cyclists*, Kutztown, PA: RBR, www.roadbikerider.com

Strickland, B. (2001). The quotable cyclist. Great moments of bicycling wisdom, inspiration and humor. Halcotsville, NY: Breakaway Books.

Weschler, L. (n.d.). *Drinking too much*. www.ultracycling.com/nutrition/drinking_too_much.html

Wilmore, J.H., & Costill, D.L. (1994). *Physiology of sport and exercise*.

INDEX

Note: The italicized *f* and *t* following page numbers refer to figures and tables, respectively. References to centuries include 200Ks; references to double centuries include 300Ks.

A

accessories. *See also specific accessories*
  computers and monitors 92-93
  food and water carriers 91-92, 91*t*
  on-the-road essentials 90-91
  touring equipment 182-184, 184*f*, 214-215, 214*f*
accidents 239-241
Achilles tendon stretch 47
active recovery 100, 117, 127
adaptation 21
Adventure Cycling Association 175
aerobar bags 92
aerobic base training
  cross-training 25-27
  functions of 22-23
  indoor riding 27-30
  outdoor riding 23-25
aerobic energy 118-119
aerobic (oxidative) system 20-21, 21*f*
aid stations 130, 142
alcoholic beverages 72, 145
altitude sickness 237-238
amino acids 63
anaerobic energy 119
ankle injuries 228-229
annual bike check-ups 97
anticipation, for safety 114
arm warmers 89
assessment. *See* self-assessment
asthma 235
athletic maturity 149-150, 197, 202
ATP-CP (phosphagen) system 20-21, 21*f*

B

back injuries 229
back massage 54, 55
back rotation stretch 46, 143*f*
balance in life 183
basal metabolic rate (BMR) 60
baseline conditioning
  aerobic training 22-30
  flexibility training 42-55, 43*t*, 50*t*
  program integration 55-56
  resistance training 30-42
  in training pyramid 150*f*, 152

beam bikes 78
bench press 39, 41
bento bags 92
bike comfort
  clothing for 86-90, 86*f*
  flexibility training and 82
  points of contact and 83-86
bike fit. *See also* injury prevention
  assessment 79, 80*f*, 82*f*
  documentation 82, 83*t*
  feet and cleats 81
  handlebars and stem 81-82
  leg geometry 79-80, 80*f*
  reassessment 82, 168
bike lanes and paths 6
bikes
  coach John's 78
  components 76-77, 77*f*
  event preparation 136-137, 137*t*, 138*t*
  frames 73-76, 213
  maintenance 93-97, 192-193, 224
  for multiday events 181, 184*f*, 213-214, 214*f*
  reassessment 168
  types 73-75, 74*f*, 75*f*
  women's 73-74
BMR 60
body geometry 79-82
bone strength 31
bonking 69
Bonner, Ken 196
brake hoods and levers 76, 82
breakfast 67
brevets
  described 7-8, 160-161, 197
  equipment 213-219
  final preparation 219-220
  mental preparation 200-201
  nutrition 219, 220-223
  planning 130
  recovery 224
  ride strategies 220-224
  self-assessment 197, 199-200
  time limits 200*t*
  training 207-212, 207*t*

brisk rides
    century training 100, 117, 152
    double century training 152
    multiday event training 176, 203
bucket list 151
Burke, Edmund 23
butt comfort 84

C
California Triple Crown 7
calories
    burned in cycling 61*t*
    daily needs 60-62, 62*f*
    in macronutrients 63, 65, 70*t*
carbohydrates 62-63, 64
cardiovascular exercise 1, 2*t*
Carpenter, Paul 133
carriers, for gear 182, 184, 184*f*, 214-215, 214*f*
cat stretch 43
centuries and 200Ks
    adversity during 133
    clothing 86-90, 86*f*
    described 5-7
    equipment preparation 136-137, 137*t*, 138-139*t*
    mental preparation 135-136
    multiple in a season. *See* double centuries and
        300Ks)
    nutrition 137-138
    planning 129-134
    preride checklist 139-140*t*
    recovery 144-145, 153
    ride strategies 140-143
    self-assessment 9-10, 13
    time to complete 99
    training programs
        8-week 101-106, 105*f*, 106*f*
        15-week 107-115, 113*f*, 115*f*
        improvement 152-156, 153*t*
        maintenance 152, 157-159
        workout types 100
chains, cleaning 93-94
charity rides 10
checklists
    event packing list 138-139*t*
    preride 95-96, 139-140*t*
    ride equipment 137*t*
    using 184
check-ups, for bike 95-97
chest stretch 45
cleats 81, 85, 85*f*. *See also* injury prevention
clothing
    centuries 86-90, 86*f*
    double centuries 168-170
    injury prevention and 227-229
    multiday events 182, 215-216
    short trips 89
club rides 4-5, 4*t*
cold-related injuries 235-237, 236*t*
commuting 24, 151
components 76-77, 77*f*

computers 92
core strength
    exercises 32-34
    need for 30
    in training schedules 100, 117-118, 152, 176, 203
cramps 233
credit-card touring 7, 197. *See also* multiday tours
cross-country skiing 25, 26
cross-training 25-27
cue sheets 130, 131*f*, 141
curiosity, as motivator 196
cycling community 4
cycling questionnaire 148-149*f*

D
Daily Value (DV) 65
delayed onset muscle soreness (DOMS) 232
descending 190-191
dinner 68
dogs 238
DOMS 232
double centuries and 300Ks
    clothing 168-170
    described 7
    equipment preparation 167-170
    mental preparation 167
    nutrition 170-171
    ride strategies 167, 171-172
    self-assessment 147-149, 148-149*f*, 171
    training programs
        century a month 152, 157-159
        double centuries 162-167
        two centuries per season 152-156, 153*t*
        workout types 152
drop bags 201
dumbbell weights
    leg exercises using 35, 37
    sizes 31-32, 32*t*
    upper body exercises using 39-41
DV 65
dynamic stretching 50-52, 50*t*

E
EIB 235
Ellis, John Lee 11, 160
emergency contacts 90, 130
emergency response 239-241, 240*t*
endurance rides. *See* long rides
energy systems 20-21, 21*f*
environmental injuries 233-238
equipment. *See also* bikes
    accessories 90-93, 182-184, 184*f*, 214-215, 214*f*
    clothing 86-90, 86*f*, 168-170, 182, 215-216,
        227-229
    event preparation 136-137, 137*t*, 138-139*t*
    gear carriers 182, 184, 184*f*, 214-215, 214*f*
    lights 170, 217-219, 217*t*
    maintenance of 93-97, 192-193, 224
    testing 23

essentials to carry 90-91
events. *See also specific events*
    participants 4
    selecting 9-12
    types 4-8, 4*t*
event scenarios
    brevets 201
    centuries 133-134
    multiday events 184, 201
event-specific training. *See* training
exercise ball bridging 34
exercise balls
    core exercises using 34
    leg exercises using 36-37
    sizes 31, 31*t*
    upper body exercises using 39
exercise induced bronchospasm (EIB) 235
eye injuries 233

F
fan trainers 29
fast-twitch muscle fibers 20
fat, dietary 62, 63
fatigue 232
feet
    cleats and 81, 85, 85*f*
    injuries to 228-229
fenders 214
first aid kit 240*t*
fitness benefits 1-2, 2*t*
flat tires 94-95
flexibility training
    bike comfort and 82
    during ride 142, 142*f*, 143*f*
    dynamic stretching 50-52, 50*t*
    need and time for 42
    postride 144, 145
    as recovery strategy 126, 188, 189
    static stretching 43-49, 43*t*
    in training schedules 100, 117-118, 152, 176, 203
fluid trainers 29
flying, with bike 132
foam rollers
    core exercises using 33
    self-massage using 52-55, 127
    size 31
food. *See* nutrition
food carriers 91-92
food journals 58, 59*f*
food labels 70
food plans 66-68
food pyramids 58-60
food supplements 66
foot comfort 81, 85
foot injuries 228-229
fork rake 213
frame geometry 75, 84
frame packs 182
frames 73-76, 213

free radicals 65
frostbite or frostnip 236
FTP 120
fueling. *See* nutrition
functional threshold power (FTP) 120

G
gastrocnemius stretch 47
Gazmararian, Julie 107
gear. *See* bikes; equipment
gearing 76, 214
glasses 88
gloves 86
gluteus medius massage 54
gluteus medius stretch 49
glycemic index 64, 64*t*
glycogen stores 62, 64, 69
glycolytic (lactic acid) system 20-21, 21*f*
goal setting 3, 11-12, 15-16, 15*f*
goniometer 79-80, 80*f*, 82*f*
Grainger, Michelle 232
grocery shopping 70
groin stretch 49
group riding
    pace lines 124, 142
    pace of 186, 223
    safety during 24

H
Haldeman, Lon 3, 75-76
hamstring curls 36, 38
hamstring massage 54
hamstring stretch 44, 142*f*
hand comfort 86
hand injuries 230-231
handlebar adjustments 81-82, 227
handlebar bags 92, 182
heart rate monitors 92-93, 118-119, 121*t*, 186
heat-related injuries 233-235
Hegmann, Jenny L. 71
Heiden, Eric 27
helmets 86-87, 86*f*
hiking 25
hill climb workouts 28
hip flexor stretch 46
hip rolls 50
hitting the wall 69
hot tubs 127
Howard, John 3
Hughes, John 14, 78, 221-222
hydration 68, 69, 142
hydration systems 91, 91*t*, 182
hyponatremia 68
hypothermia 235-236

I
ice, for sore muscles 127, 188
iliotibial band (ITB) massage 53
inchworm stretch 51

individuality
    baseline conditioning 55
    nutrition 57
    as training principle 21, 128
indoor riding 27-30
injury prevention
    environmental injuries 233-238
    guidelines 241
    muscle balance 31
    overuse injuries 225-233, 226*t*, 231*t*
    traumatic injuries 239-241
in-line skating 27
instructing 151
intensity levels 152, 153*t*, 176*t*, 203*t*
intensity workouts 122-125
isolated leg workouts 28
isolation 22
ITB massage 53

J
jerseys 88-89, 182
jumping rope 42

K
knee injuries 31, 227-228

L
lactate threshold (LT) 118-119
lactic acid (glycolytic) system 20-21, 21*f*
lat pull-down 41
Leadville 100 26
League of American Bicyclists 175
leg geometry 79-80
leg-length discrepancy 81, 226
leg press, machine single-leg 38
leg strength 30-31, 34-38
leg warmers 89
Lekisch, Peter 27
lights 170, 217-219, 217*t*
long rides
    brevet training 208
    century training 100, 116, 152
    double century training 152
    multiday event training 176, 203
LT 118-119
lunch 67
lunges 35
lunge walk 51

M
macronutrients 62-65, 70*t*
magnetic trainers 29
maintenance
    equipment 93-97, 192-193, 224
    training 152, 157-159
maps 174-175
Marino, John 3
massage 52-55, 127, 189
maximum heart rate 119

McGehee, Dan 183
Mediterranean diet pyramid 58
mental factors
    brevets 200-201, 223
    centuries 135-136, 143
    double centuries 167
    multiday tours 184, 185-186, 200-201, 223
mentoring 151, 159
Merckx, Eddy 97
micronutrients 65
military press 39, 41
minerals 65
monthly bike check-ups 96
mood, in overtraining 18
motivation, curiosity as 196
mountain bikes 76
mountain biking 27
multiday tours
    on bucket list 151
    carrying gear 181, 184*f*
    clothing 182, 215-216
    described 7
    equipment 181-184, 184*f*, 213-219, 214*f*
    equipment maintenance 192-193
    final preparation 219-220
    maps 174-175
    mental preparation 184, 200-201
    nutrition 184-185, 219, 220-223
    recovery after 224
    ride strategies 185-193, 185*f*, 201, 220-224
    self-assessment 173-174, 197
    supported vs. unsupported 174, 174*t*, 197, 198-199
    training
        weekend tour 175-181, 176*t*
        weeklong tour 202-206, 203*t*
multiple centuries. *See* double centuries and 300Ks
muscle fibers 20
muscle imbalances 31
muscle soreness 127, 232
MyPyramid 60, 66

N
neck injuries 229-230
neck stretch 45
night riding
    lights 170, 217-219, 217*t*
    techniques 207, 223
Nordic skiing 25, 26
nutrition
    brevets 219, 220-223
    caloric needs 60-62, 61*t*, 62*f*
    cold weather 237
    daily diet 66-68, 170
    food journals 58, 59*f*
    food pyramids 58-60
    glycemic index 64, 64*t*
    grocery shopping 70

individuality in 57
macronutrients 62-65, 70*t*
micronutrients 65
multiday tours 184-185, 188, 201, 219, 220-223
postride 144
practicing 23
preevent 137-138, 171
preworkout 67-68
as recovery strategy 126, 171
restaurant meals 71-72
during rides 69, 71, 125, 126*t*, 142, 170-171
supplements 66

O

osteopenia 31
outdoor riding (base training) 23-25
overhead stretch 45
overtraining 18, 128, 152
overuse injuries 225-233, 226*t*, 231*t*
oxidative (aerobic) system 20-21, 21*f*

P

pace lines 124, 142. *See also* group riding
pacing
    brevets 223
    centuries 140-141
    multiday tours 186-188, 223
panniers 214*f*, 215
Paris-Brest-Paris (PBP) 8, 160
pedals 85, 85*f*
Penseyres, Pete 75, 85, 151
perceived exertion 120-121, 121*t*, 186
periodization 150-152, 150*f*
permanent 7
personal rides 5
phosphagen (ATP-CP) system 20-21, 21*f*
piriformis massage 54
piriformis stretch 49
planning. *See* goal setting; season planning; self-
    assessment; *specific events*
plumb bob 80, 80*f*
plyometric training 42
points of contact 83-86
power meters 93, 120, 121*t*, 186
prehabilitation 31
preride checklist 95-96, 139-140*t*
priorities 12-13
problem solving 167, 187
progressive overload 21, 128
protein 62, 63-65
Pruitt, Andy 82
pyramid workouts 29

Q

quadriceps massage 54
quadriceps stretch 44, 143*f*
qualitative data 17
quantitative data 17

R

Race Across America (RAAM)
    equipment 75, 85
    history 3
    training 26, 27
racing bikes 74-76, 75*f*
rack trunk bags 182
rain, riding in 216
rain jackets 89
randonnées. *See* brevets
Randonneurs USA 157, 160
rating of perceived exertion (RPE) 120-121, 121*t*, 186
Recommended Daily Intake (RDI) 65
recovery rides
    brevet training 208
    century training 100, 117, 127
    double century training 152
    multiday event training 176, 203
recovery time
    base training 24-25
    between centuries 153
    century training 101, 128
    double century training 162
    from multiday events 224
    during multiday tours 188-189
    postride 144-145, 171
    techniques 125-127, 126*t*
    as training principle 22, 128
rehearsal rides, for brevets 208
relaxation techniques 135-136, 167, 184
repairs 90-91, 95
resistance training
    benefits 30-31
    equipment 31-32, 31*t*, 32*t*
    exercises
        core strength 32-34
        leg strength 34-38
        upper body strength 38-42
    sets and reps 32
    in training schedules 100, 117-118, 152, 176, 203
rest. *See* recovery time
restaurant meals 71-72
resting heart rate 128
rest stops (aid stations) 130, 142
reversibility 22
ride strategies
    brevets 220-224
    centuries 140-143
    double centuries 167, 171-172
    multiday tours 185-193, 185*f*, 201, 220-224
Ritz, Muffy 14, 26
road obstacles 141
roller bent-leg raise 33
rollers (trainers) 30
roller straight-leg raise 33
routines, for multiday tours 186, 188-189
rowing, with dumbbells 40
rowing machines 27, 41

RPE 120-121, 121*t,* 186
running 25
RUSA R-12 11

S
saddles
    adjustments 79-80, 80*f*
    injury prevention and 226-227
    types 84, 84*f*
saddle sores 84, 88, 226-227
safety
    anticipation 114
    descending 190-191
    dogs 238
    emergency contacts 90, 130
    group riding 24
    helmets 86-87, 86*f*
    road obstacles 141
    traffic 6
    two-lane roads 169
    visibility 18
    wet roads 216
sag support 130
saturated fat 63
saunas 127
season planning 11, 12-13
seat bags 92, 182
self-assessment
    centuries 9-10
    double centuries 147-149, 148-149*f,* 171
    multiday events 173-174, 197
    strengths and weaknesses 13
self-massage 52-55, 127, 189
Shermer, Michael 3
shift levers 76, 213
shoes 85
shorts 88
shoulder injuries 229-230
sidewalks 6
skin cancer 233
sleep 126, 224
slow-twitch muscle fibers 20
snacks 67-68
snowshoeing 25-27
social aspects 2-3
socks 89
soleus stretch 48
special-interest events 10
specificity 21-22, 128
spontaneity 11
sport bikes 74*f,* 75
sports drinks 68
sport-themed workouts 29
squat jump 42
static stretching 43-49, 43*t*
stationary trainers 29-30
stem 81-82
step-ups 36
store food 71

strengths, assessing 13
strength training. *See* resistance training
stress 2
stretching. *See* flexibility training
studio bikes 29
sumo squat 52
sunburn 233
supplements 66
Swenson, Carl 26
swimming 27
Swiss food pyramid 59-60

T
taper 101, 134-135, 150*f*
team sports, recreational 27
technique. *See* group riding; pacing; problem solving; safety
tempo rides
    baseline conditioning 28
    century training 100, 117, 152
    double century training 152
    multiday event training 176, 203
Texas Time Trials 8
300Ks. *See* double centuries and 300Ks
time management 186, 201, 224
time trial (TT) 119
tires 84, 94-95, 214
tools 90-91
touring. *See* multiday tours
touring bikes 74-76, 75*f,* 184*f,* 213-214, 214*f*
traffic safety 6, 18
trailers 215
trainers, stationary 29-30
training. *See also* baseline conditioning; recovery rides;
    recovery time; *specific events*
    brevets 207-212, 207*t*
    centuries
        8-week program 101-106, 105*f,* 106*f*
        15-week program 107-115, 113*f,* 115*f*
        improvement program 152-156, 153*t*
        maintenance program 152, 157-159
    double centuries 152, 162-167
    injury prevention and 228, 229, 230
    intensity levels 152, 153*t,* 176*t,* 203*t*
    intensity workouts 122-125
    maximizing 116-118
    monitoring effort 118-122, 121*t*
    multiday tours 175-181, 176*t,* 202-206, 203*t*
    principles of 21-22, 149-152, 150*f*
    priorities and 12-13
    staying with program 107
    structured vs. relaxed 11, 14, 15
    taper in 134-135
    workout types 100, 152
training logs 16-17*f,* 16-18
training pyramid 150-152, 150*f*
training zones 118
traumatic injuries 239-241
travel, to event 132

TT 119
turning, in traffic 18
12-hour events 8
24-hour events 8
200Ks. *See* centuries and 200Ks
two-lane roads 169

U

ultra events. *See* brevets; double centuries and 300Ks;
    multiday tours
UltraMarathon Cycling Association 157
Ultra Midwest 157
UMCA Year-Rounder (Y-R) 11
unsaturated fat 63
upper body strength 38-42

V

variation 22, 128
virtual reality trainers 29
visibility 18
visualization 136, 167, 184
vitamins 65
volunteering 159

W

wall squats 37
washing bikes 93-94
water intoxication 68
weaknesses, assessing 13
weight loss 61, 63, 68
wet roads 216
wheels 76-77, 77*f*, 213
windbreakers 89
wind chill 235, 236*t*
women's bikes 73-74
Wooldridge, Ann 85
workouts. *See* training
wrist injuries 230-231

ABOUT THE AUTHORS

John Hughes has been an endurance cyclist since 1975, spending 15 of those years as a coach and trainer. For 12 years he served as the managing director of the UltraMarathon Cycling Association (UMCA), the founding organization of the transcontinental Race Across America (RAAM). As UMCA director, Hughes published and edited *Ultra Cycling* magazine. He developed the popular century challenge, encouraging cyclists to ride a century every month.

Hughes has twice competed in RAAM and has twice won the Furnace Creek 508, a 508-mile RAAM qualifying event. Among his other accomplishments are seven 1,200-kilometer randonnées, including a course record for the Boston-Montreal-Boston route. For 10 years Hughes organized and led supported tours of the West and Southwest. He also explored the West on self-supported tours on a loaded touring bike.

Hughes has been certified as a USA Cycling sport coach and a National Strength and Conditioning Association personal trainer. Hughes has coached numerous riders, from people preparing for their first centuries to top RAAM finishers. He lives in Boulder, Colorado.

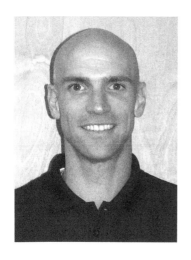

Dan Kehlenbach has been coaching cyclists and other endurance athletes since 1995. He has certifications through USA Cycling as a level 2 coach and the National Strength and Conditioning Association as a strength and conditioning specialist (CSCS). He earned his master's degree in sports medicine from the United States Sports Academy in Daphne, Alabama.

Kehlenbach spent four years with the U.S. Coast Guard, serving as the strength and conditioning instructor for the recruit training program in Cape May, New Jersey. He also represented the Coast Guard in cycling races, duathlons, triathlons, and running events.

As a contributing editor for *UltraCycling*, the official magazine of the UMCA, Kehlenbach wrote numerous articles on training and conditioning, specializing in articles that demystify the complexities of sport science.